TEXAS

Contemporary World Studies

PEOPLE, PLACES, AND SOCIETIES

Guided Reading Workbook

Houghton Mifflin Harcourt

Contents

Guided Reading Workbook

How to Use This Book

The *Guided Reading Workbook* was developed to help you get the most from your reading. Using this book will help you master geography content while developing your reading and vocabulary skills. Reviewing the next few pages before getting started will make you aware of the many useful features in this book.

Section summary pages allow you to interact with the content and key terms and places from each section of a chapter. The summaries explain each section of your textbook in a way that is easy to understand.

Section numbers make it easy to find your place in the workbook.

The main idea statements help focus your attention as you read the summaries.

Definitions for the key terms and places from your textbook are given.

Headings under each section summary match those of your textbook, which can help you find the material you need.

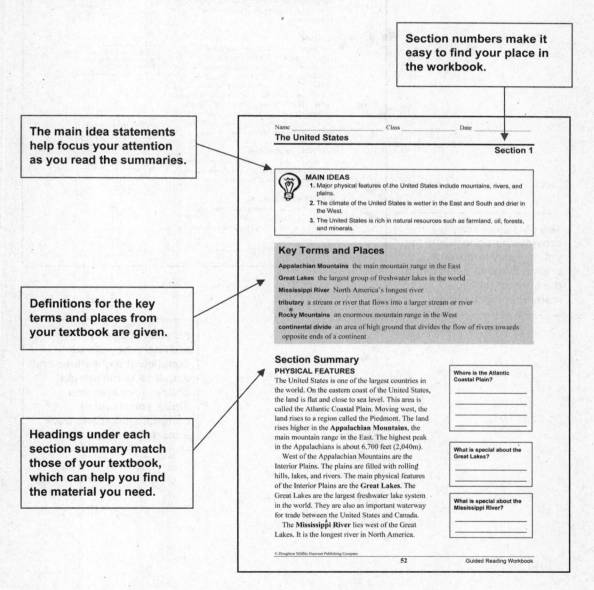

Name _____ Class _____ Date _____

The United States

Section 1

MAIN IDEAS
1. Major physical features of the United States include mountains, rivers, and plains.
2. The climate of the United States is wetter in the East and South and drier in the West.
3. The United States is rich in natural resources such as farmland, oil, forests, and minerals.

Key Terms and Places

Appalachian Mountains the main mountain range in the East

Great Lakes the largest group of freshwater lakes in the world

Mississippi River North America's longest river

tributary a stream or river that flows into a larger stream or river

Rocky Mountains an enormous mountain range in the West

continental divide an area of high ground that divides the flow of rivers towards opposite ends of a continent

Section Summary
PHYSICAL FEATURES
The United States is one of the largest countries in the world. On the eastern coast of the United States, the land is flat and close to sea level. This area is called the Atlantic Coastal Plain. Moving west, the land rises to a region called the Piedmont. The land rises higher in the **Appalachian Mountains**, the main mountain range in the East. The highest peak in the Appalachians is about 6,700 feet (2,040m).

West of the Appalachian Mountains are the Interior Plains. The plains are filled with rolling hills, lakes, and rivers. The main physical features of the Interior Plains are the **Great Lakes**. The Great Lakes are the largest freshwater lake system in the world. They are also an important waterway for trade between the United States and Canada.

The **Mississippi River** lies west of the Great Lakes. It is the longest river in North America.

Where is the Atlantic Coastal Plain?
_____
_____
_____

What is special about the Great Lakes?
_____
_____

What is special about the Mississippi River?
_____
_____

© Houghton Mifflin Harcourt Publishing Company

52

Guided Reading Workbook

The key terms and places from your textbook have been boldfaced, allowing you to quickly find and study them.

The challenge activity provides an opportunity for you to apply important critical thinking skills using the content that you learned in the section.

Name _____ Class _____ Date _____
Section 1, *continued*

Tributaries of the Mississippi River deposit rich silt that produces fertile farmlands. These farmlands cover most of the Interior Plains.

West of the Mississippi River lie the Great Plains. These are vast areas of grasslands. Further west, the land begins to rise, eventually leading to the **Rocky Mountains**. Many of these mountains reach higher than 14,000 feet (4,267m). Along the crest of the Rocky Mountains is a ridge that divides North America's rivers. This is called a **continental divide**. Rivers east of the divide mostly flow eastward, and most rivers west of the divide flow westward.

Farther west, mountain ranges include the Cascade Range and the Sierra Nevada. Mountains also stretch north along the Pacific coast. Mount McKinley in Alaska is the highest mountain in North America.

CLIMATE
The eastern United States is divided into three climate regions. The Northeast has a humid continental climate. To the south, the climate is humid subtropical. Farthest south, in the tip of southern Florida, the climate is tropical savanna.

The climate in the Interior Plains varies. It is hot and dry in the Great Plains. But in most of the Midwest, the climate is humid continental. In the West, climates are mostly dry. Alaska has subarctic and tundra climates, while Hawaii is tropical.

NATURAL RESOURCES
Our lives are affected by natural resources every day. Much of our paper, food, gas, and electricity come from natural resources in the United States.

CHALLENGE ACTIVITY
Critical Thinking: Drawing Inferences Write three paragraphs describing what makes the physical geography of the United States so diverse.

© Houghton Mifflin Harcourt Publishing Company   53   Guided Reading Workbook

About how high are the highest mountains in the Rockies?

What is the highest mountain in North America?

Circle the names of the three climate regions in the eastern United States.

List four products that come from natural resources found in the United States.

As you read each summary, be sure to complete the questions and activities in the margin boxes. They help you check your reading comprehension and track important content.

*The third page of each section allows you to demonstrate your understanding
of the key terms and places introduced in the section.*

Some pages have a word bank. You can use it to help find answers or complete writing activities.

Name _____ Class _____ Date _____
Section 1, *continued*

Appalachian Moutains	continental divide	Great Plains
Rocky Mountains	Great Lakes	Mississippi River
tributary		

DIRECTIONS Read each sentence and fill in the blank with the word
in the word pair that best completes the sentence.

1. Grasslands cover most of the _____, making the region
a good place to grow wheat and other grains. (Rocky Mountains/Great Plains)

2. The Missouri and Ohio Rivers are two major tributaries of the
_____. (Great Lakes/Mississippi River)

3. The _____ separate(s) the flow of North America's
rivers, sending some water east into the Mississippi River and some water west
into the Pacific Ocean. (tributary/continental divide)

A variety of activities helps you check your knowledge of key terms and places.

DIRECTIONS On the line provided before each statement, write **T** if a
statement is true and **F** if a statement is false. If the statement is false,
write the term from the word bank that would make the statement
correct on the line after each sentence.

_____ 4. The <u>Rocky Mountains</u> are the main mountain range in the East.

_____

_____ 5. The <u>Mississippi River</u> is (are) an important waterway for trade between
the United States and Canada.

_____

Writing activities require you to include key words and places in what you write. Remember to check to make sure that you are using the terms and places correctly.

DIRECTIONS Write three words or phrases that describe the term.

6. tributary _____

54 Guided Reading Workbook

A Geographer's World

MAIN IDEAS
1. Geography is the study of the world, its people, and the landscapes they create.
2. Geographers look at the world in many different ways.
3. Maps and other tools help geographers study the planet.

Key Terms and Places

geography the study of the world, its people, and the landscapes they create

landscape the human and physical features that make a place unique

social science a field that studies people and the relationships among them

region a part of the world with one or more common features distinguishing it from surrounding areas

map a flat drawing that shows part of Earth's surface

globe a spherical model of the entire planet

Section Summary
WHAT IS GEOGRAPHY?

For every place on Earth, you can ask questions to learn about it: What does the land look like? What is the weather like? What are people's lives like? Asking questions like these is how you study geography. **Geography** is the study of the world, its people, and the **landscapes** they create.

Geographers (people who study geography) ask questions about how the world works. For example, they may ask why a place gets tornadoes. To find answers, they gather data by observing and measuring. In this way, geography is like science.

Geography can also be like a social science. **Social science** studies people and how they relate to each other. This information cannot be measured in the same way. To study people, geographers may visit places and talk to the people about their lives.

> Underline the sentence that states how geography is like science.

LOOKING AT THE WORLD

Geographers must look carefully at the world around them. Depending on what they want to learn, they look at the world at different levels.

Geographers may study at the local level, such as a city or town. They may ask why people live there, what work they do, and how they travel. They can help a town or city plan improvements.

Geographers may also study at the regional level. A **region** is an area with common features. A region may be big or small. Its features make it different from areas around it. The features may be physical (such as mountains) or human (such as language).

Sometimes geographers study at the global level. They study how people interact all over the world. Geographers can help us learn how people's actions affect other people and places. For example, they may ask how one region influences other regions.

> Circle the three levels that geographers study.

THE GEOGRAPHER'S TOOLS

Geographers need tools to do their work. Often, they use maps and globes. A **map** is a flat drawing that shows Earth's surface. A **globe** is a spherical (round) model of the whole planet.

Maps and globes both show what Earth looks like. Because a globe is round, it can show Earth as it really is. To show the round Earth on a flat map, some details have to change. For example, a place's shape may change a little. But maps have benefits. They are easier to work with. They can also show small areas, such as cities, better.

Geographers also use other tools, such as satellite images, computers, notebooks, and tape recorders.

> In what way are maps and globes similar?
> _____

> Underline two sentences that tell the benefits of using maps.

CHALLENGE ACTIVITY

Critical Thinking: Solving Problems Pick a foreign country you would like to study. You want to develop the most complete picture possible of this place and its people. Make a list of questions to ask and tools you would use to find the answers.

DIRECTIONS On the line provided before each statement, write **T** if the statement is true and **F** if the statement is false. If the statement is false, write the correct term on the line after each sentence that makes the sentence a true statement.

_____ 1. A <u>globe</u> is a flat drawing of Earth's surface.

_____

_____ 2. The study of the world, its people, and the landscapes they create is called <u>geography</u>.

_____

_____ 3. Geography is sometimes called a <u>social science</u> because it studies people and the relationships among them.

_____

_____ 4. An example of a small <u>region</u> that geographers might study is Chinatown in San Francisco.

_____

_____ 5. A <u>map</u> is a spherical model of the entire planet.

_____

_____ 6. The combination of human and physical features that make a place unique is called a <u>landscape</u>.

_____

_____ 7. <u>Satellite images</u> help geographers to create, update, and compare maps.

_____

A Geographer's World

MAIN IDEAS
1. The five themes of geography help us organize our studies of the world.
2. The six essential elements of geography highlight some of the subject's most important ideas.

Key Terms and Places

absolute location a specific description of where a place is

relative location a general description of where a place is

environment an area's land, water, climate, plants and animals, and other physical features

Section Summary
THE FIVE THEMES OF GEOGRAPHY

Geographers use themes in their work. A theme is a topic that is common throughout a discussion or event. Many holidays have a theme, such as the flag and patriotism on the Fourth of July.

There are five major themes of geography: Location, Place, Human-Environment Interaction, Movement, and Regions. Geographers can use these themes in almost everything they study.

Location describes where a place is. This may be specific, such as an address. This is called an **absolute location.** It may also be general, such as saying the United States is north of Central America. This is called a **relative location.**

Place refers to an area's landscape. The landscape is made up of the physical and human features of a place. Together, these features give a place its own identity apart from other places.

Human-Environment Interaction studies how people and their environment affect each other. The **environment** includes an area's physical features, such as land, water, weather, and animals. Geographers study how people change their environment (by building, for example). They also

List the five major themes of geography:
_____
_____
_____
_____
_____

study how the environment causes people to adapt (by dressing for the weather, for example).

Movement involves learning about why and how people move. Do they move for work or pleasure? Do they travel by roads or other routes?

Studying Regions helps geographers learn how places are alike and different. This also helps them learn why places developed the way they did.

> Describe two ways that people and their environment affect each other.
>
> _____
> _____
> _____
> _____
> _____

THE SIX ESSENTIAL ELEMENTS

It is important to organize how you study geography, so you get the most complete picture of a place. Using the five major themes can help you do this. Using the six essential elements can, also.

Geographers and teachers created the six elements from eighteen basic ideas, called standards. The standards say what everyone should understand about geography. Each element groups together the standards that are related to each other.

The six elements are: The World in Spatial Terms (spatial refers to where places are located); Places and Regions; Physical Systems; Human Systems; Environment and Society; Uses of Geography. The six elements build on the five themes, so some elements and themes are similar. Uses of Geography is not part of the five themes. It focuses on how people can use geography to learn about the past and present, and plan for the future.

> What do the five themes and six elements of geography help you do? Underline the sentence that explains this.

CHALLENGE ACTIVITY

Critical Thinking: Analyze Analyze a place you regularly visit, such as a vacation spot or a park in your neighborhood. Write a question about the place for each geography theme to help someone not familiar with the themes understand them.

absolute location	environment	element
interaction	relative location	

DIRECTIONS Write a word or phrase that has the same meaning as the term given.

1. absolute location _____

_____

2. element _____

_____

3. environment _____

_____

4. interaction _____

_____

5. relative location _____

_____

DIRECTIONS Choose at least four of the vocabulary words from the word bank. Use these words to write a story or poem that relates to the section.

_____

_____

_____

_____

_____

_____

_____

_____

_____

A Geographer's World

Section 3

MAIN IDEAS

1. Physical geography is the study of landforms, water bodies, and other physical features.
2. Human geography focuses on people, their cultures, and the landscapes they create.
3. Other branches of geography examine specific aspects of the physical or human world.

Key Terms and Places

physical geography the study of the world's physical features, such as landforms, bodies of water, climates, soils, and plants

human geography the study of the world's people, communities, and landscapes

cartography the science of making maps

meteorology the study of weather and what causes it

Section Summary

PHYSICAL GEOGRAPHY

The field of geography has many branches, or divisions. Each branch has a certain focus. No branch alone gives us a picture of the whole world. When looked at together, the different branches help us understand Earth and its people better.

Geography has two main branches: physical geography and human geography. **Physical geography** is the study of the world's physical features, such as landforms, bodies of water, and weather.

Physical geographers ask questions about Earth's many physical features: Where are the mountains and flat areas? Why are some areas rainy and others dry? Why do rivers flow a certain way? To get their answers, physical geographers measure features—such as heights of mountains and temperatures of places.

> What do the different branches of geography help us do when they are looked at together? Underline the sentence that answers this.

> List the two main branches of geography:
> _____
> _____

Physical geography has important uses. It helps us understand how the world works. It also helps us predict and prepare for dangers, such as big storms.

HUMAN GEOGRAPHY

Human geography is the study of the world's people, communities, and landscapes. It is the other main branch of geography.

Human geographers study people in the past or present. They ask why more people live in some places than in others. They also ask other questions, such as what kinds of work people do.

People all over the world are very different, so human geographers often study a smaller topic. They might study people in one region, such as central Africa. They might study one part of people's lives in different regions, such as city life.

Human geography also has important uses. It helps us learn how people meet basic needs for food, water, and shelter. It helps people improve their lives. It can also help protect the environment.

> Why do human geographers often study one smaller topic?
> _____
> _____

> Circle three basic needs that people have to meet.

OTHER FIELDS OF GEOGRAPHY

Other branches of geography study one aspect of the world. Some of these are smaller parts of physical geography or of human geography.

Here are a few other branches to know about. **Cartography** is the science of making maps. Hydrology is the study of water on Earth. **Meteorology** is the study of weather and what causes it.

> What is meteorology?
> _____
> _____

CHALLENGE ACTIVITY

Critical Thinking: Drawing Inferences Examine a map of an unfamiliar city using a road atlas or an online map. Write a paragraph telling a visitor what physical and human features to look for in each quadrant (NE, SE, NW, SW).

| cartography | human geography | hydrology |
| meteorology | physical geography | |

DIRECTIONS Read each sentence and fill in the blank with the word
in the word pair that best completes the sentence.

1. _____ is the study of weather and what causes it.
   (cartography/meteorology)

2. Geographers might study _____ if they wanted to know

   how Victoria Falls formed. (physical geography/human geography)

3. Without _____, geographers would not be able to use maps

   to study where things are in the world. (cartography/meteorology)

4. The study of Earth's people, including their ways of life, homes, cities, beliefs,

   and customs is called _____.

   (physical geography/human geography)

5. Studying the world's river systems and how to protect the world's water supply

   are important parts of _____. (hydrology/meteorology)

DIRECTIONS Look up the vocabulary terms in the word bank in a
dictionary. Write the dictionary definition of the word that is closest to
the definition used in your textbook.

_____

_____

_____

_____

_____

Planet Earth

MAIN IDEAS
1. Earth's movement affects the amount of energy we receive from the sun.
2. Earth's seasons are caused by the planet's tilt.

Key Terms

solar energy energy from the sun

rotation one complete spin of Earth on its axis

revolution one trip of Earth around the sun

latitude the distance north or south of Earth's equator

tropics regions close to the equator

Section Summary

EARTH'S MOVEMENT

Energy from the sun, or **solar energy,** is necessary for life on Earth. It helps plants grow and provides light and heat. Several factors affect the amount of solar energy Earth receives. These are rotation, revolution, tilt, and latitude.

Earth's axis is an imaginary rod running from the North Pole to the South Pole. Earth spins around on its axis. One complete **rotation** takes 24 hours, or one day. Solar energy reaches only half of the planet at a time. As Earth rotates, levels of solar energy change. The half that faces the sun receives light and heat and is warmer. The half that faces away from the sun is darker and cooler.

As Earth rotates, it also moves around the sun. Earth completes one **revolution** around the sun every year, in 365 1/4 days. Every four years an extra day is added to February. This makes up for the extra quarter of a day.

Earth's axis is tilted, not straight up and down. At different times of year, some locations tilt toward the sun. They get more solar energy than locations tilted away from the sun.

> **List the four factors that affect the amount of solar energy Earth receives.**
> _____
> _____

> **What would happen if Earth did not rotate?**
> _____
> _____

> **Underline the sentence that describes Earth's revolution around the sun.**

> **Where you live, does more solar energy reach Earth in winter or in summer?**
> _____

Latitude refers to imaginary lines that run east and west around the planet, north and south of the Earth's equator. Areas near the equator receive direct rays from the sun all year and have warm temperatures. Higher latitudes receive fewer direct rays and are cooler.

Why are areas near the equator warmer than those in higher latitudes? _____

THE SEASONS

Many locations on Earth have four seasons: winter, spring, summer, and fall. These are based on temperature and how long the days are.

The seasons change because of the tilt of Earth's axis. In summer the Northern Hemisphere is tilted toward the sun. It receives more solar energy than during the winter, when it is tilted away from the sun.

Because Earth's axis is tilted, the hemispheres have opposite seasons. Winter in the Northern Hemisphere is summer in the Southern Hemisphere. During the fall and spring, the poles point neither toward nor away from the sun. In spring, temperatures rise and days become longer as summer approaches. In fall the opposite occurs.

What would the seasons be like in the Northern and Southern hemispheres if Earth's axis weren't tilted? _____

In some regions, the seasons are tied to rainfall instead of temperature. One of these regions, close to the equator, is the **tropics.** There, winds bring heavy rains from June to October. The weather turns dry in the tropics from November to January.

Circle the name of the warm region near the equator.

CHALLENGE ACTIVITY

Critical Thinking: Drawing Conclusions Imagine that you are a travel agent. One of your clients is planning a trip to Argentina in June, and another is planning a trip to Chicago in August. What kinds of clothing would you suggest they pack for their trips and why?

latitude	revolution	rotation
solar energy	tropics	

DIRECTIONS On the line provided before each statement, write **T** if a statement is true and **F** if a statement is false. If the statement is false, write the term from the word bank that would make the statement correct on the line after each sentence.

_____ 1. The hemisphere of Earth that is tilted away from the sun receives less direct <u>rainfall</u> than the other hemisphere receives.

_____

_____ 2. An umbrella might be more useful to a person in the <u>tropics</u> than a winter coat.

_____

_____ 3. Earth's path, or orbit, around the sun is its <u>rotation</u>.

_____

_____ 4. One <u>revolution</u> of Earth takes 24 hours.

_____

_____ 5. Plants in a high latitude receive less direct solar energy during the year than plants at a <u>lower latitude</u> because they are farther from the equator.

_____

MAIN IDEAS

1. Salt water and freshwater make up Earth's water supply.
2. In the water cycle, water circulates from Earth's surface to the atmosphere and back again.
3. Water plays an important role in people's lives.

Key Terms

freshwater water without salt

glacier large area of slow-moving ice

surface water water that is stored in Earth's streams, rivers, and lakes

precipitation water that falls to Earth's surface as rain, snow, sleet, or hail

groundwater water found below Earth's surface

water vapor water that occurs in the air as an invisible gas

water cycle the circulation of water from Earth's surface to the atmosphere and back

drought a long period of lower-than-normal precipitation

Section Summary
EARTH'S WATER SUPPLY

Approximately three-quarters of Earth's surface is covered with water. There are two kinds of water—salt water and **freshwater.** About 97 percent of Earth's water is salt water. Most of it is in the oceans, seas, gulfs, bays, and straits. Some lakes, such as the Great Salt Lake in Utah, also contain salt water.

Salt water cannot be used for drinking. Only freshwater is safe to drink. Freshwater is found in lakes and rivers and stored underground. Much is frozen in **glaciers.** Freshwater is also found in the ice of the Arctic and Antarctic regions.

One form of freshwater is **surface water.** This is stored in streams, lakes, and rivers. Streams form when **precipitation** falls to Earth as rain, snow,

> Circle the places where we find salt water.

> Underline the places where we find freshwater.

sleet, or hail. These streams then flow into larger streams and rivers.

Most freshwater is stored underground. **Groundwater** bubbles to the surface in springs or can be reached by digging deep holes, or wells.

THE WATER CYCLE

Water can take the form of a liquid, gas, or solid. In its solid form, water is snow and ice. Liquid water is rain or water found in lakes and rivers. **Water vapor** is an invisible form of water in the air.

Water is always moving. When water on Earth's surface heats up, it evaporates and turns into water vapor. It then rises from Earth into the atmosphere. When it cools down, it changes from water vapor to liquid. Droplets of water form clouds. When they get heavier, these droplets fall to Earth as precipitation. This process of evaporation and precipitation is called the **water cycle.**

Some precipitation is absorbed into the soil as groundwater. The rest flows into streams, rivers, and oceans.

| Underline the words that define water vapor. |

| What are the two main processes of the water cycle?

_____

_____ |

WATER AND PEOPLE

Problems with water include shortages, pollution, and flooding. Shortages are caused by overuse and by **drought,** when there is little or no precipitation for a long time. Chemicals and waste can pollute water. Heavy rains can cause flooding.

Water quenches our thirst and allows us to have food to eat. Flowing water is an important source of energy. Water also provides recreation, making our lives richer and more enjoyable. Water is essential for life on Earth.

| What water problems affect human beings?

_____

_____ |

CHALLENGE ACTIVITY

Critical Thinking: Solving Problems You are campaigning for public office. Write a speech describing three actions you plan to take to protect supplies of freshwater.

| drought | freshwater | glacier | groundwater |
| precipitation | surface water | water cycle | water vapor |

DIRECTIONS Read each sentence and fill in the blank with the word in the word pair that best completes the sentence.

1. Some _____ is locked in Earth's glaciers. (drought/freshwater)

2. Less than one percent of Earth's water supply comes from

   _____ stored in streams, rivers, and lakes.

   (surface water/water vapor)

3. Water can be a solid (ice), a liquid, or a gas called _____. (precipitation/water vapor)

4. The water brought to the surface from deep holes dug in the ground is

   _____. (freshwater/groundwater)

5. _____ is water that falls from clouds as rain, snow, sleet, or hail. (Precipitation/Water cycle)

DIRECTIONS Use the terms from the word bank to write a summary of what you learned in the section.

_____

_____

_____

_____

_____

Planet Earth

 MAIN IDEAS
1. Earth's surface is covered by many different landforms.
2. Forces below Earth's surface build up our landforms.
3. Forces on the planet's surface shape Earth's landforms.
4. Landforms influence people's lives and culture.

Key Terms

landforms shapes on Earth's surface, such as hills or mountains

continents large landmasses

plate tectonics a theory suggesting that Earth's surface is divided into more than 12 slow-moving plates, or pieces of Earth's crust

lava magma, or liquid rock, that reaches Earth's surface

earthquake sudden, violent movement of Earth's crust

weathering the process of breaking rock into smaller pieces

erosion the movement of sediment from one location to another

Section Summary

LANDFORMS

Geographers study **landforms** such as mountains, valleys, plains, islands, and peninsulas. They study how landforms are made and how they influence people.

> Give two examples of landforms.
>
> _____
> _____

FORCES BELOW EARTH'S SURFACE

Below Earth's surface, or crust, is a layer of liquid and a solid core. The planet has seven **continents,** large landmasses made of Earth's crust. All of Earth's crust rests on 12 plates. These plates are constantly in motion. Geographers call the study of these moving pieces of crust **plate tectonics.**

All of these plates move at different speeds and in different directions. As they move, they shape Earth's landforms. Plates move in three ways: They collide, they separate, and they slide past each other.

> Underline the sentence that lists the three different ways in which Earth's plates move.

The energy of colliding plates creates new landforms. When two ocean plates collide, they may form deep valleys on the ocean's floor. When ocean plates collide with continental plates, mountain ranges are formed. Mountains are also created when two continental plates collide.

> **Underline what happens when two ocean plates collide with one another.**

When plates separate, usually on the ocean floor, they cause gaps in the planet's crust. Magma, or liquid rock, rises through the cracks as **lava.** As it cools, it forms underwater mountains or ridges. Sometimes these mountains rise above the surface of the water and form islands.

Plates can also slide past each other. They grind along faults, causing **earthquakes.**

> **What causes earthquakes?**
> _____
> _____

FORCES ON EARTH'S SURFACE

As landforms are created, other forces work to wear them away. **Weathering** breaks larger rocks into smaller rocks. Changes in temperature can cause cracks in rocks. Water then gets into the cracks, expands as it freezes, and breaks the rocks. Rocks eventually break down into smaller pieces called sediment. Flowing water moves sediment to form new landforms, such as river deltas.

> **Circle the three forces that can cause erosion.**

Another force that wears down landforms is **erosion.** Erosion takes place when sediment is moved by ice, water, and wind.

LANDFORMS INFLUENCE LIFE

Landforms influence where people live. For example, people might want to settle in an area with good soil and water. People change landforms in many ways. For example, engineers build tunnels through mountains to make roads. Farmers build terraces on steep hillsides.

CHALLENGE ACTIVITY

Critical Thinking: Drawing Inferences Find out about a landform in your area that was changed by people. Write a report explaining why and how it was changed.

| continents | earthquake | erosion | landforms |
| lava | plate tectonics | weathering | |

DIRECTIONS Look at each set of four vocabulary terms. On the line provided, write the letter of the term that does not relate to the others.

_____ 1. a. erosion   b. weathering   c. landform   d. continent

_____ 2. a. lava   b. erosion   c. earthquake   d. plate tectonics

DIRECTIONS Answer each question by writing a sentence that contains at least one word from the word bank.

3. What are two ways that the movement of tectonic plates affect the Earth?

_____

_____

_____

4. What is the most common cause of erosion?

_____

_____

_____

DIRECTIONS Choose four of the terms from the word bank. Look them up in a dictionary. Write the definition of the word that is closest to the definition that is used in your textbook.

_____

_____

_____

_____

Climate, Environment, and Resources

MAIN IDEAS

1. While weather is short term, climate is a region's average weather over a long period.
2. The amount of sun at a given location is affected by Earth's tilt, movement, and shape.
3. Wind and water move heat around Earth, affecting how warm or wet a place is.
4. Mountains influence temperature and precipitation.

Key Terms and Places

weather the short-term changes in the air for a given place and time

climate a region's average weather conditions over a long period

prevailing winds winds that blow in the same direction over large areas of Earth

ocean currents large streams of surface seawater

front a place where two air masses of different temperature or moisture content meet

Section Summary

UNDERSTANDING WEATHER AND CLIMATE

Weather is the condition of the atmosphere at a certain time and place. **Climate** is a region's average weather over a long time. Climate is affected mostly by two factors: sun and latitude. Energy from the sun falls more directly on the equator, so the hottest temperatures are near the equator. In general it gets colder as you move away from the equator to a higher latitude.

> What are two important forces that affect climate?
> _____
> _____

SUN AND LOCATION

Heat from the sun moves around the Earth, partly through winds. Wind is caused by the rising and sinking of air. Cold air sinks, and warm air rises. At different latitudes winds tend to blow in the same direction. These **prevailing winds** can be from the west or east. Near the poles and in the subtropics, prevailing winds are easterlies. In the middle

> What causes wind?
> _____
> _____

latitudes are the westerlies. Prevailing winds control an area's climate.

WIND AND WATER

Winds pick up moisture over oceans and dry out passing over land. At about 30° North and South latitude, dry winds cause many of the world's deserts.

Ocean currents—large streams of surface water—also move heat around. The Gulf Stream is a warm current that flows from the Gulf of Mexico across the Atlantic Ocean to western Europe.

Water heats and cools more slowly than land. Therefore, water helps to moderate the temperature of nearby land, keeping it from getting very hot or very cold.

A **front** is a place where two different air masses meet. In the United States and other regions, warm and cold air masses meet often, causing severe weather. These can include thunderstorms, blizzards, and tornadoes. Tornadoes are twisting funnels of air that touch the ground. Hurricanes are large tropical storms that form over water. They bring destructive high winds and heavy rain.

> **Which heats and cools more slowly—land or water?**
>
> _____

> **What often happens when warm and cold air masses meet?**
>
> _____
>
> _____

MOUNTAINS

Mountains also affect climate. Warm air blowing against a mountainside rises and cools. Clouds form, and precipitation falls on the side facing the wind. However, the air is dry by the time it goes over the mountain. This effect creates a rain shadow, a dry area on the side of the mountain facing land.

CHALLENGE ACTIVITY

Critical Thinking: Sequencing Write a short description of the process leading up to the formation of a rain shadow. Draw and label a picture to go with your description.

| air mass | climate | front | ocean currents |
| precipitation | prevailing winds | rain shadow | weather |

DIRECTIONS On the line provided before each statement, write **T** if a statement is true and **F** if a statement is false. If the statement is false, write the correct term on the line after each sentence that makes the sentence a true statement.

_____ 1. <u>Climate</u> describes the atmospheric conditions in a place at a specific time. It changes rapidly.

_____

_____ 2. Weather is the temperature and <u>wind</u> from hour to hour or day to day.

_____

_____ 3. <u>Fronts</u> can cause severe weather. They may form when air masses of different temperatures come together.

_____

_____ 4. <u>Rain shadows</u> form on the side of a mountain away from the wind.

_____

_____ 5. The Gulf Stream is an example of a/an <u>prevailing wind</u>.

_____

DIRECTIONS Choose five of the vocabulary words from the word bank. Use these words to write a summary of what you learned in the section.

_____

_____

_____

_____

_____

_____

Climate, Environment, and Resources

MAIN IDEAS

1. Geographers use temperature, precipitation, and plant life to identify climate zones.
2. Tropical climates are wet and warm, while dry climates receive little or no rain.
3. Temperate climates have the most seasonal change.
4. Polar climates are cold and dry, while highland climates change with elevation.

Key Terms and Places

monsoon winds that shift direction with the seasons and create wet and dry periods

savanna an area of tall grasses and scattered trees and shrubs

steppe a semi-dry grassland or prairie

permafrost permanently frozen layers of soil

Section Summary

MAJOR CLIMATE ZONES

We can divide Earth into five climate zones: tropical, temperate, polar, dry, and highland. Tropical climates appear near the equator, temperate climates are found in the middle latitudes, and polar climates occur near the poles. Dry and highland climates can appear at different latitudes.

> Underline the names of the five climate zones.

TROPICAL AND DRY CLIMATES

Humid tropical climates occur near the equator. Some are warm and rainy throughout the year. Others have **monsoons**—winds that shift directions and create wet and dry seasons. Rain forests need a humid climate to thrive and support thousands of species.

Moving away from the equator, we find tropical savanna climates. A **savanna** is an area of tall grasses and scattered trees and shrubs. A long, hot dry season is followed by short periods of rain.

> What happens when monsoon winds change direction?
>
> _____
>
> _____

Deserts are hot and dry. At night, the dry air cools quickly; desert nights can be cold. Only a few living things survive in a desert. Sometimes **steppes**—dry grasslands—are found near deserts.

TEMPERATE CLIMATES

Away from the ocean in the middle latitudes are humid continental climates. Most have four distinct seasons, with hot summers and cold winters. In this climate, weather often changes quickly when cold and warm air masses meet.

A Mediterranean climate has hot, sunny summers and mild, wet winters. They occur near the ocean, and the climate is mostly pleasant. People like to vacation in these climates. Only small, scattered trees survive in these areas.

East coasts near the tropics have humid subtropical climates, because of winds bringing in moisture from the ocean. They have hot, wet summers and mild winters. Marine west coast climates occur farther north and also get moisture from prevailing winds coming in from the ocean.

> Underline the name of the climate that can have four distinct seasons.

> What do people typically like to do in Mediterranean climates?
> _____

POLAR AND HIGHLAND CLIMATES

Subarctic climate occurs south of the Arctic Ocean. Winters are long and cold, and summers are cool. There is enough precipitation to support forests. At the same latitude near the coasts, tundra climate is also cold, but too dry for trees to survive. In parts of the tundra, soil is frozen as **permafrost.**

Ice cap climates are the coldest on Earth. There is little precipitation and little vegetation.

Highland, or mountain, climate changes with elevation. As you go up a mountain, the climate may go from tropical to polar.

> Can there be forests in subarctic climates? Explain.
> _____

CHALLENGE ACTIVITY
Critical Thinking: Comparing and Contrasting

Create a table showing the differences and similarities between any two types of climate.

DIRECTIONS Write three words or phrases that describe the term.

1. savanna _____

2. steppe _____

3. polar climate _____

4. monsoon _____

5. permafrost _____

DIRECTIONS Look at each set of four terms. On the line provided, write the letter of the term that does not relate to the others.

_____ 6. a. coastal
      b. polar
      c. temperate
      d. tropical

_____ 7. a. humid continental
      b. marine west coast
      c. Mediterranean
      d. steppe

_____ 8. a. subarctic
      b. tundra
      c. desert
      d. ice cap

_____ 9. a. monsoon
      b. muggy
      c. prairies
      d. rain forest

_____ 10. a. forest
      b. tundra
      c. highland
      d. grassland

Guided Reading Workbook

Climate, Environment, and Resources

MAIN IDEAS
1. The environment and life are interconnected and exist in a fragile balance.
2. Soils play an important role in the environment.

Key Terms and Places

environment a plant or animal's surroundings

ecosystem any place where plants and animals depend upon each other and their environment for survival

habitat the place where a plant or animal lives

extinct to die out completely

humus decayed plant or animal matter

desertification the slow process of losing soil fertility and plant life

Section Summary
THE ENVIRONMENT AND LIFE

Plants and animals cannot live just anywhere. They must have the right surroundings, or **environment.** Climate, land features, and water are all part of a living thing's environment. If an area has everything a living thing needs, it can be a **habitat** for that species.

Many plants and animals usually share a habitat. Many small animals eat plants, and then some large animals eat the small animals. Species are connected in many ways. A community of connected species is called an **ecosystem.** Ecosystems can be as small as a pond or as large as the entire Earth.

Geographers study how changes in environments affect living things. Natural events and human actions change environments. Natural events include forest fires, disease, and climate changes. Human actions include clearing land and polluting.

> How large can an ecosystem be?
> _____

> Underline two human actions that can cause changes in an environment.

If a change to the environment is extreme, a species might become **extinct,** or die out completely.

SOIL AND THE ENVIRONMENT

Without soil, much of our food would not exist. Soil forms in layers over hundreds or thousands of years. The most fertile layer, the topsoil, has the most humus. **Humus** is decayed plant or animal matter.

The next layer, the subsoil, has less humus and more material from rocks. Soil gets minerals from these rocks. Below the subsoil is mostly rock.

An environment's soil affects which plants can grow there. Fertile soils have lots of humus and minerals. Fertile soils also need to contain water and small air spaces.

Soils can lose fertility from erosion by wind or water. Soil can also lose fertility from planting the same crops repeatedly. If soil becomes worn out and can no longer support plants, **desertification** can occur.

CHALLENGE ACTIVITY

Critical Thinking: Drawing Inferences Consider the interconnections in your environment. As you go through a normal day, keep a list of the sources you rely on for energy, food, and water.

| What does it mean to become extinct? |
| Which has more humus—topsoil or subsoil? |
| Underline four things found in fertile soil |

broken rock	consequence	desertification	ecosystem
environment	erosion	extinct	fertile soils
habitat	humus	nutrients	topsoil

DIRECTIONS Read each sentence and fill in the blank with the word
in the word pair that best completes the sentence.

1. Organic material called _____ enriches the soil.
   (topsoil/humus)

2. When soil gets worn out, it may lead to _____.
   (erosion/desertification)

3. A prairie is a type of _____. A forest is another type.
   (ecosystem/environment)

4. If there are too many changes in conditions, a species may die out, or become

   _____. (consequence/extinct)

5. Most plant roots are found in the _____, or the uppermost
   layer of soil. (broken rock/topsoil)

6. A place where animals and plants live is called a/an _____.
   (environment/habitat)

7. All plants and animals are adapted to a certain _____, or
   surroundings. (environment/erosion)

DIRECTIONS Choose five of the words from the word bank. On a
separate sheet of paper, use these words to write a poem or story that
relates to the section.

Climate, Environment, and Resources

MAIN IDEAS
1. Earth provides valuable resources for our use.
2. Energy resources provide fuel, heat, and electricity.
3. Mineral resources include metals, rocks, and salt.
4. Resources shape people's lives and countries' wealth.

Key Terms and Places

natural resource any material in nature that people use and value

renewable resources resources that can be replaced naturally

nonrenewable resources resources that cannot be replaced

deforestation the loss of forestland

reforestation planting trees to replace lost forestland

fossil fuels nonrenewable resources formed from the remains of ancient plants and animals

hydroelectric power the production of electricity by moving water

Section Summary
EARTH'S VALUABLE RESOURCES

Anything in nature that people use and value is a **natural resource.** These include such ordinary things as air, water, and soil. Resources such as trees are called **renewable resources** because Earth replaces them naturally. Those that cannot be replaced, such as oil, are called **nonrenewable resources.**

Air and water are renewable resources, but pollution can damage both. Some people get their water from underground wells, which can run out if too many people use them.

Soil is needed for all plant growth, including trees in forests. We get lumber, medicine, nuts, and rubber from forests. Soil and trees are renewable, but must be protected. The loss of forests is called **deforestation.** When we plant trees to replace lost forests, we call it **reforestation.**

> Are air and water renewable or nonrenewable resources?
>
> _____

> Underline the resources we can get from a forest.

Guided Reading Workbook

ENERGY RESOURCES

Most of our energy comes from **fossil fuels,** which are formed from the remains of ancient living things. These include coal, oil, and natural gas.

We use coal mostly for electricity, but it causes air pollution. An advantage of coal is that Earth still has a large supply. Another fossil fuel is petroleum, or oil. It is used to make gasoline and heating oil. Oil can be turned into plastics and other products. Oil also causes pollution, but we depend on it for much of our energy. The cleanest fossil fuel is natural gas, which is used mainly for cooking and heating.

Renewable energy resources include **hydroelectric power**—the creation of electricity by moving water. This is accomplished mainly by building dams on rivers. Other renewable energy sources are wind, solar, and nuclear energy. Nuclear energy produces dangerous waste material that must be stored for thousands of years.

> **Where does gasoline come from?**
> _____

> **What is the cleanest-burning fossil fuel?**
> _____

MINERAL RESOURCES

Minerals are solid substances in the Earth's crust formed from nonliving matter. Like fossil fuels, minerals are nonrenewable. Types of minerals include metals, rocks and gemstones, and salt. Mineral uses include making steel from iron, making window glass from quartz, and using stone as a building material. We also use minerals to make jewelry, coins, and many other common objects.

> **List two uses of minerals.**
> _____
> _____

RESOURCES AND PEOPLE

Some places are rich in natural resources. Resources such as fertile farmland, forests, and oil have helped the United States become a powerful country with a strong economy.

CHALLENGE ACTIVITY

Critical Thinking: Drawing Inferences Write a short essay explaining why we still use coal, even though it causes pollution.

deforestation	electricity	fossil fuels
hydroelectric power	natural resources	nonrenewable resources
petroleum	reforestation	renewable resources

DIRECTIONS Answer each question by writing a sentence that
contains at least one word from the word list.

1. What problem is caused when trees are cut down faster than they can grow back?
   How can this problem be fixed?

   _____

   _____

   _____

2. What are some examples of alternatives to fossil fuels? List two types and
   explain how they work.

   _____

   _____

   _____

3. What may happen to a country that only has a few natural resources?

   _____

   _____

   _____

DIRECTIONS Write three examples of each term.

4. natural resources _____

5. renewable resources _____

6. fossil fuels _____

The World's People

MAIN IDEAS
1. Culture is the set of beliefs, goals, and practices that a group of people share.
2. The world includes many different culture groups.
3. New ideas and events lead to changes in culture.

Key Terms

culture the set of beliefs, values, and practices a group of people have in common

culture trait an activity or behavior in which people often take part

culture region an area in which people have many shared culture traits

ethnic group a group of people who share a common culture and ancestry

cultural diversity having a variety of cultures in the same area

cultural diffusion the spread of culture traits from one region to another

Section Summary

WHAT IS CULTURE?

Culture is the set of beliefs, values, and practices a group of people have in common. Everything in day-to-day life is part of culture, including language, religion, clothes, music, and foods. People everywhere share certain basic cultural features, such as forming a government, educating children, and creating art or music. However, people practice these things in different ways, making each culture unique.

Underline the sentence that lists some parts of culture.

Culture traits are activities or behaviors in which people often take part, such as language and popular sports. People share some culture traits, but not others. For example, people eat using forks, chopsticks, or their fingers in different areas.

What are some basic cultural features that people share? _____ _____ _____

CULTURE GROUPS

There are thousands of different cultures in the world. People who share a culture are part of a culture group that may be based on things like age or religion.

A **culture region** is an area in which people have many shared culture traits such as language, religion, or lifestyle. A country may have several different culture regions, or just a single region, as Japan has.

A culture region may be based on an **ethnic group,** a group of people who share the same religion, traditions, language, or foods. **Cultural diversity** is having a variety of cultures in the same area. It can create a variety of ideas and practices, but it can also lead to conflict.

> How can cultural diversity affect the people in an area?
>
> _____
>
> _____

CHANGES IN CULTURE

Cultures are constantly changing. They can change through the development of new ideas or contact with other societies. New ideas such as the development of electricity, motion pictures, and the Internet have changed what people do and how they communicate. When two cultures come in close contact, both usually change. For example, the Spanish and Native American cultures changed when the Spanish conquered parts of the Americas.

> Underline the sentences that describe how cultures change.

Cultural diffusion is the spread of culture traits from one part of the world to another. It can happen when people move and bring their culture with them. New ideas and customs, such as baseball or clothing styles, can spread from one place to another as people learn about them.

> What are two ways cultural diffusion occurs?
>
> _____

CHALLENGE ACTIVITY

Critical Thinking: Drawing Inferences Consider all of the parts of your culture that have been influenced by other cultures. During a normal day, keep a list of all the things you use or do that you think have been influenced by other cultures.

cultural diffusion	cultural diversity	culture trait
culture	culture region	ethnic group

DIRECTIONS On the line provided before each statement, write **T** if a statement is true and **F** if a statement is false. If the statement is false, write the term that would make the statement correct on the line after each sentence.

_____ 1. The language you speak and the sports you play are examples of <u>culture traits</u>.

_____

_____ 2. <u>Cultural diversity</u> creates an interesting mix of ideas, but sometimes it can lead to conflict.

_____

_____ 3. When more than one cultural group lives in an area, this is called <u>cultural diffusion</u>.

_____

_____ 4. The spread of culture traits to different parts of the world is called <u>cultural diversity</u>.

_____

_____ 5. All aspects of your daily life are part of your <u>ethnic group</u>.

_____

DIRECTIONS Use all of the terms from the word bank to write a summary of what you learned in the section.

_____

_____

_____

_____

_____

The World's People

MAIN IDEAS
1. The study of population patterns helps geographers learn about the world.
2. Population statistics and trends are important measures of population change.

Key Terms

population the total number of people in a given area

population density a measure of the number of people living in an area, usually expressed as persons per square mile or square kilometer

birthrate the annual number of births per 1,000 people

migration the process of moving from one place to live in another

Section Summary
POPULATION PATTERNS

Population is the total number of people in a given area. Geographers study population patterns to learn about the world.

Some places are crowded with people, while others are almost empty. **Population density** is a measure of the number of people living in an area, usually expressed as persons per square mile or square kilometer. It describes how crowded a place is, which in turn affects how people live. In places with a high density, there is little open space, buildings are taller, and roads are more crowded than they are in places with lower density. They also often have more products available for a variety of shoppers.

High-density areas often have fertile soil, available water, and a favorable climate for agriculture. Areas that are less dense often have harsh land or climate that makes survival harder.

> Underline the two sentences that describe the effects of population density on a place.

> What is the land and climate often like in areas of high population density?
> _____
> _____

POPULATION CHANGE

The number of people living in an area affects jobs, housing, schools, medical care, available food, and many other things. Geographers study population changes and world trends to understand how people live in different parts of the world.

Three statistics are important to studying a country's population over time. **Birthrate** is the annual number of births per 1,000 people. Death rate is the annual number of deaths per 1,000 people. The rate of natural increase is found by subtracting the death rate from the birthrate.

| Underline the sentence that tells how to calculate the rate of natural increase. |

Some areas have low rates of natural increase, such as Europe and North America. Some countries in Africa and Asia have very high rates of natural increase. High rates can make it hard for countries to develop economically because they need to provide jobs, education, and medical care for a growing population.

| How can high rates of natural increase make it hard for a country to develop economically? _____ _____ |

Migration is the process of moving from one place to live in another. People may leave a place because of problems there, such as war, famine, drought, or lack of jobs. Other people may move to find political or religious freedom or economic opportunities in a new place.

The world's population has grown very rapidly in the last 200 years. Better health care and food supplies have helped more babies survive and eventually have children of their own. Many industrialized countries currently have slow population growth while other countries have very fast growth. Fast growth can put a strain on resources, housing, and government aid.

| How has the world's population changed during the last 200 years? _____ _____ |

CHALLENGE ACTIVITY

Critical Thinking: Identify Cause and Effect

Find out the population density of your city or town. Write down ways that this density affects your life and the lives of others.

birthrate	migration	population
population density	population trends	sparse

DIRECTIONS Read each sentence and fill in the blank with the word in the word pair that best completes the sentence.

1. The study of human _____ focuses on the total number of people in a given area. (population/migration)

2. Studying the _____ is one way to track the percentage of natural increase in the population. (population density/birthrate)

3. Calculating the _____ can tell us how crowded or sparse an area is. (population trends/population density)

4. _____ can cause one country's population to decline while it increases another country's population. (Birthrate/Migration)

5. One _____ shows that many of the world's industrialized nations have slow population growth. (birthrate/population trend)

DIRECTIONS Look up three terms from the word bank in a dictionary. On a separate sheet of paper, write the dictionary definition of the term that is closest to the definition used in your textbook. Then write a sentence using each term correctly.

The World's People

MAIN IDEAS
1. The features common to all cultures are called cultural universals.
2. All societies have social institutions that help their groups survive.
3. Every culture expresses itself creatively in a variety of ways.
4. All societies use technology to help shape and control the environment.

Key Terms and Places

cultural universal features societies have developed that are common to all cultures

social institution an organized pattern of belief and behavior that focuses on meeting a societal need

heritage the wealth of cultural elements that has been passed down over generations

universal theme a message about life or human nature that is meaningful across time and in all places

technology the use of knowledge, tools, and skills to solve problems

science a way of understanding the world through observation and the testing of ideas

Section Summary

WHAT DO ALL CULTURES HAVE IN COMMON?

All people have the same basic needs. Societies have developed **cultural universals** to meet the basic needs of their members.

BASIC SOCIAL INSTITUTIONS

Social institutions are organized patterns of belief and behavior that focus on meeting the needs of the society's members. The most basic social institutions are family, education, religion, government, and economy.

Family is the most basic social institution. The family cares for the children and for the elderly. They also teach accepted behaviors and cultural values. Societies pass on knowledge through education. Schools also teach the norms that support or sustain a society.

> List the most basic social institutions.
>
> _____
> _____
> _____
> _____
> _____

Religion provides a way for societies to explain the meanings of life and death and the difference between good and bad behavior. In all world regions, religion has inspired great works of devotion, including art and architecture.

Government is a system of leaders and laws that help people live together in their community or country. A society's economy is its system of using resources to meet needs.

> **What is the purpose of religion?**
>
> _____
>
> _____

CREATIVE EXPRESSIONS

Societies, like individuals, express themselves creatively. There are three main types of creative expression. Performing arts include music, theater, and dance. Visual arts include painting, sculpture, and architecture. Literary arts are related in words and language such as literature and folklore. Creative expressions reflect a specific **heritage,** or wealth of cultural elements that have been passed down through generations. Some creative expressions communicate universal themes. A **universal theme** is a message about life that is true throughout time and in all places.

> **What are the three main types of creative expressions?**
>
> _____
>
> _____
>
> _____

SCIENCE AND TECHNOLOGY

Technology is the use of knowledge, tools, and skills to solve problems. **Science** is a way of understanding the world through observation and the testing of ideas. Technology use can be determined by environmental factors as well as by governments or religious beliefs. Advances in science and technology have made life easier.

> **How do scientists understand the world?**
>
> _____
>
> _____

CHALLENGE ACTIVITY

Critical Thinking: Classify Pick a creative expression that you admire or use. Classify it as one of the three basic types of creative expression and describe why it is important.

| cultural universal | social institution | heritage |
| universal theme | technology | science |

DIRECTIONS Write three words or phrases to describe each term.

1. cultural universal _____

2. social institution _____

3. universal theme _____

4. heritage _____

5. science _____

6. technology _____

The World's People

> **MAIN IDEAS**
> 1. Globalization links the world's countries together through culture and trade.
> 2. The world community works together to solve global conflicts and crises.

Key Terms and Places

globalization the process in which countries are increasingly linked to each other through culture and trade

popular culture culture traits that are well known and widely accepted

interdependence the reliance of one country on the resources, goods, or services of another country

United Nations (UN) an organization of the world's countries that promotes peace and security around the globe

humanitarian aid assistance to people in distress

Section Summary

GLOBALIZATION

People around the world are more closely linked than ever before. **Globalization** is the process in which countries are increasingly linked to each other through culture and trade. Improvements in technology and communication have increased globalization.

> Underline the sentence that describes two ways countries are linked together.

    Popular culture consists of culture traits that are well known and widely accepted. These traits can include food, sports, music, and movies. The United States has a great influence on popular culture through sales of American products and the use of English for business, science, and education around the world. The United States is in turn greatly influenced by other countries.

> What are four traits that can be considered part of popular culture?
> _____
> _____

    World businesses are connected through trade. Companies may make products in many different countries or may use products from around the world. **Interdependence** occurs when countries depend on each other for resources, goods, or services. Companies and consumers depend on goods produced elsewhere.

A WORLD COMMUNITY

Because places around the world are connected closely, what happens in one place affects others. The world community works together to promote cooperation between countries.

When conflicts occur, countries from around the world try to settle them. The **United Nations (UN)** is an association of nearly 200 countries dedicated to promoting peace and security.

Crises such as earthquakes, floods, droughts, or tsunamis can leave people in great need. Groups from around the world provide **humanitarian aid,** or assistance to people in distress. Some groups help refugees or provide medical care.

CHALLENGE ACTIVITY

Critical Thinking: Contrast Talk to a parent or other adult about their knowledge of other countries and their connections to them when they were young. Write a short essay that contrasts their global connections with yours.

> **What two groups might depend on goods produced elsewhere?**
> _____
> _____

> **Underline the sentence that describes the main goals of the United Nations.**

crisis	globalization	humanitarian aid
interdependence	popular culture	United Nations (UN)

DIRECTIONS Read each sentence and fill in the blank with the word
in the word pair that best completes the sentence.

1. Groups from around the world come together to provide

   _____ in times of crisis. (humanitarian aid/globalization)

2. _____ occurs when countries depend on each other for
   resources, goods, or services. (Globalization /Interdependence)

DIRECTIONS On the line provided before each statement, write **T** if
the statement is true and **F** if the statement is false. If the statement is
false, write the term that would make the statement correct on the line
after each sentence.

_____ 3. The process in which countries are linked to one another through culture
         and trade is called popular culture.

         _____

_____ 4. Culture traits such as food, music, movies, and sports are examples of
         globalization.

         _____

_____ 5. As a result of globalization, there is more interdependence among
         countries.

         _____

_____ 6. The United Nations (UN) promotes peace and security around the world.

         _____

Government and Economic Systems

MAIN IDEAS
1. Limited governments of the world include democracies.
2. Unlimited governments of the world include totalitarian governments.
3. Most human rights abuses occur under unlimited governments of the world.

Key Terms

democracy a form of government in which the people elect leaders and rule by majority

direct democracy government in which citizens meet in popular assembly to discuss issues and vote for leaders

limited government government that has legal limits on its power, usually in the form of a constitution

unlimited government government in which power is concentrated in the hands of a single leader or small group

totalitarian government government that controls all aspects of society

Section Summary

GOVERNMENTS OF THE WORLD

A **democracy** is a form of government in which the people elect leaders and rule by majority. Citizens are free to choose representatives to make and enforce laws. In a **direct democracy**, citizens meet regularly in assembly to discuss issues and vote for leaders. Ancient Athens is an example of a direct democracy. A democracy is a form of **limited government,** in that the government has legal limits on its power, usually in the form of a constitution.

Today nearly half of the more than 190 countries in the world are democratic or partly democratic. These democracies share some similar characteristics. They have social welfare systems that seek to improve the quality of their citizens' lives. They protect their citizens rights and freedoms. They can usually withstand national crises such as war or civil unrest.

> Circle an example of a direct democracy.

> What is a constitution?
> _____
> _____

UNLIMITED GOVERNMENTS

In an **unlimited government**, power is concentrated in the hands of a single leader or group.

Totalitarian governments exercise control over all aspects of society—the government, economy, and even people's beliefs and actions. In these societies, citizens have no way to change the government. Examples of totalitarian governments include the Soviet Union under Joseph Stalin and China under Mao Zedong.

A totalitarian government is the most extreme kind of authoritarian government, one in which its people are subject to state control. In unlimited governments, citizens have limited political and economic freedoms. Rulers often use force to put down opposition movements. For example, Saddam Hussein of Iraq used torture and violence against his political opponents and his own people.

> List two examples of totalitarian governments.
> _____
> _____

HUMAN RIGHTS ABUSES

Human rights abuses include torture, slavery, and murder. Most abuses occur in countries with unlimited governments. However, human rights abuses are also common in countries in the process of establishing democracy. Abuses in democratic countries often occur as a result of inaction.

The United States takes a three-part approach to its work on human rights: learning the truth and stating the facts, taking consistent positions about human rights abuses, and partnering with other organizations committed to human rights.

> What are some examples of human rights abuses.
> _____
> _____
> _____
> _____
> _____

CHALLENGE ACTIVITY

Critical Thinking: Comparing and Contrasting

Write a paragraph comparing and contrasting limited and unlimited governments.

Guided Reading Workbook

democracy	direct democracy	limited government
unlimited government	totalitarian government	constitution

DIRECTIONS On the line provided before each statement, write **T** if a statement is true and **F** if a statement is false. If the statement is false, write a term that would make the statement correct on the line after each sentence.

_____ 1. <u>Ancient Athens</u> is an example of an unlimited government.

_____

_____ 2. A <u>democracy</u> is a form of government in which one person or a few people hold power.

_____

_____ 3. A government in which the state has control over all aspects of society is called a <u>totalitarian government</u>.

_____

_____ 4. An <u>unlimited government</u> is one in which the people elect leaders and rule by majority.

_____

_____ 5. A <u>constitution</u> enforces the legal limits of a government's power.

_____

_____ 6. <u>Communist China</u> is an example of a direct democracy.

_____

Government and Economic Systems

MAIN IDEAS
1. The duties and roles of citizenship help to make representative government work.
2. Good citizens accept their responsibilities for maintaining a strong democracy.
3. The type of government in some societies influences the roles of the citizens in those societies.

Key Terms

representative government a government in which people are the ultimate source of government authority

draft a law that requires men of certain ages and qualifications to join the military

jury duty a required service of citizens to act as a member of a jury

nonrepresentative government a government in which government power is unlimited and citizens have few, if any, rights

Section Summary
DUTIES AND ROLES OF CITIZENSHIP

In the United States, citizens are the ultimate source of government authority. This is called a **representative government**. For this type of government to work, citizens have to peform certain duties.

In order for our society to work, citizens must obey the law. In the United States, you must go to school until the age of 16. School is important because it provides citizens with critical thinking skills to help them choose leaders and understand issues. Education also provides workforce skills.

Citizens must pay taxes. When we pay taxes on purchases, we are paying or public services such as road repair, police protection, and national security.

When the country needs people to fight wars, it may issue a **draft**. A draft requires men of certain ages and qualifications to serve in the military. Citizens must also serve on a jury if they are called

> Who is the source of government authority in a representative government?
> _____

> Why is it important for citizens to go to school?
> _____
> _____
> _____
> _____

to do so. This service is called **jury duty.** The Constitution guarantees citizens the right to a trial by their peers—their fellow citizens.

RIGHTS AND RESPONSIBILITES

In a representative government, citizens also have responsibilities—tasks we should do as citizens but that are not required by law.

In order to give consent to our lawmakers in government, we should vote. Voting is a way to show our decision makers whether we agree with their opinions on issues. Becoming informed about key issues, candidates, and current events will help you make informed choices when you vote.

You might also take part in government by joining political parties or serving for political office. Another way to help society is by volunteering in your community.

By knowing your own rights as a citizen, you can make sure you respect the rights of the people around you. You should also know if someone else's rights are being violated.

What are some of our responsibilities as citizens?

_____

_____

_____

_____

CITIZENSHIP IN OTHER SOCIETIES

Other representative governments may have similar roles and responsibilities for their citizens. These may not be the same as those of U.S. citizens.

Nonrepresentative governments are governments in which citizens have few, if any, rights. The government maintains all the power.

CHALLENGE ACTIVITY

Critical Thinking: Drawing Inferences Imagine that you are about to turn 18. Make a list of the responsibilities you have as a United States citizen.

representative government	draft	jury duty
nonrepresentative government	candidate	citizen

DIRECTIONS Answer each question by writing a sentence that contains at least one term from the word bank.

1. How does a representative government work?

_____

_____

_____

2. When might the United States issue a draft?

_____

_____

_____

3. Name some duties and responsibilities of a United States citizen.

_____

_____

_____

4. What is a nonrepresentative government?

_____

_____

_____

5. Explain how the Constitution guarantees citizens a right to a trial by their peers.

_____

_____

_____

_____

Government and Economic Systems

MAIN IDEAS

1. Scarcity shapes how societies use factors.
2. There are three basic types of economic systems.
3. Contemporary societies have mixed economies.
4. The United States benefits from a free enterprise system.
5. Geographers categorize countries based on levels of economic development and range of economic activities.

Key Terms and Places

scarcity a problem of having unlimited human wants in a world of limited resources

factors of production basic economic resources needed to produce goods and services

free enterprise system an economic system in which few limits are placed on business activities

agricultural industries businesses that focus on growing crops and raising livestock

manufacturing industries businesses that make finished products from raw materials

wholesale industries businesses that sell to other businesses

retail industries businesses that sell directly to consumers

developed countries countries with strong economies and a high quality of life

developing countries countries with weak economies and a lower quality of life

Section Summary

SCARCITY AND RESOURCE USE

The condition created when humans' unlimited wants conflict with the world's limited resources is called **scarcity**. Economists study **factors of production**—land, labor, capital, and entrepreneurship.

> Underline the four main factors of production.

ECONOMIC SYSTEMS

Traditional economies rely on long-established customs such as hunting and fishing. In a command economy, the government controls the economy. A market economy is based on private ownership, free trade, and competition.

MODERN ECONOMIES

Most countries have one of three types of mixed economies: communist, capitalist, and socialist. In a communist society, the government owns all factors of production. In a capitalist economy, individuals and businesses own the factors of production. In socialist economies, the government controls some of the basic factors of production.

THE FREE ENTERPRISE SYSTEM

In the American **free enterprise system,** individuals are free to exchange goods and services, and own and operate businesses with little government intervention.

What is a free enterprise system?
_____
_____
_____
_____

ECONOMIC ACTIVITIES AND DEVELOPMENTS

Every nation has a variety of economies. In **agricultural industries,** people focus on growing crops and raising livestock. In **manufacturing industries,** people make finished materials from raw materials. In tertiary industries, people work in **wholesale**—businesses that sell to other businesses. Others work in **retail industries**—businesses that sell directly to consumers.

The world's most powerful nations are **developed countries,** countries with strong economies and a high quality of life. **Developing nations** are those with weak economies.

CHALLENGE ACTIVITY

Critical Thinking: Compare and Contrast How is the American free enterprise system different from communist and socialist economies? Write a paragraph explaining the differences.

scarcity	agricultural industries	developing countries
factors of production	retail industries	manufacturing industries
developed countries	free enterprise system	wholesale industries

DIRECTIONS Read each sentence and fill in the blank with the word
in the word pair that best completes the sentence.

1. Businesses known as _____ make finished products from
   raw materials. (manufacturing industries/retail industries)

2. Unlimited human wants create _____ in the world because
   of limited resources. (developed countries/scarcity)

3. In a _____, few limits are placed on business activities.
   (factor of production/free enterprise system)

4. _____ industries focus on growing crops and raising
   livestock. (Agricultural/Wholesale)

5. Countries with weak economies and a lower quality of life are known as
   _____. (developing countries/developed countries)

DIRECTIONS Look up three terms from the word bank in an
encyclopedia. On a separate sheet of paper, write the dictionary
definition of the term that is closest to the definition used in your
textbook. Then write a sentence using each term correctly.

MAIN IDEAS
1. Major physical features of the United States include mountains, rivers, and plains.
2. The climate of the United States is wetter in the East and South and drier in the West.
3. The United States is rich in natural resources such as farmland, oil, forests, and minerals.

Key Terms and Places

Appalachian Mountains the main mountain range in the East

Great Lakes the largest group of freshwater lakes in the world

Mississippi River North America's longest river

tributary a stream or river that flows into a larger stream or river

Rocky Mountains an enormous mountain range in the West

continental divide an area of high ground that divides the flow of rivers towards opposite ends of a continent

Section Summary

PHYSICAL FEATURES

The United States is one of the largest countries in the world. On the eastern coast of the United States, the land is flat and close to sea level. This area is called the Atlantic Coastal Plain. Moving west, the land rises to a region called the Piedmont. The land rises higher in the **Appalachian Mountains**, the main mountain range in the East. The highest peak in the Appalachians is about 6,700 feet (2,040m).

West of the Appalachian Mountains are the Interior Plains. The plains are filled with rolling hills, lakes, and rivers. The main physical features of the Interior Plains are the **Great Lakes**. The Great Lakes are the largest freshwater lake system in the world. They are also an important waterway for trade between the United States and Canada.

The **Mississippi River** lies west of the Great Lakes. It is the longest river in North America.

Where is the Atlantic Coastal Plain?
_____
_____
_____
_____

What is special about the Great Lakes?
_____
_____

What is special about the Mississippi River?
_____
_____

Tributaries of the Mississippi River deposit rich silt that produces fertile farmlands. These farmlands cover most of the Interior Plains.

West of the Mississippi River lie the Great Plains. These are vast areas of grasslands. Further west, the land begins to rise, eventually leading to the **Rocky Mountains**. Many of these mountains reach higher than 14,000 feet (4,267m). Along the crest of the Rocky Mountains is a ridge that divides North America's rivers. This is called a **continental divide**. Rivers east of the divide mostly flow eastward, and most rivers west of the divide flow westward.

Farther west, mountain ranges include the Cascade Range and the Sierra Nevada. Mountains also stretch north along the Pacific coast. Mount McKinley in Alaska is the highest mountain in North America.

> **About how high are the highest mountains in the Rockies?**
> _____
> _____

> **What is the highest mountain in North America?**
> _____
> _____

CLIMATE

The eastern United States is divided into three climate regions. The Northeast has a humid continental climate. To the south, the climate is humid subtropical. Farthest south, in the tip of southern Florida, the climate is tropical savanna.

The climate in the Interior Plains varies. It is hot and dry in the Great Plains. But in most of the Midwest, the climate is humid continental. In the West, climates are mostly dry. Alaska has subarctic and tundra climates, while Hawaii is tropical.

> **Circle the names of the three climate regions in the eastern United States.**

NATURAL RESOURCES

Our lives are affected by natural resources every day. Much of our paper, food, gas, and electricity come from natural resources in the United States.

> **List four products that come from natural resources found in the United States.**
> _____
> _____
> _____
> _____

CHALLENGE ACTIVITY

Critical Thinking: Drawing Inferences Write three paragraphs describing what makes the physical geography of the United States so diverse.

Guided Reading Workbook

Appalachian Moutains	continental divide	Great Plains
Rocky Mountains	Great Lakes	Mississippi River
tributary		

DIRECTIONS Read each sentence and fill in the blank with the word
in the word pair that best completes the sentence.

1. Grasslands cover most of the _____, making the region
   a good place to grow wheat and other grains. (Rocky Mountains/Great Plains)

2. The Missouri and Ohio Rivers are two major tributaries of the

   _____. (Great Lakes/Mississippi River)

3. The _____ separate(s) the flow of North America's
   rivers, sending some water east into the Mississippi River and some water west
   into the Pacific Ocean. (tributary/continental divide)

DIRECTIONS On the line provided before each statement, write **T** if a
statement is true and **F** if a statement is false. If the statement is false,
write the term from the word bank that would make the statement
correct on the line after each sentence.

_____ 4. The <u>Rocky Mountains</u> are the main mountain range in the East.

   _____

_____ 5. The <u>Mississippi River</u> is (are) an important waterway for trade between
   the United States and Canada.

   _____

DIRECTIONS Write three words or phrases that describe the term.

6. tributary _____

The United States

Section 2

MAIN IDEAS
1. The United States is the world's first modern democracy.
2. The people and culture of the United States are very diverse.

Key Terms and Places

colony a territory inhabited and controlled by people from a foreign land

Boston a major seaport in the British colonies during the mid-1700s

New York a major seaport in the British colonies during the mid-1700s

plantation a large farm that grows mainly one crop

pioneers the first settlers in the West

bilingual having the ability to speak two languages

Section Summary
FIRST MODERN DEMOCRACY

Europeans began settling in North America in the 1500s and setting up **colonies**. New cities such as **Boston** and **New York** became major seaports in the British colonies. Thousands of enslaved Africans were brought to the colonies and forced to work on **plantations**.

In 1774, many British colonists were unhappy with British rule. As a result, the Continental Congress adopted the Declaration of Independence in July 1776. To win independence, colonists fought the British in the Revolutionary War. The British were defeated in 1781 at the Battle of Yorktown in Virginia.

After the war, the United States began to expand west. The first settlers were called **pioneers**.

The United States faced two world wars during the 1900s. After World War II, the United States and the Soviet Union became rivals in the Cold War, which lasted until the 1990s.

> **Name two major seaports in the British colonies.**
> _____
> _____

> **What happened in July 1776?**
> _____
> _____
> _____

> **What kind of government does the United States have?**
> _____
> _____

The United States has a limited, democratic government based on the U.S. Constitution. The president and Congress are elected by U.S. citizens. Citizens may vote starting at age 18.

American citizens have many rights and responsibilities. Citizens are encouraged to play an active role in government. The democratic process suffers unless people participate.

PEOPLE AND CULTURE

The majority of Americans are descendants of European immigrants. The United States is also home to people of many different cultures and ethnic groups. The United States is a diverse nation, where many languages are spoken, different religions are practiced, and a variety of foods are eaten.

For thousands of years, Native Americans were the only people living in the Americas. Descendants of enslaved Africans live throughout the country, with the highest population of African Americans living in the South. Other people migrated to the United States from different regions of the world. These include Asian countries, such as China, India, and the Philippines. Many Hispanic Americans originally migrated to the United States from Mexico, Cuba, and other Latin American countries.

> Who were the first people who lived in the Americas?
> _____
> _____

> Underline the sentence that explains from where many Hispanic Americans originally migrated.

When people migrate to the United States, they bring parts of their culture with them, including their religions, food, and music. Some Americans are **bilingual**. Other than English, Spanish is the most widely spoken language in the United States.

People of different ethnic groups make the United States a very diverse country.

CHALLENGE ACTIVITY

Critical Thinking: Drawing Inferences Imagine that you are about to turn 18. Make a list of the responsibilities you have as a United States citizen.

Section 2, *continued*

bilingual	Boston	colony	New York
pioneers	plantation		

DIRECTIONS Look at the set of four terms following each number.
On the line provided, write the letter of the term that does not relate to
the others.

_____ 1. a. cotton   b. plantation   c. bilingual   d. enslaved Africans

_____ 2. a. seaport   b. colony   c. Boston   d. New York

_____ 3. a. pioneers   b. west   c. gold   d. troops

_____ 4. a. New York   b. independence   c. Yorktown   d. Revolutionary War

DIRECTIONS Answer each question by writing a sentence that
contains at least one term from the word bank.

5. What is one reason that the population of the United States is so culturally
diverse today?

_____

_____

_____

6. What was America like before the Revolutionary War?

_____

_____

_____

The United States

Section 3

MAIN IDEAS
1. The United States has four regions—the Northeast, South, Midwest, and West.
2. The United States has a strong economy and a powerful military but is facing the challenge of world terrorism.

Key Terms and Places

megalopolis a string of large cities that have grown together

Washington, D.C. the United States capital

Detroit located in Michigan and is the nation's leading automobile producer

Chicago the third-largest city in the United States and one of the busiest shipping ports on the Great Lakes

Seattle Washington's largest city and home of a major software company

terrorism violent attacks that cause fear

Section Summary
REGIONS OF THE UNITED STATES

Geographers often divide the United States into four main regions. These are the Northeast, the South, the Midwest, and the West.

The Northeast is the smallest region in the United States, as well as the most densely populated. Natural resources in the Northeast include rich farmland, coal, and fishing. Major seaports make it possible to ship products to markets around the world.

The Northeast is covered by a string of large cities called a **megalopolis**. It stretches from Boston to **Washington**, **D.C.** Other major cities are New York, Philadelphia, and Baltimore.

The South includes coastlines along the Atlantic Ocean and the Gulf of Mexico. The coastal plains provide farmers with rich soils for growing cotton, tobacco, and citrus fruits.

Technology, education, and oil are also important industries in the South. Warm weather and beautiful beaches make tourism an important part of the South's economy.

> **What are the four main regions of the United States?**
> _____
> _____
> _____
> _____

> **List 5 cities that make up the megalopolis in the Northeast.**
> _____
> _____
> _____
> _____
> _____

> **Underline the sentences that describe the industries that contribute to the South's economy.**

The Midwest is one of the world's most productive farming regions. Rich soils deposited by the region's rivers are perfect for raising livestock and producing corn, dairy products, and soybeans.

Most of the major cities in the Midwest, such as **Chicago** and **Detroit**, are located on rivers or the Great Lakes. This makes it easier to transport farm products, coal, and iron ore.

The West is the largest region. California's mild climate and wealth of resources make it home to more than 10 percent of the country's population.

Ranching, farming, coal, oil, gold, silver, copper, forestry, and fishing are important industries in the West. **Seattle**, Washington's largest city, is home to many of these industries.

> **Where are the major cities of the Midwest located?**
> _____
> _____

> **What is the largest region in the United States?**
> _____
> _____

CHANGES IN THE NATION

The United States has faced many challenges in recent years. Trade, technology, and an abundance of natural resources have helped make the U.S. economy strong. However, by the end of 2007, the United States faced a recession, or a sharp decrease in economic activity. The housing market collapsed, some banks and businesses failed, and millions of jobs were lost.

Terrorism continued to threaten the nation's safety. After the deadliest terrorist attack in U.S. history on September 11, 2001, the United States and other world leaders began working together to combat terrorism.

In 2008, in the highest voter turnout for any election in U.S. history, Barack Obama was elected president. He became the nation's first African American president.

> **What are two major issues the United States has faced in recent years?**
> _____
> _____

CHALLENGE ACTIVITY

Critical Thinking: Drawing Inferences Think about the physical features, climates, natural resources, industries, and economies of the regions in the United States. Choose the region you would most like to live in and explain why.

| Chicago | Detroit | megalopolis | terrorism |
| Seattle | strip mining | Washington, D.C. | |

DIRECTIONS On the line provided before each statement, write **T** if a statement is true and **F** if a statement is false. If the statement is false, write the term from the word bank that would make the statement correct on the line after each sentence.

_____ 1. Seattle and New York are part of a megalopolis in the northeastern region of the United States.

_____

_____ 2. Most major cities in the Midwest, such as Detroit and Chicago, are located on rivers or the Great Lakes.

_____

_____ 3. Because strip mining leads to soil erosion and other problems in the West, laws have been passed to protect the land there.

_____

_____ 4. Terrorist acts in the United States have encouraged leaders around the world to work together to combat the problem of terrorism.

_____

_____ 5. Forestry and fishing are two important economic activities in the Detroit area.

_____

DIRECTIONS Choose four of the terms from the word bank. On a separate sheet of paper use these terms to write a description of the United States.

Canada

MAIN IDEAS
1. A huge country, Canada has a wide variety of physical features, including rugged mountains, plains, and swamps.
2. Because of its northerly location, Canada is dominated by cold climates.
3. Canada is rich in resources like fish, minerals, fertile soils, and forests.

Key Terms and Places

Rocky Mountains mountains that extend north from the United States into western Canada

St. Lawrence River an important international waterway that links the Great Lakes to the Atlantic Ocean

Niagara Falls falls created by the waters of the Niagara River

Canadian Shield region of rocky uplands, lakes, and swamps

Grand Banks large fishing ground off the Atlantic coast near Newfoundland and Labrador

pulp softened wood fibers

newsprint cheap paper used mainly for newspapers

Section Summary
PHYSICAL FEATURES

Canada is the second-largest country in the world. Only Russia is larger. The United States and Canada share several physical features. Among them are the mountains along the Pacific coast and the **Rocky Mountain**s as well as broad plains that stretch across both countries. The two nations also share a natural border formed by the **St. Lawrence River**.

Niagara Falls is another physical feature that the two countries share. The falls are created by the Niagara River as it drops over a rocky ledge.

One of Canada's unique features is the **Canadian Shield**. This rocky region covers about 1.8 million square miles of Canada. Canadian territory extends north to the Arctic Ocean where the land is covered

> Underline the sentence that describes Canada's size compared to other countries in the world.

> List three physical features that are in both Canada and the United States.
> _____
> _____

with ice all year. Very few people live in this harsh environment.

CLIMATE

Canada's climate is greatly affected by its location. The country is far to the north of the equator. It is also at higher latitudes than the United States. Because of this, it generally has cool to freezing temperatures year-round.

The coldest part of Canada is close to the Arctic Circle. Both central and northern Canada have subarctic climates. The far north has tundra and ice cap climates. About half of Canada has very cold climates.

> How has Canada's location influenced its climate?
> _____
> _____
> _____
> _____

RESOURCES

Canada has many natural resources. These resources include fish, minerals, and forests. One of Canada's richest fishing areas is the **Grand Banks** near Newfoundland and Labrador, off the Atlantic coast. Large schools of fish once swam there, but too much fishing has reduced the number of fish in this part of the ocean.

> Circle the names of three types of natural resources that Canada has.
> _____
> _____

Canada has many mineral resources. It also has oil and gas. Many of Canada's mineral resources come from the Canadian Shield, a region of rocky uplands, lakes, and swamps. Canada has more nickel, zinc, and uranium than any other country. Alberta produces most of Canada's oil and natural gas.

All across Canada, forests provide lumber and **pulp** to make paper. The United States, the United Kingdom, and Japan get much of their **newsprint** from Canada.

CHALLENGE ACTIVITY

Critical Thinking: Drawing Inferences How are Canada's natural resources connected to its climate and physical features? Write two paragraphs explaining the connections.

Canadian Shield	Grand Banks	Hudson Bay
newsprint	Niagara Falls	pulp
Rocky Mountains	St. Lawrence River	tundra
uplands		

DIRECTIONS Read each sentence and fill in the blank with the word
in the word pair that best completes the sentence.

1. The _____ forms a natural border between the United States
   and Canada. (Canadian Shield/St. Lawrence River)

2. _____ refers to softened wood fibers used to make paper.
   (Pulp/Newsprint)

3. The _____ extend from the western United States into
   western Canada. (Grand Banks/Rocky Mountains)

4. The Canadian Shield is a region of lakes, swamps, and rocky

   _____. (tundra/uplands)

5. _____ is a physical feature that the United States and Canada
   share. (Hudson Bay/Niagara Falls)

DIRECTIONS Choose five of the terms from the word bank. Use these
terms to write a summary of what you learned in the section.

_____

_____

_____

_____

_____

Canada

MAIN IDEAS

1. Beginning in the 1600s, Europeans settled the region that would later become Canada.

2. Immigration and migration to cities have shaped Canadian culture.

Key Terms and Places

provinces administrative divisions of a country

Quebec province of Canada, first settled by the French

British Columbia province of Canada on the Pacific Coast

Toronto Canada's largest city

Section Summary

HISTORY

Indians and Inuit were the first people to live in Canada. Over time, some native peoples divided into groups known as the First Nations. The Cree, one of those groups, lived on the plains. They survived by hunting bison. The Inuit lived in the far north. They learned to survive in the harsh, cold climate by hunting seals, whales, and other animals.

The Vikings were the first Europeans to come to Canada, but they did not stay. European explorers and fishermen came in the late 1400s. Europeans soon began to trade with Native Canadians. The French built the first permanent settlements in what became Canada. They called the lands they claimed New France. In the 1700s Britain defeated France in the French and Indian War. Although the British took control, most French settlers stayed. Their way of life did not change much. Many descendants of these French settlers live in **Quebec** today.

The British divided their territory into two colonies called Upper and Lower Canada. Canada stayed divided until 1867, when the British passed a law making it a dominion, a territory or area of influence. This act gave Canada its own

> Circle the names of Canada's first people and Canada's first permanent European settlers.

> How did the French and Indian War affect the French colonists in New France?
>
> _____
> _____

> What is a dominion?
>
> _____
> _____

government. The British also divided the country into **provinces**. In 1885, Canadians completed a railroad across Canada. It connected **British Columbia** with the eastern provinces. Canada increased in size by buying lands in the north where many Native Canadians lived.

CULTURE

Canadians come from many places. Some are descendants of early French and British settlers. In the late 1800s and early 1900s many immigrants came from Europe and the United States. Most farmed, while others worked in mines, forests, and factories. Some hoped to find gold in Canada's Yukon Territory. Many Asian immigrants have come to Canada, especially from China, Japan, and India. Many Chinese immigrants came to work on the railroads. Immigrants helped Canada's economy grow. British Columbia was the first Canadian province to have a large Asian minority.

> Circle the countries where some of Canada's immigrants came from prior to World War II.

After World War II a new wave of immigrants came to large cities like **Toronto**. Many came from Asia. Others came from Europe, Africa, the Caribbean, and Latin America. Like earlier immigrants, they came for jobs and new opportunities. In recent years, Canadians have also moved from farms in rural areas to large cities like Vancouver and Ontario. Many of these people have moved to cities to find jobs.

CHALLENGE ACTIVITY

Critical Thinking: Making Inferences How has immigration helped Canada's economy grow? Imagine that you are a person preparing to move to Canada. Write a letter to a friend explaining your reasons for moving and how you expect to contribute to the Canadian economy.

DIRECTIONS On the line provided before each statement, write **T** if a statement is true and **F** if a statement is false. If the statement is false, write the term that would make the statement correct on the line after each sentence.

_____ 1. Since World War II, <u>Quebec</u> has become one of the most culturally diverse cities in the world.

_____

_____ 2. Quebec and Ontario are examples of Canadian <u>colonies</u>.

_____

_____ 3. The Canadians built a transcontinental railroad to connect <u>British Columbia</u> with eastern Canada.

_____

_____ 4. <u>Toronto</u> remains a mainly French-speaking region.

_____

_____ 5. A <u>dominion</u>, such as the Dominion of Canada, is a territory or area of influence.

_____

DIRECTIONS Write three adjectives or descriptive phrases that describe the term.

6. British Columbia _____

7. New France _____

8. Canadian Pacific Railroad _____

9. Vancouver's Chinatown _____

10. First Nations _____

Canada

MAIN IDEAS

1. Canada has a democratic government with a prime minister and a parliament.
2. Canada has four distinct geographic and cultural regions.
3. Canada's economy is largely based on trade with the United States.

Key Terms and Places

regionalism a strong connection that people feel toward their region

maritime on or near the sea

Montreal Canada's second-largest city, one of the world's largest French-speaking cities

Ottawa Canada's national capital

Vancouver city on the Pacific coast with strong trade ties to Asia

Section Summary

CANADA'S GOVERNMENT

Canada has a democratic central government led by a prime minister. This job is like that of a president. The prime minister is the head of Canada's national government. The prime minister also leads Parliament, Canada's governing body. Parliament is made up of the House of Commons and the Senate. Canadians elect members of the House of Commons. The prime minister appoints senators. Provincial governments are like state governments. A premier leads each province.

> Circle the title of the person who is the leader of Canada's national government.

CANADA'S REGIONS

Canada has four regions. Each has its own cultural and physical features. In Quebec province, located in the Heartland region, **regionalism** has created problems between French and English speakers.

The eastern provinces are on the Atlantic coast. They include the **Maritime** Provinces—New Brunswick, Nova Scotia and Prince Edward Island—as well as Newfoundland and Labrador.

> Underline the names of the three Maritime Provinces.

Most people live in cities near the coast. Forestry and fishing are the major economic activities.

More than half of all Canadians live in the Heartland provinces of Ontario and Quebec. This region includes **Montreal**, Toronto, and **Ottawa**. Quebec is a center of French culture. Ontario is Canada's top manufacturing province.

The Western Provinces include British Columbia on the Pacific coast and the prairie provinces—Manitoba, Saskatchewan, and Alberta. Farming is important there, especially growing wheat. In British Columbia, **Vancouver** is a major center for trade with Asia.

The Canadian North consists of the Yukon and Northwest territories and Nunavut, the Inuit homeland. The region is very cold and not many people live there. Nunavut has its own local government.

> List two ways in which the Eastern and Heartland Provinces are different from each other.
> _____
> _____
> _____
> _____

CANADA'S ECONOMY

Many of Canada's economic activities are connected to its natural resources. Mining and manufacturing are key industries along with producing minerals. Most Canadians hold service jobs. Tourism is the fastest-growing service industry. Trade is also important. The United States is Canada's leading trading partner. The United States buys much of its lumber from Canada.

> Which type of economic activity employs the most workers?
> _____
> _____

CHALLENGE ACTIVITY

Critical Thinking: Drawing Conclusions Why do you think Canada and the United States are such strong trading partners? What are the advantages and disadvantages of this strong trading relationship? Explain your answer in a one-page essay.

Section 3, *continued*

heartland	Inuit	Maritime
Montreal	motto	Ottawa
regionalism	Toronto	Vancouver

DIRECTIONS Look at each set of four vocabulary terms. On the line provided, write the letter of the term that does not relate to the others.

_____ 1. a. culture
        b. regionalism
        c. connection
        d. industrial

_____ 2. a. coast
        b. heartland
        c. Atlantic
        d. maritime

_____ 3. a. Montreal
        b. Toronto
        c. Ottawa
        d. Windsor

_____ 4. a. Yukon
        b. Vancouver
        c. Nunavut
        d. tundra

_____ 5. a. Alberta
        b. Manitoba
        c. Saskatchewan
        d. Nova Scotia

DIRECTIONS Choose five terms from the word bank. On the lines below use these terms to write a poem or story that relates to the section.

_____

_____

_____

_____

_____

_____

_____

_____

_____

Mexico

MAIN IDEAS

1. Mexico's physical features include plateaus, mountains, and coastal lowlands.
2. Mexico's climate and vegetation include deserts, tropical forests, and cool highlands.
3. Key natural resources in Mexico include oil, silver, gold, and scenic landscapes.

Key Terms and Places

Río Bravo Rio Grande, forms part of Mexico's border with the U.S.

peninsula piece of land surrounded on three sides by water

Baja California peninsula stretching from northern Mexico into the Pacific Ocean

Gulf of Mexico body of water that forms Mexico's eastern border

Yucatán Peninsula land separating the Gulf of Mexico from the Caribbean Sea

Sierra Madre "mother range" made up of three mountain ranges in Mexico

Section Summary

PHYSICAL FEATURES

Mexico shares a long border with the United States. Part of this border is formed by a river called the **Río Bravo,** known as the Rio Grande in the United States. Mexico's western border is the Pacific Ocean, where a long **peninsula** called **Baja California** stretches south from northern Mexico. In the east, the **Yucatán Peninsula** separates the **Gulf of Mexico** from the Caribbean Sea.

The interior of Mexico is mostly the high, rugged Mexican Plateau, which rises in the west to the Sierra Madre Occidental. In the east it meets the Sierra Madre Oriental. **Sierra Madre** means "mother range." The country's capital, Mexico City, lies at the southern end of the plateau in the Valley of Mexico. The city has earthquakes, and to the south there are active volcanoes.

> Underline the names of Mexico's two peninsulas.

> Where is Mexico City located?
> _____
> _____

From the central highlands, the land slopes down to Mexico's sunny beaches. In the east the Gulf coastal plain is wide, and there are many farms.

The Yucatán Peninsula is mostly flat. The limestone rock there has eroded to form caves and steep depressions called sinkholes, many of which are filled with water.

> How is the terrain in the Yucatán Peninsula different from that of the Sierra Madre?
>
> _____
>
> _____

CLIMATE AND VEGETATION

Mexico has many climates with different types of vegetation. The mountains and plateaus are cool, and freezing temperatures can reach all the way to Mexico City. The mountain valleys are mild, and the southern coast is also pleasant. Summer rains support tropical rain forests, where animals such as jaguars, monkeys, and anteaters live. The Yucatán Peninsula is hot and dry, supporting only scrub forests. The north is also dry, much of it covered by the Sonoran and Chihuahuan deserts.

> Underline the names of the deserts in the north of Mexico.

NATURAL RESOURCES

Oil is an important resource. Mexico sells a lot of oil to the United States. Before oil was discovered, minerals were the most valuable resource. Today Mexico mines more silver than any other country. Copper, lead, gold, and zinc are also mined.

Another important resource is water. Unfortunately, this resource is scarce in parts of Mexico, especially the north. However, the water surrounding Mexico draws many tourists to the country's scenic beaches.

> What is Mexico's most important mineral product?
>
> _____
>
> _____

CHALLENGE ACTIVITY

Critical Thinking: Making Predictions Write a paragraph making a prediction about which of Mexico's resources will be most important in Mexico's future. Support your prediction with information you learned in the section.

DIRECTIONS On the line provided before each statement, write **T** if a statement is true and **F** if a statement is false. If the statement is false, write the term that would make the statement correct on the line after each sentence.

_____ 1. In the Yucatán Peninsula, erosion of limestone rock has created many caves and <u>sinkholes</u>.

_____

_____ 2. The climate in southern Mexico is mostly warm and humid, or humid <u>peninsula</u>.

_____

_____ 3. Baja California is a narrow <u>plateau</u> that stretches into the Pacific Ocean.

_____

_____ 4. <u>Petroleum</u> is one of Mexico's most important natural resources.

_____

_____ 5. The <u>Gulf of Mexico</u> is Mexico's eastern border.

_____

DIRECTIONS Write three words or phrases that describe the term.

6. peninsula _____

7. Río Bravo _____

8. plateau _____

9. Sierra Madre _____

10. Yucatán Peninsula _____

Mexico

MAIN IDEAS
1. Early cultures of Mexico included the Olmec, the Maya, and the Aztec.
2. Mexico's period as a Spanish colony and its struggles since independence have shaped its culture.
3. Spanish and native cultures have influenced Mexico's customs and traditions today.

Key Terms and Places

empire a land with different territories and peoples under a single ruler

mestizos the Spanish name for people of mixed European and Indian ancestry

missions church outposts

haciendas huge expanses of farm or ranch land

Section Summary
EARLY CULTURES

People grew corn, beans, and squash in Mexico as early as 5,000 years ago. About 1500 BC the Olmec settled on the southern coast of the Gulf of Mexico. They built temples and statues. About AD 250 the Maya built cities in Mexico and Central America. They were astronomers and left written records. Maya civilization collapsed after AD 900.

> Underline the achievements of the Olmec and Maya.

Later, the Aztecs moved into central Mexico. In 1325 they founded their capital, Tenochtitlán. They built an **empire** through conquest of other tribes.

COLONIAL MEXICO AND INDEPENDENCE

In 1519 a Spanish soldier, Hernán Cortés, arrived in Mexico with guns, horses, and about 600 soldiers. The Spanish also brought diseases, which hurt the Aztecs. This helped Cortés defeat the Aztecs in 1521. He called the land New Spain.

> How long did it take Cortés to conquer the Aztecs?
>
> _____

Many people in New Spain were of mixed European and Indian ancestry and were called **mestizos**. The Catholic Church was important in the colony. Priests tried to convert the Indians, traveling far north to build **missions**.

Spain was eager to mine gold and silver in Mexico. The native people and enslaved Africans did most of the mining. They also worked the huge farms and ranches, called **haciendas**, that were owned by people of Spanish ancestry.

Mexico gained independence in 1821. Miguel Hidalgo started the revolt by asking for equality in 1810. Later, Texas broke away from Mexico and joined the United States. The two countries fought over its border in the Mexican War. Mexico lost the war and almost half its territory.

In the mid-1800s, the popular president Benito Juárez made many reforms. But in the early 1900s the government helped the hacienda owners take land from the peasants. People were angry and started the Mexican Revolution in 1910. In 1920 a new government took land from the large landowners and gave it back to the peasants.

Who owned the haciendas?
_____

What did the government do that made people angry?
_____
_____

CULTURE

In Mexico language is tied to ethnic groups. Speaking an American Indian language identifies a person as Indian. Mexicans have combined Indian religious practices with Catholic practices. One example is a holiday called Day of the Dead. On this day, Mexicans follow native traditions for remembering ancestors. The holiday is celebrated on November 1 and 2—the same dates as similar Catholic holidays.

Underline the Indian aspects of the Day of the Dead

CHALLENGE ACTIVITY

Critical Thinking: Sequencing Make a time line with important dates and events in Mexican history.

ancestors	chinampas	conquistadors	empire
haciendas	mestizos	missions	revolt

DIRECTIONS Read each sentence and circle the word in the word pair
that best completes each sentence.

1. The Aztecs grew corn, beans, and peppers on raised fields called (ancestors/
chinampas).

2. In 1521 Hernán Cortés and his (conquistadors/mestizos) conquered the Aztecs.

3. During colonial times, Catholic priests at (haciendas/missions) taught the Indians
Spanish and learned their language.

4. To seek independence from Spain, Miguel Hidalgo began a/an (revolt/empire)
in 1810.

DIRECTIONS Look at each set of four vocabulary terms. On the line
provided, write the letter of the term that does not relate to the others.

_____ 5. a. haciendas
      b. ranches
      c. peasants
      d. smog

_____ 7. a. empire
      b. inflation
      c. Aztecs
      d. conquistadors

_____ 6. a. Olmec
      b. revolt
      c. independence
      d. equality

_____ 8. a. ancestors
      b. Day of the Dead
      c. chinampas
      d. celebration

DIRECTIONS Choose five of the words from the word bank. On a
separate sheet of paper, use these words to write a summary of what
you have learned in the section.

Mexico

MAIN IDEAS
1. Government has traditionally played a large role in Mexico's economy.
2. Mexico has four distinct culture regions.

Key Terms and Places

inflation a rise in prices that occurs when currency loses its buying power

slash-and-burn agriculture the practice of burning forest to clear land for planting

cash crop a crop that farmers grow mainly to sell for a profit

Mexico City the world's second-largest city and Mexico's capital

smog a mixture of smoke, chemicals, and fog

maquiladoras U.S.- and foreign-owned factories in Mexico

Section Summary

GOVERNMENT AND ECONOMY

Although Mexico is a democracy, one political party ran the government for 71 years. This ended in 2000 when Vicente Fox was elected president. Like other developing countries, Mexico has foreign debts, unemployment, and **inflation**. Due to the North American Free Trade Agreement (NAFTA), Mexico now sells more products to its neighbors. Trucks bring **cash crops** like fruits and vegetables to the United States. Some farmers who don't own much land and only grow enough to feed their families use **slash-and-burn agriculture**.

Mexicans work in oil fields and in factories. Many Mexicans also come to the U.S. looking for work. Tourists visit Mexico to enjoy its attractions.

> How is Mexico like other developing countries?
> _____
> _____

> How did NAFTA change trade for Mexico?
> _____
> _____

MEXICO'S CULTURE REGIONS

Mexico has four culture regions that differ from one another in population, resources, and climate.

The Greater **Mexico City** region includes the capital and about 50 nearby cities. More than 19 million people make Mexico City the world's second-largest city. Many people move there to look for work, and air pollution has become a problem. The mountains trap the **smog**—a mixture of smoke, chemicals, and fog. Poverty is also a problem.

Many cities in Mexico's central region were colonial mining or ranching centers. Mexico's colonial heritage can be seen today in the churches and public squares of this region. Family farmers grow vegetables and corn in the fertile valleys. In recent years, cities such as Guadalajara have attracted new industries from Mexico City.

> **Underline information about the current economy of Mexico's central region. Circle information about its past economy.**

Trade with the United States has helped northern region cities like Monterrey and Tijuana grow. Foreign-owned factories, called **maquiladoras**, have been built in this region. Many Mexicans cross the border to shop, work, or live in the United States. Some cross the border legally. The U.S. government tries to prevent illegal immigration.

> **What has helped Monterrey and Tijuana grow?**
>
> _____
>
> _____

Many people in the southern Mexico region speak Indian languages and follow traditional customs. Sugarcane and coffee, two major export crops, grow well in the humid southern climate. Oil production in the region has brought population growth to southern Mexico. Maya ruins, sunny beaches, and clear blue waters make tourism a major industry in the Yucatán Peninsula. Many of today's cities were tiny villages just 20 years ago.

> **Underline information about the people in Mexico's southern region.**

CHALLENGE ACTIVITY

Critical Thinking: Compare and Contrast Make a four-columned chart—one column for each cultural region in Mexico. Make three rows and write information for each region about History, Population and Economy, and Geography and Natural Resources. When you are done, circle things that are similar among the regions.

cash crop	inflation	slash-and-burn agriculture
Mexico City	smog	maquiladoras

DIRECTIONS Answer each question by writing a sentence that
contains at least one term from the word bank.

1. Why is Mexico called a developing country?

_____

_____

_____

2. Why is northern Mexico's economy growing today?

_____

_____

_____

3. What problems exist in Mexico City today?

_____

_____

_____

4. How do many farmers in southern Mexico earn a living?

_____

_____

_____

DIRECTIONS Look up the terms *smog*, *cash crop*, and *inflation* in a
dictionary. On a separate sheet of paper, write the dictionary definition
of the term that is closest to the definition used in your textbook.

Central America and the Caribbean

MAIN IDEAS
1. Physical features of the region include volcanic highlands and coastal plains.
2. The climate and vegetation of the region include forested highlands, tropical forests, and humid lowlands.
3. Key natural resources in the region include rich soils for agriculture, a few minerals, and beautiful beaches.

Key Terms and Places

isthmus narrow strip of land that connects two larger land areas

Caribbean Sea sea surrounded by Central America, the Greater and Lesser Antilles, and South America

archipelago large group of islands

Greater Antilles group of large islands in the Caribbean Sea

Lesser Antilles group of small islands in the Caribbean Sea

cloud forest moist, high-elevation tropical forest where low clouds are common

Section Summary

PHYSICAL FEATURES

Central America is an **isthmus** that connects North and South America. It is made up of seven small countries: Belize, Guatemala, El Salvador, Honduras, Nicaragua, Costa Rica, and Panama. At its widest, the isthmus separates the Pacific Ocean and the **Caribbean Sea** by 125 miles (200 km). A chain of mountains and volcanoes runs through the middle of the isthmus. On both sides, a few short rivers run through the coastal plains to the sea. The lack of good water routes and ruggedness of the land make travel difficult.

The Caribbean islands separate the Atlantic Ocean from the Caribbean Sea. On the east lie the **Lesser Antilles**, an **archipelago** of islands that stretch from the Virgin Islands to Trinidad and Tobago. West and north of these are the **Greater Antilles**, which include Cuba, Jamaica, Puerto Rico,

> Underline the names of the seven countries that make up Central America.

> What two bodies of water are separated by the Caribbean islands?
> _____
> _____

and Hispaniola. Many of these islands are actually
the tops of underwater volcanoes. They are located
along the edges of tectonic plates that move against
each other, causing earthquakes and volcanic
eruptions. The Bahama Islands, located in the
Atlantic Ocean, southeast of Florida, were formed
by coral reefs.

What causes earthquakes and volcanoes in the region?
_____
_____

CLIMATE AND VEGETATION

Most of the region is generally sunny and warm.
Most of Central America's Pacific coast, where
plantations and ranches are found, has a tropical
savanna climate. The Caribbean coast has areas of
tropical rain forest. The inland mountains are cool
and humid. Some mountainous areas have dense
cloud forests, or moist, high-elevation tropical
forests where low clouds are common. Many animal
and plant species live there.

Where are cloud forests found?
_____
_____

   Temperatures in the region do not change much
from day to night or from winter to summer.
Change in seasons is marked by changes in rainfall.
Winters are generally dry, but it rains nearly every
day in the summer. From summer to fall, hurricanes
bring heavy rains and wind, which occasionally
cause flooding and great destruction.

RESOURCES

The region's best resources are its land and climate,
which make tourism an important industry. Warm
climate and rich volcanic soil make the region a
good place to grow coffee, bananas, sugarcane, and
cotton. However, the region has few mineral or
energy resources.

What two factors make the region a good place to grow crops?
_____
_____

CHALLENGE ACTIVITY

Critical Thinking: Comparing and Contrasting
Write a description of the year-round climate in
your region and compare and contrast it with that of
the Central American and Caribbean region.

archipelago	Caribbean Sea	cloud forest	Greater Antilles
isthmus	Lesser Antilles	reefs	volcanic ash

DIRECTIONS Read each sentence and fill in the blank with the word in the word pair that best completes the sentence.

1. The land that the seven countries of Central America are on is an

   _____, a narrow strip of land that connects two larger land

   areas. (archipelago/isthmus)

2. A large group of islands, such as the Caribbean Islands, is called an

   _____. (archipelago/isthmus)

3. The _____ is the body of water between Central America and
   the Caribbean Islands. (Greater Antilles/Caribbean Sea)

4. Cuba is part of the _____, one of the two main island
   groups in the Caribbean. (Greater Antilles/Caribbean Sea)

5. The many smaller islands of the Caribbean are called the

   _____. (Lesser Antilles/Greater Antilles)

6. A _____ is a moist, high-elevation tropical forest where low
   clouds are common. (cloud forest/tropical savanna climate)

DIRECTIONS On a separate sheet of paper, write a letter to someone who lives in a desert region. Describe how the geography of the Central America and Caribbean area differs from the desert. Include at least four terms from the word bank to describe the Central America and Caribbean region.

MAIN IDEAS
1. The history of Central America was mostly influenced by Spain.
2. The culture of Central America is a mixture of Native American and European traditions.
3. The countries of Central America today have challenges and opportunities.

Key Terms and Places

ecotourism the practice of using an area's natural environment to attract tourists

civil war a conflict between two or more groups within a country

Panama Canal a waterway connecting the Pacific Ocean, the Caribbean Sea, and the Atlantic Ocean

Section Summary
HISTORY

The Maya people built a civilization in the region from about AD 250 to 900. Many of their descendents, and some of their customs, can still be found. In the 1500s Spain controlled the entire region except for Belize, which became a British colony. The Europeans established gold mines and large tobacco and sugarcane plantations and forced the Central American Indians to do the hard work. They also brought enslaved Africans to work.

In 1821 Honduras, El Salvador, Costa Rica, Guatemala, and Nicaragua gained independence and were a single country until 1839. Panama was part of Colombia until 1903. Belize separated from Britain in 1981. Independence did not help most people, as wealthy landowners took control. In the early to mid-1900s the U.S.-based United Fruit Company controlled most of the banana production in the region. Many people resented the role of foreign companies and thought it was unfair for a few people to have so much power. In the mid- to late 1900s people fought for land reform in Guatemala, El Salvador and Nicaragua.

> Underline the country that controlled most of the region in the 1500s.

> Underline the sentences that explain why people in the region objected to large foreign companies.

CULTURE

Most people in Central America are mestizos, people of mixed Indian and European ancestry. Some Indian people live in areas such as the highlands, and people of African ancestry live mainly along the eastern coast. English is the official language in Belize. Spanish is also spoken there and in the other countries. Many people speak Indian languages.

The Spanish brought Roman Catholicism to people in the region, but Indian traditions are also followed. Corn, tomatoes, chocolate, and hot peppers are foods of the region.

> Underline the languages that are spoken in the region.

CENTRAL AMERICA TODAY

Guatemala has the region's largest population. Most people are mestizos, but many are descendents of the Maya. Conflict there killed some 200,000 people from 1960 to 1996. Coffee is the most important crop.

Belize has the region's lowest population. Recently, **ecotourism** has become a large industry, as more people visit the Maya ruins and coral reefs.

Honduras is mountainous, making transportation difficult. It has little farmland, but fruit is exported.

In the 1980s the poor people of El Salvador fought a **civil war** against the few rich families that owned much of the best land, which is very fertile. The war ended in 1992, and people are rebuilding.

> Underline the countries that fought a civil war in the last century.

Nicaragua was ruled by Sandinistas from 1979 to 1990. After a civil war, it became a democracy.

Costa Rica has been more peaceful than most of its neighbors, which helps its economy. Coffee, bananas, and tourism are its largest industries.

Most Panamanians live near the **Panama Canal**, built and controlled by the United States. In 1999 the U.S. gave control of the canal to Panama.

> Which country has been more peaceful than most of the other countries in the region?
>
> _____

CHALLENGE ACTIVITY

Critical Thinking: Sequencing Make a time line that shows important events in Central American history.

Guided Reading Workbook

| civil wars | ecotourism | Europeans | independence |
| Maya | Panama Canal | plantations | |

DIRECTIONS On the line before each statement, write **T** if the statement is true and **F** if the statement is false. If the statement is false, change the underlined term to make the sentence true. Then write the correct term on the line after the sentence

_____ 1. The <u>Europeans</u> began building large cities with pyramids and temples in many Central American countries.

_____

_____ 2. Most of Central America came under the control of Europeans, who established <u>ecotourism</u> to grow crops such as tobacco and sugarcane.

_____

_____ 3. The Spanish colonies declared <u>independence</u> from Spain, but little changed, leading to wars more than a century later.

_____

_____ 4. As agreed to with the United States, Panama took over the <u>Maya</u>, which links the Pacific Ocean, Caribbean Sea, and Atlantic Ocean.

_____

_____ 5. Belize is one country that supports its economy with <u>plantations</u>, using its natural environment to attract tourists.

_____

DIRECTIONS Write a poem or short story about the history or culture of Central America. Use at least four terms from the word bank.

Central America and the Caribbean

MAIN IDEAS

1. The history of the Caribbean islands includes European colonization followed by independence.
2. The culture of the Caribbean islands shows signs of past colonialism and slavery.
3. Today the Caribbean islands have distinctive governments with economies that depend on agriculture and tourism.

Key Terms and Places

dialect regional variety of a language

commonwealth self-governing territory associated with another country

refugee someone who flees to another country, usually for political or economic reasons

Havana the capital of Cuba

cooperative organization owned by its members and operated for their benefit

Section Summary

HISTORY

The Caribbean islands were the first land Christopher Columbus saw in 1492, though he thought he had sailed to islands near India. By the 1700s the islands were colonized by the Spanish, English, French, Dutch, and Danish. They brought enslaved Africans to work on their sugarcane plantations.

> Underline the sentence that tells who colonized the Caribbean Islands.

Haiti gained independence in 1804. Cuba became independent in 1902. Other islands became independent after World War II. Some, such as Martinique and Guadeloupe, never did. Most people on these French islands do not want independence.

CULTURE

Most islanders are descended from Europeans, Africans, or a mixture of the two. There are also some Asians. Some people speak English, French, or Spanish—others speak Creole, a **dialect**, or regional variety of a language.

Today, islands colonized by France and Spain have many Catholics. In Cuba and elsewhere, people practice a blend of Catholicism and traditional African religion called Santería. Caribbeans enjoy the Carnival holiday. It comes before the Christian season of Lent and features parades and costumes. Some of the region's foods, such as okra and yams, were brought by enslaved Africans. They also made souse, a dish made from the leftover pig parts given to them by slaveholders.

THE CARIBBEAN ISLANDS TODAY

Puerto Rico is a **commonwealth**, a self-governing territory associated with the United States. Some Puerto Ricans are happy about this, while others would like to become a state or a separate country. Though richer than others in the region, Puerto Ricans are not as well off as other U.S. citizens.

> Underline the sentence that describes the general economic status of people living in Puerto Rico.

Haiti, occupying the western part of Hispaniola, is the poorest country in the Americas. Dishonest governments have caused violence, which many Haitians have tried to escape by becoming **refugees.**

> What is the poorest country in the Americas?
>
> _____

The eastern part of Hispaniola is the Dominican Republic. Its industries are tourism and agriculture.

Havana is the capital of Cuba, the largest, most populous island in the Caribbean. Cuba has been run by a Communist government since Fidel Castro came to power in 1959. The government runs the economy, newspapers, and television. Most farms are organized as **cooperatives,** owned by the people who work on them and run for their benefit.

> Underline the sentences that describe Cuba's government.

Some of the rest of the Caribbean islands, such as Jamaica, are independent countries, while others, such as the Virgin Islands, are territories of other countries. Most rely on tourism for their income.

CHALLENGE ACTIVITY

Critical Thinking: Drawing Inferences Imagine you are a Haitian refugee. Write a paragraph describing the reasons you left Haiti and your hopes for the future.

| Creole | commonwealth | cooperative | dialect |
| Havana | Hispaniola | refugee | revolt |

DIRECTIONS Look at each set of words. On the line provided, write the letter of the term that does not relate to the others.

_____ 1. a. dialect   b. language   c. religion   d. Creole

_____ 2. a. treasury   b. territory   c. Puerto Rico   d. commonwealth

_____ 3. a. refugee   b. poverty   c. tourism   d. violence

_____ 4. a. Hispaniola   b. Havana   c. Cuba   d. Castro

_____ 5. a. cooperative   b. territory   c. members   d. organization

DIRECTIONS Write a summary of what you learned in Section 3. Use five of the terms from the word bank.

_____

_____

_____

_____

_____

_____

_____

_____

_____

Caribbean South America

MAIN IDEAS
1. Caribbean South America has a wide variety of physical features and wildlife.
2. The region's location and elevation both affect its climate and vegetation.
3. Caribbean South America is rich in resources, such as farmland, oil, timber, and rivers for hydroelectric power.

Key Terms and Places

Andes mountains on the western side of Colombia

cordillera a mountain system made up of roughly parallel ranges

Guiana Highlands plateaus stretching from Venezuela to Suriname

Llanos plains region between the highlands and Andes

Orinoco River longest river in the region, flows through Venezuela to the Atlantic Ocean

Section Summary

PHYSICAL FEATURES AND WILDLIFE

Caribbean South America includes rugged mountains, highlands, and plains drained by huge river systems. The region's highest point is in western Colombia, where the snow-capped **Andes** reach 18,000 feet. These mountains form a **cordillera**, or a system of roughly parallel mountain ranges. Some peaks in the Andes are active volcanoes. The **Guiana Highlands** are a series of plateaus stretching from Venezuela to Suriname. Some areas have flat-topped layers called *tepuís*, made of sandstone that has resisted erosion.

The **Llanos** is a region of plains that lies between the Andes and the Guiana Highlands. The Llanos is mostly grassland and often floods. The **Orinoco River**, the region's longest, flows for about 1,600 miles and empties into the Atlantic Ocean in eastern Venezuela. The Orinoco and its tributaries drain the plains and highlands. Two other rivers, the Cauca and the Magdalena, drain the Andean region.

> Where are the Guiana Highlands?
> _____
> _____

> Underline the sentence that explains what the Llanos is.

> What two rivers drain the Andean region?
> _____
> _____

Wildlife in Caribbean South America includes meat-eating fish called piranhas, jaguars, ocelots, monkeys, and hundreds of bird species.

CLIMATE AND VEGETATION

Most of Caribbean South America is warm year-round due to its location near the equator. The coldest temperatures are found at high elevations in the Andes. Temperatures can fall as much as four degrees for every additional 1,000 feet above sea level. The grassy Llanos has low elevation, giving it a tropical savanna climate with wet and dry seasons. Humid tropical rain forests cover much of southern Colombia. Heavy rainfall produces huge trees and vegetation so thick that sunlight barely penetrates to the jungle floor.

> **How much can temperature change at higher elevations?**
> _____
> _____

RESOURCES

Resources in Caribbean South America include rich soils, oil reserves in both Venezuela and Colombia, timber from the forests, fish and shrimp from coastal waters, and plentiful supplies of hydroelectric power.

> **Circle the resources of Caribbean South America that are mentioned in the paragraph.**

CHALLENGE ACTIVITY

Critical Thinking: Evaluating Write a brief report that identifies the factors that affect the climate of Caribbean South America and explains how the climate changes throughout the region.

Andes	cordillera	Guiana Highlands
Llanos	Orinoco River	

DIRECTIONS Read each sentence and choose the correct term from the word bank to replace the underlined phrase. Write the term in the space provided and then define the term in your own words.

1. This is the <u>longest river in Caribbean South America</u>. _____

   Your definition: _____

   _____

2. Between the highlands and the Andes lies the <u>region of vast plains with very few</u>

   <u>trees</u>. _____

   Your definition: _____

   _____

3. This is a <u>mountain system made up of parallel ranges</u>. _____

   Your definition: _____

   _____

4. On the western side of Colombia stretch the <u>mountains, many of which are active</u>

   <u>volcanoes</u>. _____

   Your definition: _____

   _____

5. Wind and rain have eroded the <u>Venezuelan highlands</u>, leaving behind unusual

   formations called *tepuís*. _____

   Your definition: _____

   _____

Caribbean South America

MAIN IDEAS

1. Native cultures, Spanish conquest, and independence shaped Colombia's history.
2. In Colombia today, the benefits of a rich culture and many natural resources contrast with the effects of a long period of civil war.

Key Terms and Places

Cartagena major Caribbean naval base and port during the Spanish empire

Bogotá capital of Colombia, located high in the eastern Andes

guerrillas members of an irregular military force

Section Summary

COLOMBIA'S HISTORY

Before the Spanish conquest around 1500, the Chibcha people lived in Colombia. The Chibcha had a well-developed civilization. They made pottery, wove fabrics, and made fine objects from gold and other metals. To expand their new empire, the Spanish defeated the Chibcha and seized much of their treasure. The Spanish claimed the land, started a colony, and built large estates, forcing the Chibcha and enslaved Africans to work on them. They also built a large fort and commercial port at the city of **Cartagena**.

By the late 1700s many people in the Spanish colonies began struggling for independence. The people who lived in the land that is now Ecuador, Panama, Venezuela, and Colombia formed a Republic called Gran Colombia. The republic broke up, and in 1830 New Granada, which included Colombia and Panama, was created. Even after independence there was trouble in Colombia. People could not agree about how much power the Catholic Church or the central government should have. Violence in Colombia broke out from time to time and continues to the present day. Part of the

> **Who was forced to work for the Spanish in Colombia?**
> _____
> _____

> **Underline the names of the countries that were part of Gran Colombia.**

problem is Colombia's rugged geography, which isolates people into separate regions. Many people identify with their region more than their nation.

COLOMBIA TODAY

Most Colombians live in the fertile valleys and river basins among the mountain ranges, where the climate is moderate. **Bogotá**, the capital, is located high in the eastern Andes. Few people live in the rain forests of the south. Each region has a distinct geography as well as a distinct culture. Most people are Roman Catholic and speak Spanish. Dances and songs reflect the cultures of each region. Culture on the Caribbean coast is influenced by African culture while South American Indian culture survives in remote mountain areas. Most people are mestizos or of Spanish, African, or Indian descent.

Colombia's major export is oil. It also supplies most of the world's emeralds. Other minerals include iron ore, coal, and gold. Colombia's most famous agricultural product is coffee, but it also grows bananas, sugarcane, corn, rice, and flowers.

Today, different groups fight each other and the government. One army of **guerrillas**, an irregular military force, wants to overthrow the government. Guerrillas have seized land from farmers and are involved in growing the illegal coca plant, which is used to make the dangerous drug cocaine. Colombia's government continues to fight the guerrillas with laws and military action. The United States government provides money and equipment to help in this effort.

Where do most Colombians live?
_____

Circle Colombia's exports.

Who is helping the Colombian government to fight the guerrillas?
_____

CHALLENGE ACTIVITY

Critical Thinking: Drawing Inferences On a separate piece of paper, write a paragraph describing how life in Colombia might be different if there were no mountains there.

Bogotá	Cartagena	guerillas

DIRECTIONS Answer each question by writing a sentence that contains at least one term from the word bank.

1. Why is civil war a major problem in Colombia today?

_____

_____

_____

2. What did the Spanish do after conquering the Chibcha culture?

_____

_____

_____

3. Where is Colombia's capital city located?

_____

_____

_____

Caribbean South America

Section 3

MAIN IDEAS
1. Spanish settlement shaped the history and culture of Venezuela.
2. Oil production plays a large role in Venezuela's economy and government today.
3. The Guianas have diverse cultures and plentiful resources.

Key Terms and Places

llaneros Venezuelan cowboys

Lake Maracaibo a lake near the Caribbean Sea, rich in oil deposits

Caracas the capital of Venezuela and the economic and cultural center of the country

strike a group of workers stopping work until their demands are met

referundum a recall vote

Section Summary

HISTORY AND CULTURE OF VENEZUELA

The Spanish came to Venezuela in the early 1500s looking for gold, but found little. So they grew indigo, a plant used to make blue dye. They forced Indians and enslaved Africans to do the hard work. In the early 1800s the Venezuelan people, led by Simon Bolívar, revolted against their Spanish rulers and fought for independence, which they officially gained in 1830. Military dictators ran the country throughout the 1800s. Oil was discovered in the 1900s but brought wealth only to the powerful.

> **When did Venezuela officially become independent?**
> _____

Venezuelans are of native Indian, African, and European descent. European descendents tend to live in the cities, and African descendents tend to live on the coast. Most people are Spanish-speaking Roman Catholics, but Indian languages and religious beliefs have been kept alive. Venezuelans enjoy soccer, baseball, rodeos, and the national dance, the *joropo*.

> **Underline the sentence that identifies the different groups who live in Venezuela.**

VENEZUELA TODAY

Many people in rural Venezuela are farmers or ranchers. The ranchers are called **llaneros**—cowboys of the Llanos. Venezuela's economy is based on oil, found mostly near the Orinoco River and **Lake Maracaibo**. The oil industry has made some people wealthy and attracted many immigrants; however, the vast majority of the population lives in poverty. **Caracas**, Venezuela's capital, is the country's economic and cultural center. It has modern subways and buildings, but it is surrounded by slums.

Military dictators ran Venezuela until 1959, when the first president was elected. Since then the government has dealt with economic and political problems. In 2002 President Hugo Chavez started to distribute the country's oil income equally among all Venezuelans. Millions of Venezuelans went on **strike** to protest the president's actions. The country's economy suffered greatly. In 2004 Venezuelans opposed to President Chavez called for a **referendum**, a vote that would remove him from office, but it failed. Recently Chavez created new policies to try to end poverty, illiteracy, and hunger in Venezuela.

> **Why do you think there is significant poverty in Venezuela?**
>
> _____

> **What was the result of Venezuela's referendum in 2004?**
>
> _____

THE GUIANAS

The Guianas consist of the countries of Guyana, Suriname, and French Guiana. These countries have diverse populations with many people descended from Africans, but each country is different. Guyana has many immigrants from India who came to work on sugarcane plantations. Today most people run small farms or businesses. Suriname's population includes Creoles, or people of mixed heritage, and people from China, Indonesia, Africa, and South Asia. Suriname's economy is similar to Guyana's. French Guiana is a territory of France. Most people live in coastal areas, and the country relies heavily on imports.

> **Circle names of the countries that make up the Guianas.**

Critical Thinking: Identifying Points of View

Why would some Venezuelans think Hugo Chavez should no longer be president? Write a short paragraph to explain your answer.

Name _____ Class _____ Date _____

Section 3, *continued*

Caracas	Lake Maracaibo	llaneros
referendum	Strike	

DIRECTIONS On the line provided before each statement, write **T** if a statement is true and **F** if a statement is false. If the statement is false, write the term from the word bank on the line that makes the sentence a true statement.

_____ 1. The Orinoco River Basin and <u>Lake Maracaibo</u> are particularly rich in oil.

_____

_____ 2. <u>Guyana</u> is the economic center and capital city of Venezuela.

_____

_____ 3. In 2002, millions of Venezuelans protested their president's control of oil by calling for a <u>strike</u>, or a recall vote.

_____

_____ 4. <u>Llaneros</u> are cowboys who herd cattle on ranches in the Llanos region.

_____

_____ 5. Venezuela's economy suffered, and many people lost their jobs when oil workers went on <u>referendum</u>.

_____

Guided Reading Workbook

Atlantic South America

MAIN IDEAS
1. Physical features of Atlantic South America include large rivers, plateaus, and plains.
2. Climate and vegetation in the region range from cool, dry plains to warm, humid forests.
3. The rain forest is a major source of natural resources.

Key Terms and Places

Amazon River 4,000-mile-long river that flows eastward across northern Brazil

Río de la Plata an estuary that connects the Paraná River and the Atlantic Ocean

estuary a partially enclosed body of water where freshwater mixes with salty seawater

Pampas wide, grassy plains in central Argentina

deforestation the clearing of trees

soil exhaustion soil that has become infertile because it has lost nutrients needed by plants

Section Summary
PHYSICAL FEATURES

The region of Atlantic South America includes four countries: Brazil, Argentina, Uruguay, and Paraguay. A major river system in the region is the Amazon. The **Amazon River** extends from the Andes Mountains in Peru to the Atlantic Ocean. The Amazon carries more water than any other river in the world.

The Paraná River, which drains much of the central part of South America, flows into an **estuary** called the **Río de la Plata** and the Atlantic Ocean.

The region's landforms mainly consist of plains and plateaus. The Amazon Basin in northern Brazil is a huge, flat floodplain. Farther south are the Brazilian Highlands and an area of high plains called the Mato Grosso Plateau.

> **What four countries make up Atlantic South America?**
> _____
> _____
> _____
> _____

> **What is the Amazon Basin?**
> _____
> _____

The low plains region, Gran Chaco, stretches across parts of Paraguay and northern Argentina. The grassy plains of the **Pampas** are found in central Argentina. Patagonia is a region of dry plains and plateaus south of the Pampas. These plains rise in the west to form the Andes Mountains.

> Circle the names of three plains regions in Atlantic South America.

CLIMATE AND VEGETATION

Atlantic South America has many climates. Southern and highland areas have cool climates while northern and coastal areas have tropical and moist climates.

Patagonia has a cool, desert climate. To the north in the Pampas, the climate is humid subtropical. In Argentina, the Gran Chaco has a humid tropical climate. Central Brazil has a tropical savanna climate, but to the northeast the climate is hot and dry. In southeast Brazil, the climate is cooler and more humid. In northern Brazil, where the Amazon Basin is located, the climate is humid tropical.

> What type of climate does northern Brazil have?
>
> _____
>
> _____

NATURAL RESOURCES

The Amazon rain forest is one of Atlantic South America's greatest natural resources. It provides food, wood, rubber, plants for medicines, and other products. **Deforestation** has become an issue that threatens the resources of the rain forest.

Land near the coastal areas in the region is used for commercial farming. However, planting the same crop year after year has caused **soil exhaustion** in some areas.

Other resources in Atlantic South America include gold, silver, copper, iron, and oil. Dams on some rivers also provide hydroelectric power.

> What threatens the Amazon rain forest?
>
> _____
>
> _____

CHALLENGE ACTIVITY

Critical Thinking: Drawing Inferences Write an essay describing ways to preserve the Amazon rain forest while still helping people who rely on its resources to survive.

Amazon River	deforestation	estuary
floodplain	Gran Chaco	marshlands
Pampas	Río de la Plata	soil exhaustion

DIRECTIONS Answer each question by writing a sentence that contains at least one term from the word bank.

1. Into what body of water does the Paraná River flow?

_____

_____

2. What two large plains regions are located in Argentina?

_____

_____

3. How would you describe the world's largest river system?

_____

_____

4. What problems are affecting the natural resources of Atlantic South America?

_____

_____

5. How would you describe the climate and vegetation of Atlantic South America?

_____

_____

Atlantic South America

MAIN IDEAS
1. Brazil's history has been affected by Brazilian Indians, Portuguese settlers, and enslaved Africans.
2. Brazil's society reflects a mix of people and cultures.
3. Brazil today is experiencing population growth in its cities and new development in rain forest areas.

Key Terms and Places

São Paulo the largest urban area in South America, located in southeastern Brazil

megacity a giant urban area that includes surrounding cities and suburbs

Rio de Janeiro Brazil's second-largest city, located northeast of São Paulo

favelas huge slums

Brasília the capital of Brazil

Manaus a major port and industrial city, located 1,000 miles from the mouth of the Amazon River

Section Summary

HISTORY

Brazil is the largest country in South America. It has a population of more than 186 million people. The first people in Brazil were American Indians who arrived in the region thousands of years ago.

In 1500 Portuguese explorers became the first Europeans to find Brazil. Colonists brought Africans to the region to work as slaves on sugar plantations. These plantations helped make Portugal rich.

Gold and precious gems were discovered in the late 1600s and early 1700s in the southeast, and a mining boom drew people to Brazil from all over the world. Brazil became a major coffee producer in the late 1800s. Brazil gained independence from Portugal without a fight in 1822. Since the end of Portuguese rule, Brazil has been governed by both dictators and elected officials. Today Brazil has an elected president and legislature.

> Who were the first people to live in Brazil?
>
> _____
>
> _____

> What discovery brought people to Brazil from all over the world?
>
> _____
>
> _____

PEOPLE AND CULTURE

Nearly 40 percent of Brazil's people are of mixed African and European descent. Brazil also has the largest Japanese population outside of Japan. Brazil's official language is Portuguese.

Brazil has the world's largest population of Roman Catholics. Some Brazilians practice macumba, a religion that combines beliefs and practices of African and Indian religions with Christianity.

Brazilians celebrate Carnival, a celebration that mixes traditions from Africa, Brazil, and Europe. Immigrant influences can also be found in Brazilian foods.

> **What percentage of Brazil's people are of mixed African and European descent?**
> _____

> **What is macumba?**
> _____
> _____

BRAZIL TODAY

Brazil can be divided into four regions. The southeast is the most populated. More than 17 million people live in the city of **São Paulo**, which is considered a **megacity**, or giant urban area that includes surrounding cities and suburbs. **Rio de Janeiro** is Brazil's second-largest city, also located in the southeast. The southeast has a good economy, but it also has poverty. Many people live in city slums, or **favelas**.

The northeast is Brazil's poorest region. Drought has made farming difficult. However, many tourists are attracted to the region. Tourism is an important industry.

The interior region is a frontier land, with much potential for farming. The capital of Brasil, **Brasília**, is located there.

The Amazon region covers the northern part of Brazil. **Manaus** is a major port and industrial city 1,000 miles from the mouth of the Amazon River. The Amazon rain forest is a valuable resource to people who live and work there, but deforestation threatens the wildlife and Brazilian Indians living there.

> **What is Brazil's second-largest city?**
> _____

> **Circle the word describing an important industry in northeast Brazil.**

> **What are the four regions of Brazil?**
> _____
> _____
> _____
> _____

CHALLENGE ACTIVITY

Critical Thinking: Drawing Inferences Why do most Brazilians live in the southeast? Turn to a partner and give reasons for your answer.

Guided Reading Workbook

Brasília	Carnival	favelas
macumba	Manaus	megacity
Rio de Janeiro	São Paulo	

DIRECTIONS Read each sentence and choose the correct term from the word bank to replace the underlined phrase. Write the term in the space provided and then define the term in your own words.

1. Although <u>this city</u> was designed for only 500,000 people, more than 2 million live there. _____

   Your definition: _____

   _____

2. <u>These areas</u> within Brazil's southeastern cities are marked by poverty.

   _____

   Your definition: _____

   _____

3. <u>This cultural event</u> mixes traditions from Africa, Brazil, and Europe.

   _____

   Your definition: _____

   _____

4. Popular with tourists, <u>this major port city</u> was once Brazil's capital.

   _____

   Your definition: _____

   _____

5. São Paulo is a <u>giant city</u>. _____

   Your definition: _____

   _____

   _____

Atlantic South America

MAIN IDEAS
1. European immigrants have dominated the history and culture of Argentina.
2. Argentina's capital, Buenos Aires, plays a large role in the country's government and economy today.
3. Uruguay has been influenced by its neighbors.
4. Paraguay is the most rural country in the region.

Key Terms and Places

gauchos Argentine cowboys

Buenos Aires the capital of Argentina

Mercosur an organization that promotes trade and economic cooperation among the southern and eastern countries of South America

informal economy a part of the economy based on odd jobs that people perform without government regulation through taxes

landlocked completely surrounded by land with no direct access to the ocean

Section Summary
ARGENTINA'S HISTORY AND CULTURE

Argentina was originally home to groups of Indians. In the 1500s, Spanish conquerors spread into southern South America in search of silver and gold. They built settlements in Argentina. Spanish monarchs granted land to the colonists. Landowners forced Indians living there to work.

During the colonial era, the Pampas became an important agricultural region. Argentine cowboys called **gauchos** herded cattle and horses there.

Argentina fought for and gained independence in the 1800s. Many Indians were killed. Immigrants from Italy, Germany, and Spain began to arrive in Argentina.

During the "Dirty War" in the 1970s, many Argentines were tortured and killed after being accused of disagreeing with the government. Argentina's military government gave up power to an elected government in the 1980s.

Why did Spanish conquerors come to the region in the 1500s?
_____
_____

Immigrants began to arrive from what European countries?
_____
_____

ARGENTINA TODAY

Buenos Aires is the capital of Argentina. It is the second-largest urban area in South America. In the 1990s, government leaders made economic reforms to help businesses grow. Argentina joined **Mercosur**—an organization that promotes trade and economic cooperation among the southern and eastern countries of South America. However, heavy debt and government spending brought Argentina into an economic crisis. Many people lost their jobs and joined the **informal economy**—a part of the economy based on odd jobs that people perform without government regulation through taxes.

What is the purpose of Mercosur?
_____
_____
_____

URUGUAY

Uruguay lies between Argentina and Brazil. Its capital is Montevideo. Portugal claimed Uruguay during the colonial era, but the Spanish took over by the 1770s. Few Uruguayan Indians remained. Uruguay declared its independence from Spain in 1825. Today Uruguay is a democracy.

What is the capital of Uruguay?
_____

PARAGUAY

Paraguay is **landlocked**, which means completely surrounded by land, with no direct access to the ocean. It was claimed by the Spanish in the mid-1530s and remained a Spanish colony until 1811, when it won indepedence. Today Paraguay is a democracy. Ninety-five percent of Paraguayans are mestizos. People of European descent and Indians make up the rest of the population. Most Paraguayans speak both Spanish and Guarani. Agriculture is an important part of the economy.

Underline the definition of *landlocked*.

What type of government do Uruguay and Paraguay have today?
_____

CHALLENGE ACTIVITY

Critical Thinking: Drawing Inferences Which Atlantic South American country do you think has the strongest economy? Write a paragraph giving reasons to support your answer.

DIRECTIONS Read each sentence and fill in the blank with the word
in the word pair that best completes the sentence.

1. _____ is a popular dish in Argentina. (Mestizo/Parrilla)

2. The _____ in Argentina is based on odd jobs performed
without government regulation through taxes. (Mercosur/informal economy)

3. A few rich families and companies control much of _____
wealth. (Paraguay's/Uruguay's)

4. _____ is the official language in Uruguay and Paraguay.
(Spanish/Portuguese)

5. An important export for both Argentina and Uruguay is

_____ (beef/silver)

DIRECTIONS Look at each set of four terms following each number.
On the line provided, write the letter of the term that does not relate to
the others.

_____ 6. a. Argentina   b. Montevideo   c. gauchos   d. Buenos Aires

_____ 7. a. trade   b. Mercosur   c. cooperation d. rural

_____ 8. a. Paraguay   b. Guarini   c. coastal   d. landlocked

_____ 9. a. agriculture   b. urban   c. Asunción   d. Uruguay

_____ 10. a. economy   b. Spanish   c. mestizo   d. Portuguese

Pacific South America

MAIN IDEAS
1. The Andes are the main physical feature of Pacific South America.
2. The region's climate and vegetation change with elevation.
3. Key natural resources in the region include lumber, oil, and minerals.

Key Terms and Places

altiplano a broad, high plateau that lies between the ridges of the Andes

strait a narrow body of water that connects two larger bodies of water

Atacama Desert a very dry desert in northern Chile

El Niño an ocean weather pattern that affects the Pacific coast

Section Summary

PHYSICAL FEATURES

The Andes Mountains run through all of the Pacific South American countries, with some peaks above 20,000 feet. In the south, the mountains are rugged and covered by ice caps. In the north, they are rounded, and the range splits into two ranges. A high plateau, called the **altiplano**, lies between the two ranges. Earthquakes and volcanoes sometimes disturb Andean glaciers, causing ice and mud slides.

The region has Amazon tributaries, but few other major rivers. Rivers flowing into the altiplano never reach the sea, but fill two large lakes. Between the southern tip of Chile and Tierra del Fuego lies the Strait of Magellan. A **strait** is a waterway linking two large bodies of water. Ecuador's Galápagos Islands in the Pacific Ocean have wildlife not found anywhere else in the world.

> Underline the sentences that explain the differences between the Andes Mountains in the south and in the north.

CLIMATE AND VEGETATION

Climate varies more with elevation than with latitude in this region. There are five climate zones, starting at the hot and humid zone near sea level, where bananas and sugarcane are grown. Coffee is

> What is the main reason climate varies in the region?
> _____

the main crop of the second climate zone, with cooler, moist air and mountain forests. Many large cities are located there. Many people also live in the third, cooler climate zone. Some grow potatoes and wheat among the grasslands and forests. Grassland and shrubs, but no trees, grow in the fourth zone. In the highest zone, near the mountaintops, no vegetation grows, and most of this zone is covered in snow year-round.

The **Atacama Desert** in northern Chile receives rain only about once every 20 years. Fog and low clouds blow in from the Pacific Ocean, making this coastal desert one of the driest, cloudiest places on Earth. In Peru, snow melting in the Andes collects in rivers flowing down to the Pacific Ocean, allowing a small number of people to live there.

Every two to seven years, the water off the Pacific coast is warm, rather than cool. This change of pattern, called **El Niño**, causes the fish off the coast to find cooler waters, leaving local fishermen with less to catch. El Niño also causes extreme and unusual weather around the world.

> Underline specific details that describe the five climate zones in the region.

> How often does it rain in the Atacama Desert?
> _____

NATURAL RESOURCES

The region's natural resources include lumber from forests in southern Chile, eastern Peru, and Ecuador. Bolivia produces the minerals tin, gold, silver, lead, and zinc. Chile exports more copper than any other country in the world. Ecuador's main export is oil, and it also has reserves of natural gas. Most of the region, however, has little good farmland, and so there are few agricultural exports.

> Underline minerals found in Bolivia.

CHALLENGE ACTIVITY

Critical Thinking: Comparing and Contrasting
Create an illustrated brochure that tells about the five climate zones in the region.

altiplano	Andes	Atacama Desert
El Niño	Galápagos Islands	Tierra del Fuego
strait	tectonic plates	

DIRECTIONS On the line provided before each statement, write **T** if a statement is true and **F** if a statement is false. If the statement is false, write the correct term from the word bank on the line after each sentence that makes the sentence a true statement.

_____ 1. The <u>Andes</u> run through Ecuador, Peru, Bolivia, and Chile.

_____

_____ 2. Earthquakes and volcanoes threaten the Andes because two <u>altiplanos</u> meet at the region's edge.

_____

_____ 3. Ecuador's <u>Galápagos Islands</u> have wildlife not found anywhere else.

_____

_____ 4. Every few years, an ocean and weather pattern called <u>Tierra del Fuego</u> warms the normally cool Pacific waters.

_____

_____ 5. The <u>strait</u> in Northern Chile is about 600 miles long.

_____

Pacific South America

MAIN IDEAS

1. The countries of Pacific South America share a history influenced by the Inca civilization and Spanish colonization.

2. The culture of Pacific South America includes American Indian and Spanish influences.

Key Terms and Places

viceroy governor of a Spanish colony

Creoles American-born descendants of Europeans

Section Summary

HISTORY

Peru's first advanced civilization reached its height in the Andes about 900 BC. The people raised crops in stone terraces built into the steep mountainsides. Near the coast, people used irrigation to control flooding and to store water. These early people supported themselves and their towns by growing crops. One early mountain culture, the Tiahuanaco, made huge stone carvings near a lake. Other people, near the Peruvian coast, scratched the outlines of animals and other shapes into the surface of the desert. These designs, called the Nazca lines, are so large that they can only be seen from high above.

> Underline the sentence that describes how people in Peru's first advanced civilization farmed on rugged land.

By the early 1500s, the Incas controlled the area from northern Ecuador to central Chile. The Inca Empire was the home of about 12 million people. They built stone-paved roads and suspension bridges across the steep Andean valleys. They used irrigation to turn the desert into farmland. Although the Incas were an advanced civilization, they had no written language, no wheeled vehicles, and no horses. Teams of runners carried messages, as in a relay race, to distant parts of the empire. One team could cover as much as 150 miles a day.

> How many people were in the Inca Empire by the early 1500s?
>
> _____

One day in the early 1500s, a new Inca ruler was on his way to be crowned. He met the Spanish explorer Francisco Pizarro, who took him captive. The new Inca ruler ordered a room to be filled with gold and silver objects, thinking it was to be his ransom. Instead, Pizarro had the Inca ruler killed. By 1535 the Spanish had conquered the entire Inca Empire. The Spanish forced many Indians to work in mines or on plantations. The Spanish **viceroy**, or governor, made the Indians follow Spanish laws and customs.

By the early 1800s people began to revolt against Spanish rule. **Creoles**, American-born descendants of Europeans, were the main leaders. These revolts helped Chile, Ecuador, Bolivia, and Peru gain independence by 1825.

> Underline the sentence that tells what the new Inca ruler did after being taken captive by Pizarro.

CULTURE

Most people in the region speak Spanish, an official language in every country in the region. However, millions of South American Indians speak a native language. Some speak only their native language, and some also speak Spanish. Bolivia, which has the highest percentage of Indians in South America, has three official languages: Spanish and two Indian languages.

> Which country has three official languages?
> _____

The religion of this region also reflects both Spanish and native Indian influences. Roman Catholic traditions come from the Spanish, but some people in the Andes still practice ancient religious customs. In June, for example, they participate in a sun worship festival that was celebrated by the Incas. They wear traditional costumes, sometimes with wooden masks. They also play wooden flutes and other traditional instruments.

> Underline the sentence that identifies an ancient Inca religious festival still observed today.

CHALLENGE ACTIVITY

Critical Thinking: Comparing Write a short essay comparing the Inca civilization before and after the Spanish conquest.

Guided Reading Workbook

DIRECTIONS Read each sentence and fill in the blank with the word
in the word pair that best completes the sentence.

1. Around 900 BC, _____ supported Peru's first advanced
   civilization. (agriculture/hunting)

2. A series of ancient designs called the _____ can be recognized
   only from the sky. (Nazca lines/Tiahuanaco)

3. The Incas controlled an area that stretched from northern Ecuador to central

   _____. (Peru/Chile)

4. The fall of the Inca Empire began with Francisco Pizarro's capture of the Inca

   _____. (viceroy/king)

5. _____ refers to American-born descendants of Europeans.
   (Tiahuanaco/Creole)

DIRECTIONS Write three words or phrases that describe the term.

6. Creole _____

7. Tiahuanaco _____

8. Nazca lines _____

9. Inca Empire _____

10. viceroy _____

Pacific South America

> **MAIN IDEAS**
> 1. Ecuador struggles with poverty and political instability.
> 2. Bolivia's government is trying to gain stability and improve the economy.
> 3. Peru has made progress against poverty and violence.
> 4. Chile has a stable government and a strong economy.

Key Terms and Places

Quito the capital of Ecuador

La Paz one of Bolivia's two capital cities

Lima the capital of Peru

coup the sudden overthrow of a government by a small group of people

Santiago the capital of Chile

Section Summary

ECUADOR TODAY

Although Ecuador is a democracy, it has not had a
stable or popular government for a long time. From
1996–2007, the country had 9 different presidents.
In 2005 the president was forced out of office
because reforms had not improved conditions for
the citizens of Ecuador.

Ecuador has three economic regions. Most of the
agriculture and industry is found along the coastal
plain region. The Andes region, where the capital,
Quito, is located, is poor. Tourism is a major
industry there. The third region, the Amazon basin,
produces Ecuador's major export, oil.

> Underline the region of
> Ecuador that has tourism
> as a major industry.

BOLIVIA TODAY

Bolivia has two capitals—the supreme court meets
in Sucre and the congress meets in **La Paz**, the
highest capital in the world. After many years of
military rule, Bolivia is now a democracy. Many
people do not think the government is doing enough
to help the poor. Several presidents have had to
resign because of political protests, and

> What are Bolivia's two
> capitals?
> _____

development has been slow. Bolivia is the poorest country in South America, although it does have resources such as metals and natural gas.

PERU TODAY

Peru is the largest and most populous country in Pacific South America, and its capital, **Lima**, is the region's largest city. Lima was the colonial capital of Peru and has many beautiful buildings. Many Peruvians have moved there to find jobs in government or industry. However, many people in Lima are poor, living in slums around the city center. Often they cannot get water or electricity. Other poor people have built houses at the edge of the city in areas called "young towns." In the 1980s and 1990s, a group called the Shining Path terrorized people, especially in the highlands. The government fought it, and Peru is making economic progress. Mineral deposits are located near the coast, and hydroelectric projects provide energy. In the highlands, people grow potatoes and corn.

> Underline the sentences that describe the living conditions of poor people in Lima.

> What group terrorized people living in the highlands in the 1980s and 1990s?
> _____

CHILE TODAY

In the 1970s Chile's elected president was overthrown in a U.S.-backed military **coup**. These military leaders later imprisoned or killed thousands of their political opponents. In the late 1980s, Chileans restored democracy, and now they have one of the most stable governments in South America. About one-third of Chileans live in central Chile, near the capital, **Santiago**. This area has a Mediterranean climate good for crops such as grapes for making wine. Besides farming, fishing, and forestry, Chile's industries include copper mining, which accounts for one-third of Chile's exports.

> Underline Chile's industries.

CHALLENGE ACTIVITY

Critical Thinking: Comparing and Contrasting

You are a recent arrival to a "young town" in Lima. Write a letter to a friend in another country about Lima and your home.

Callao	coup	Guayaquil
La Paz	Lima	Quito
Santiago	Shining Path	Sucre

DIRECTIONS Look at each set of four terms following each number. On the line provided, write the letter of the term that does not relate to the others.

_____ 1. a. Sucre   b. La Paz   c. Peru   d. Bolivia

_____ 2. a. Guayaquil   b. port   c. Lima   d. coastal lowlands

_____ 3. a. coup   b. terrorist   c. violence   d. Shining Path

_____ 4. a. Chile   b. export   c. oil   d. Amazon basin

_____ 5. a. trade   b. Quito   c. economy   d. NAFTA

DIRECTIONS Answer each question by writing a sentence that contains at least one term from the word bank.

6. Where does Bolivia's congress meet?

_____

_____

7. How would you describe Pacific South America's largest city?

_____

_____

8. What happened to the president of Chile in the 1970s?

_____

_____

Southern Europe

MAIN IDEAS

1. Southern Europe's physical features include rugged mountains and narrow coastal plains.
2. The region's climate and resources support such industries as agriculture, fishing, and tourism.

Key Terms and Places

Mediterranean Sea sea that borders Southern Europe

Pyrenees mountain range separating Spain and France

Apennines mountain range running along the whole Italian Peninsula

Alps Europe's highest mountains, some of which are located in northern Italy

Mediterranean climate type of climate found across Southern Europe, with warm, sunny days and mild nights for most of the year

Section Summary

PHYSICAL FEATURES

Southern Europe is composed of three peninsulas—the Iberian, the Italian, and the Balkan—and some large islands. All of the peninsulas have coastlines on the **Mediterranean Sea**.

These peninsulas are largely covered with rugged mountains. The **Pyrenees** form a boundary between Spain and France. The **Apennines** run along the Italian Peninsula. The **Alps**—Europe's highest mountains—are in northern Italy. The Pindus Mountains cover much of Greece. The region also has coastal plains and river valleys, where most of the farming is done and where most of the people live. Crete, which is south of Greece, and Sicily, at the southern tip of Italy, are two of the larger islands in the region. Many of the region's islands are the peaks of undersea mountains.

In addition to the Mediterranean Sea, the Adriatic, Aegean, and Ionian seas are important to Southern Europe. They give the people food and an

> **What are the three peninsulas of Southern Europe?**
> _____
> _____
> _____

> **Circle the four mountain ranges in Southern Europe.**

easy way to travel around the region. The Po and the Tagus are two important rivers in Southern Europe. The Po flows across northern Italy. The Tagus, the region's longest river, flows across the Iberian Peninsula.

CLIMATE AND RESOURCES

The climate in Southern Europe is called a **Mediterranean climate**. The climate is warm and sunny in the summer and mild and rainy in the winter. Southern Europe's climate is one of its most valuable resources. It supports the growing of many crops, and it attracts tourists.

The seas are another important resource in Southern Europe. Many of the region's cities are ports, shipping goods all over the world. In addition, the seas support profitable fishing industries.

CHALLENGE ACTIVITY

Critical Thinking: Analyzing Explain how Southern Europe's climate supports the region's economy.

> What are the characteristics of a Mediterranean climate?
> _____
> _____

Name _____ Class _____ Date _____

Section 1, *continued*

Mediterranean Sea	Pyrenees	Apennines
Alps	Mediterranean climate	plains
undersea mountains		

DIRECTIONS On the line provided before each statement, write **T** if a statement is true and **F** if a statement is false. If the statement is false, write the term from the word bank that would make the statement true on the line after each sentence.

_____ 1. The <u>Alps</u> form a boundary between Spain and France.

_____

_____ 2. Islands and <u>peninsulas</u> form the region of Southern Europe.

_____

_____ 3. The <u>Apennines</u> are Europe's highest mountain range.

_____

_____ 4. The countries of Southern Europe all share a common location on the <u>Adriatic Sea</u>.

_____

_____ 5. The <u>Pyrenees</u> run along the Italian Peninsula.

_____

DIRECTIONS Read each sentence and fill in the blank with the word in the word pair that best completes the sentence.

6. Many of Southern Europe's islands are formed by _____. (undersea mountains/plains)

7. The _____ is ideal for growing a variety of crops. (Mediterranean Sea/Mediterranean climate)

Guided Reading Workbook

Southern Europe

MAIN IDEAS
1. Early in its history, Greece was the home of a great civilization, but it was later ruled by foreign powers.
2. The Greek language, the Orthodox Church, and varied customs have helped shape Greece's culture.
3. In Greece today, many people are looking for new economic opportunities.

Key Terms and Places

Orthodox Church a branch of Christianity that dates to the Byzantine Empire

Athens Greece's capital and largest city

Section Summary

HISTORY

Greece has been called the birthplace of Western culture. Ancient Greeks created statues and paintings that inspired later artists. They invented new forms of history and drama. They made advances in geometry. They developed a system of reason that is the basis for modern science, and they created democracy.

In the 300s BC, Greece was conquered by Alexander the Great. Later, it was ruled by the Romans, the Byzantines, and the Ottoman Turks. Many Greeks were not happy with Turkish rule. In the 1800s they rebelled against the Turks and drove them out. Greece then became a monarchy.

Greece experienced instability for much of the 1900s. A military dictatorship ruled from 1967 to 1974. More recently Greece has become democratic again.

> Name two achievements of ancient Greece.
>
> _____
> _____

> Circle the groups who ruled Greece before it became a monarchy.

CULTURE

The Greek people today speak a form of the same language as their ancient ancestors, but their ancient religions have disappeared. Nearly everyone in Greece is a member of the **Orthodox Church**, a

> To what church do most people in Greece belong?
>
> _____

branch of Christianity that dates to the Byzantine Empire. Religion is important to the Greek people and religious holidays are popular times for celebration and family gatherings.

The customs of the Greeks have been influenced by the country's geography and by past foreign rulers. Their customs rely on food native to Greece, and they have borrowed ideas for ingredients and food preparation from the groups who have ruled them. For centuries, the family has been central to Greek culture, and today it remains the cornerstone of Greek society.

> What is the cornerstone of Greek society?
> _____

GREECE TODAY

About three-fifths of all people in Greece live in cities. **Athens** is the largest city in Greece and its capital. Athens has both modern skyscrapers and ancient ruins. It is a major center of industry, and as a result, suffers from air pollution.

People in rural areas live much like they did in the past. Many live in isolated mountain villages. They grow crops, raise sheep and goats, and socialize in the village square.

Today, Greece's economy is growing but still lags behind other European nations. Greece has few mineral resources, and only one-fifth of the land is suitable for growing crops. However, Greece is a leading country in the shipping industry, with one of the largest shipping fleets in the world.

Another profitable industry is tourism. Many people from around the world are attracted to the ancient ruins of Athens and to the sandy beaches of Greece's islands.

> Underline two important industries in Greece.

CHALLENGE ACTIVITY

Critical Thinking: Synthesizing Explain how religion and family work together to form a central part of Greek culture.

Athens	Alexander the Great	Byzantine Empire
Roman Empire	Orthodox Church	monarchy
philosophy	democracy	

DIRECTIONS Write three words or phrases that describe the term.

1. democracy _____

2. monarchy _____

3. philosophy _____

DIRECTIONS Look at each set of vocabulary terms. On the line provided, write the letter of the term that does not relate to the others.

_____ 4. a. theater   _____ 5. a. Orthodox Church
      b. philosophy   b. Parthenon
      c. democracy   c. Byzantine Empire
      d. population   d. Christianity

DIRECTIONS Choose five of the words from the word bank. Use the words to write a summary of what you learned in the section.

_____

_____

_____

_____

_____

_____

_____

_____

_____

_____

Southern Europe

MAIN IDEAS
1. Italian history can be divided into three periods: ancient Rome, the Renaissance, and unified Italy.
2. Religion and local traditions have helped shape Italy's culture.
3. Italy today has two distinct economic regions—northern Italy and southern Italy.

Key Terms and Places

pope the spiritual head of the Roman Catholic Church

Vatican City an independent state within the city of Rome

Sicily an island at Italy's southern tip

Naples largest city in southern Italy and an important port

Milan major industrial city in northern Italy and a fashion center

Rome the capital of Italy

Section Summary
HISTORY

Ancient Rome grew from a tiny village in 700 BC to an empire that stretched from Britain in the northwest to the Persian Gulf. Ancient Rome's achievements in art, architecture, literature, law, and government still influence the world today. When the Roman Empire collapsed in the AD 400s, cities in Italy formed their own states. Later they became centers of trade. Merchants became rich and started supporting artists. The merchants' support of the arts helped lead to a period of great creativity in Europe called the Renaissance. During this time, artists and writers created some of the greatest works of art and literature in the world.

Italy remained divided until the mid-1800s when a rise in nationalism, or strong patriotic feelings for a country, led to a fight for unification. Italy was officially unified in 1861. In the 1920s Italy became a dictatorship under Benito Mussolini. This lasted

> Underline five areas in which the achievements of ancient Rome still influence the world today.

> What helped lead to the Renaissance?
> _____
> _____
> _____

until Italy's defeat in World War II, after which Italy became a democracy.

CULTURE

The Roman Catholic Church has historically been the strongest influence on Italian culture. The **pope**, who is the spiritual head of the Roman Catholic Church, lives in **Vatican City**, which is an independent state located within Rome. Religious holidays and festivals are major events.

Local traditions and regional geography have also influenced Italian culture. For example, Italian food varies widely from region to region. Those variations are based on local preferences and products. Other traditions reflect Italy's past. Italians have long been trendsetters in contemporary art forms, including painting, composing, fashion, and film.

> Underline three influences on Italian culture.

ITALY TODAY

Southern Italy is poorer than northern Italy. It has less industry and relies on agriculture and tourism for its survival. Farming is especially important in **Sicily**, an island at the southern tip of Italy. **Naples** is the largest city in southern Italy and a busy port.

Northern Italy has a strong economy, including major industrial centers, the most productive farmland, and the most popular tourist destinations. **Milan** is a major industrial center and a worldwide center for fashion design. Turin and Genoa are also industrial centers. Florence, Pisa, and Venice are popular tourist destinations. **Rome**, Italy's capital, is located between northern Italy and southern Italy.

> Why is the economy of northern Italy strong?
>
> _____
> _____

CHALLENGE ACTIVITY

Critical Thinking: Analyzing and Evaluating

Identify three important periods in Italy's history, and explain why each one is important to Italy today.

Rome	Renaissance	nationalism	dictatorship
pope	Vatican City	Sicily	Naples
Milan			

DIRECTIONS Read each sentence and fill in the blank with the word
in the word pair that best completes the sentence.

1. _____, or strong patriotic feelings for a country, led people
   across Italy to fight for unification. (Nationalism/ Renaissance)

2. The _____ is the head of the Roman Catholic church.
   (pope/prime minister)

3. _____ is an independent state located within the city of
   Rome. (Venice/Vatican City)

4. _____, Italy's capital, has ties to both northern and southern
   Italy. (Rome/Naples)

5. The island of _____ at Italy's southern tip depends on
   agriculture for its survival. (Milan/Sicily)

6. _____ is a center for industry and fashion design.
   (Naples/Milan)

DIRECTIONS Choose five of the words from the word bank. On a
separate piece of paper use these words to write a poem, story, or letter
that relates to the section.

Southern Europe

MAIN IDEAS
1. Over the centuries, Spain and Portugal have been part of many large and powerful empires.
2. The cultures of Spain and Portugal reflect their long histories.
3. Having been both rich and poor in the past, Spain and Portugal today have growing economies.

Key Terms and Places

Iberia westernmost peninsula in Europe

parliamentary monarchy form of government in which a king rules with the help of an elected parliament

Madrid capital of Spain

Barcelona center of industry, culture, and tourism in Spain

Lisbon large city in Portugal and important industrial center

Section Summary

HISTORY

Spain and Portugal lie on the Iberian Peninsula, or **Iberia**. Both countries have been part of large, powerful empires. Coastal areas of what is now Spain were first ruled by Phoenicians from the eastern Mediterranean. Later the Greeks established colonies there. A few centuries later, Iberia became part of the Roman Empire. After the fall of Rome, they were conquered by the Moors—Muslims from north Africa. For about 600 years, much of the Iberian Peninsula was under Muslim rule.

Eventually the Christian kingdoms of Spain and Portugal banded together to drive out the Muslims. Both countries went on to establish empires of their own in the Americas, Africa, and Asia. Both countries became rich and powerful until the 1800s, when most of their colonies broke away and became independent.

> **What foreign powers have ruled Spain and Portugal?**
> _____
> _____

> **Where did Spain and Portugal establish colonies?**
> _____
> _____

CULTURE

Many dialects of Spanish and Portuguese are spoken in various parts of Iberia. In addition, Catalan, which is similar to Spanish, is spoken in eastern Spain. Galician, which is more closely related to Portuguese, is spoken in northwest Spain. The Basques of the Pyrenees have their own language and customs. In both Spain and Portugal the people are mainly Roman Catholic.

Music is important to both countries. The Portuguese are famous for sad folk songs called fados. The Spanish are famous for a style of song and dance called flamenco. Much of the peninsula's art and architecture reflect its Muslim past. The round arches and elaborate tilework on many buildings were influenced by Muslim design.

> **Circle the group in Spain that has its own language and customs.**

> **What Muslim influences can be seen on buildings in Iberia?**
> _____
> _____

SPAIN AND PORTUGAL TODAY

With the gold and silver found in their colonies, Spain and Portugal were once the richest countries in Europe. When other countries started building industrial economies, Spain and Portugal continued to rely on their colonies. When their colonies broke away, the income they had depended on was lost. Today the economies of Spain and Portugal are growing rapidly.

Spain is governed by a **parliamentary monarchy**—a king rules with the help of an elected parliament. **Madrid**—the capital—and **Barcelona** are centers of industry, culture, and tourism.

Portugal is a republic whose leaders are elected. The economy is based on industries in **Lisbon** and other large cities. In rural areas farmers grow many crops but are most famous for grapes and cork.

> **Underline the definition of a parliamentary monarchy.**

CHALLENGE ACTIVITY

Critical Thinking: Comparing and Contrasting
Compare and contrast Spain and Portugal. Then explain which country you would prefer to visit.

Lisbon	republic	Madrid
fado	flamenco	parliamentary monarchy
Barcelona	Iberia	

DIRECTIONS Answer each question by writing a sentence that contains at least one word from the word bank.

1. Describe one cultural contribution of Spain or Portugal in the area of music or art.

_____

_____

2. How are Spain and Portugal governed today?

_____

_____

3. Where are the centers of industry, tourism, and culture in Spain?

_____

_____

4. Where are the industries of Portugal based?

_____

_____

DIRECTIONS Look at each set of terms. On the line provided, write the letter of the term that does not relate to the others.

_____ 5. a. Basque   b. Catalan   c. Galician   d. Lisbon

_____ 6. a. Muslim   b. Greek   c. Roman   d. Portuguese

West-Central Europe

MAIN IDEAS

1. The physical features of West-Central Europe include plains, uplands, mountains, rivers, and seas.
2. West-Central Europe's mild climate and resources support agriculture, energy production, and tourism.

Key Terms and Places

Northern European Plain broad coastal plain that stretches from the Atlantic coast into Eastern Europe

North Sea large body of water to the north of the region

English Channel narrow waterway to the north of the region that separates West-Central Europe from the United Kingdom

Danube River one of the major rivers of the region

Rhine River one of the major rivers of the region

navigable river river that is deep and wide enough for ships to use

Section Summary

PHYSICAL FEATURES

West-Central Europe has three major types of landforms: plains, uplands, and mountains. Most of the **Northern European Plain** is flat or rolling, but in the Netherlands the plains drop below sea level. The plain has the region's best farmland and largest cities. The Central Uplands are in the middle of the region. This area has many rounded hills, small plateaus, and valleys. In France, the uplands include the Massif Central, a plateau region, and the Jura Mountains, a low mountain range on the French-Swiss border. Coal fields in the Central Uplands have helped to make it a major mining and industrial area. The area has some fertile soil, but is mostly too rocky for farming.

The region has two high mountain ranges. The Alps and Pyrenees form the alpine mountain system. The Alps are the highest mountains in Europe.

> Circle the three major landform types in West-Central Europe.

> Underline the names of three mountain ranges in West-Central Europe.

Water is an important part of the region's physical geography. The Mediterranean Sea borders France to the south. The Atlantic Ocean lies to the west and the **North Sea** and the **English Channel** lie to the north. The **Danube** and the **Rhine** rivers are important waterways for trade and travel. Several of the region's rivers are **navigable**. These rivers and a system of canals link the region's interior to the seas. People and goods travel on these waterways, and cities, farms, and industrial areas line their banks.

> Circle the names of two important rivers in the region.

CLIMATE AND RESOURCES

Most of West-Central Europe has a marine west coast climate. This is a mild climate with colder winters. In the Alps and other higher elevation areas, the climate is colder and wetter. In contrast, southern France has a warm Mediterranean climate with dry, hot summers and mild, wet winters.

The mild climate is a valuable resource. Mild temperatures and ample rainfall, along with rich soil, have made the region's farmlands very productive. Farmers grow grapes, grains, and vegetables. In the Alps and the uplands, farmers raise livestock.

> Why is a mild climate a valuable resource for the region?
> _____
> _____

Energy resources are not evenly divided. France has iron ore and coal. Germany has coal, and the Netherlands has natural gas. Fast-flowing alpine rivers provide hydroelectric power. Even so, many countries have to import fuel.

> Circle the energy resources of France. Underline the energy resources of Germany and the Netherlands.

The Alps are another important resource. Tourists come to the mountains for the scenery and to ski and hike.

> In what way are the Alps an important resource for the region?
> _____

CHALLENGE ACTIVITY

Critical Thinking: Evaluating Information How have landforms and bodies of water affected activities in the region? Give support for your answer.

Guided Reading Workbook

Massif Central	Northern European Plain	Danube River
Rhine River	Jura Mountains	English Channel
North Sea	navigable river	

DIRECTIONS On the line provided before each statement, write **T** if a statement is true and **F** if a statement is false. If the statement is false, write the correct term or terms on the line after each sentence that makes the sentence a true statement.

_____ 1. The vast plain that stretches from the Atlantic coast into Eastern Europe is called the Northern European Plain.

_____

_____ 2. The two most important rivers in West-Central Europe are the Nile and the Mississippi. Many cities and industrial areas line their banks.

_____

_____ 3. A navigable river is one that is deep and wide enough for ships to use.

_____

_____ 4. The Atlantic Ocean is north of Belgium and the Netherlands.

_____

_____ 5. The Danube is the body of water between the North Sea and the Atlantic Ocean.

_____

DIRECTIONS Choose four of the vocabulary terms from the word bank. On a separate sheet of paper, use these terms to write directions for how to travel (by boat, car, train, or air) across West-Central Europe from the United Kingdom to Italy.

West-Central Europe

MAIN IDEAS

1. During its history France has been a kingdom, empire, colonial power, and republic.
2. The culture of France has contributed to the world's arts and ideas.
3. France today is a farming and manufacturing center.
4. The Benelux Countries have strong economies and high standards of living.

Key Terms and Places

Paris capital and largest city in France

Amsterdam capital of the Netherlands

The Hague seat of government in the Netherlands

Brussels capital of Belgium, headquarters of many international organizations

cosmopolitan characterized by many foreign influences

Section Summary

HISTORY OF FRANCE

France has a history as a major European power. Early in its history, the Romans and Franks conquered lands that became France. The Franks' ruler, Charlemagne, built a large empire. Later the Normans claimed northwestern France. They extended their rule to England, becoming kings of England and ruling part of France as well. English rule in France ended in 1453 after the Hundred Years' War. In the 1500s France became a colonial power with colonies in Asia, Africa, and the Americas.

In 1789 the French Revolution led to greater equality and more rights for the French. In 1799 Napoleon Bonaparte took power. He conquered most of Europe, creating a vast empire, which ended in 1815 when European powers defeated his armies. In the 1900s during World Wars I and II, Germany invaded France. In the 1950s and 1960s, many French colonies declared independence. France is now a democratic republic.

> Circle the names of three groups that ruled France during its early history.

> Underline the sentence that tells how Napoleon Bonaparte affected French history.

THE CULTURE OF FRANCE

The French share a common heritage. Most speak French and are Catholic. Recently France has become more diverse due to immigrants. The French share a love of good food and company. The French have made major contributions to the arts and ideas—including impressionism, Gothic cathedrals, and Enlightenment ideas about government.

Underline the sentences that describe the ways the French are alike.

FRANCE TODAY

France is a European and world leader. **Paris** is a center of business, finance, learning, and culture. France has a strong economy and it is the EU's top agricultural producer. Its economy also relies on tourism and the export of goods such as perfumes and wines.

THE BENELUX COUNTRIES

Belgium, the Netherlands, and Luxembourg are the Benelux Countries. Their location has led to invasions but has also promoted trade. All are densely populated, lie at low elevations between larger, stronger countries, and have strong economies and democratic governments. North Sea harbors have made the Netherlands a center for trade. Major cities include Rotterdam, **Amsterdam**, and **The Hague**. In Belgium, **Brussels** is a **cosmopolitan** city with many international organizations. Luxembourg's economy is based on banking and steel and chemical production.

Circle the names of the three Benelux Countries.

Underline the sentence that tells how the Benelux Countries are alike.

CHALLENGE ACTIVITY

Critical Thinking: Drawing Conclusions How has the location of the Benelux Countries both helped and hurt them?

DIRECTIONS Read each sentence and fill in the blank with the word in the word pair that best completes the sentence.

1. _____ is a style of painting developed by French artists that uses rippling light to create an impression of a scene. (Impressionism/Abstract expressionism)

2. _____ is the capital of France. (London/Paris)

3. The Dutch use _____, or earthen walls, in addition to dams and pumps to hold back the sea. (dikes/trenches)

4. Brussels, the capital of Belgium, is considered a _____ city because of its many foreign influences. (cosmopolitan/sprawling)

5. _____ is the capital of the Netherlands. (Amsterdam/The Hague)

DIRECTIONS Write a word or short phrase that has the same meaning as the term given.

6. *joie de vivre* _____

7. Marseille _____

8. The Hague _____

9. Brussels _____

10. Benelux _____

West-Central Europe

MAIN IDEAS

1. After a history of division and two world wars, Germany is now a unified country.

2. German culture, known for its contributions to music, literature, and science, is growing more diverse.

3. Germany today has Europe's largest economy, but eastern Germany faces challenges.

4. The Alpine Countries reflect German culture and have strong economies based on tourism and services.

Key Terms and Places

Berlin capital of Germany

chancellor prime minister elected by Parliament who runs the government

Vienna Austria's capital and largest city

cantons districts of Switzerland's federal republic

Bern capital of Switzerland

Section Summary

HISTORY OF GERMANY

The land that is now Germany was a loose association of small states for hundreds of years. In 1871 Prussia united them to create Germany, which grew into a world power. In the 1900s Germany lost two world wars. After its defeat in World War II, Germany was divided into West Germany and East Germany. West Germany kept control of western **Berlin** and Communists took eastern Berlin. They built the Berlin Wall to stop East Germans from escaping. In 1989 democracy movements swept Eastern Europe and communism collapsed. In 1990 East and West Germany were reunited.

> **Why did Communist leaders build the Berlin Wall?**
> _____
> _____

> **What events helped East and West Germany reunite?**
> _____
> _____

CULTURE OF GERMANY

Most people in Germany are ethnic Germans who speak German. Germany also has immigrants from Turkey, Italy, and Eastern Europe. Most people are either Protestant or Catholic. Germans have made important contributions to classical music, literature, chemistry, engineering, and medicine.

GERMANY TODAY

Today Germany is a leading European power. A parliament with a **chancellor** governs the nation. Berlin is the largest city. Germany is Europe's largest economy, exporting many products, including cars. Its economy is based mainly on industries such as chemicals, engineering, and steel, but agriculture is also still important. The reuniting of East and West Germany slowed economic growth.

THE ALPINE COUNTRIES

Austria and Switzerland are the Alpine Countries. Both were once part of the Holy Roman Empire, are landlocked, influenced by German culture, and prosperous. Austria once led the powerful Habsburg Empire that ruled much of Europe. After World War I the empire collapsed. Today Austria is a modern, industrialized nation. **Vienna** is a center of music and fine arts. Austria has a strong economy with little unemployment. Service industries and tourism are important.

Switzerland has been independent since the 1600s. It is a federal republic made up of 26 **cantons**. It is neutral and not a member of the EU or NATO. The Swiss speak several languages, including German and French. Its capital is **Bern**. Like Austria, Switzerland is a modern, industrialized nation. It is known for tourism and for its banks, watches, chocolate, and cheese.

CHALLENGE ACTIVITY

Critical Thinking: Drawing Inferences What are some factors that have contributed to the Alpine Countries' prosperity?

> **Most Germans belong to one or the other of which two religious groups?**
> _____
> _____

> **What economic activities have made Germany Europe's strongest economy?**
> _____
> _____

> **Underline the sentence that explains what the Alpine Countries have in common.**

> **List two important industries in the Alpine Countries.**
> _____
> _____

Berlin	chancellor	cantons	purpose
Vienna	neutral	Bern	

DIRECTIONS Read each sentence and fill in the blank with the word
in the word pair that best completes the sentence.

1. _____ is the capital of Germany. (Vienna/Berlin)

2. In Germany, a parliament elects a _____, or prime minister,
   who runs the government. (canton/chancellor)

3. Switzerland is made up of 26 districts called _____.
   (cantons/Bern)

4. _____ is the capital of Austria and also its largest city.
   (Berlin/Vienna)

5. The capital of Switzerland, _____, is centrally located
   between the country's German- and French-speaking regions. (Bern/Vienna)

DIRECTIONS Choose five terms from the word bank. Use these terms
to write a summary of what you learned in this section.

_____

_____

_____

_____

_____

_____

_____

_____

_____

Northern Europe

MAIN IDEAS
1. The physical features of Northern Europe include low mountain ranges and jagged coastlines.
2. Northern Europe's natural resources include energy sources, soils, and seas.
3. The climates of Northern Europe range from a mild coastal climate to a freezing ice cap climate.

Key Terms and Places

British Isles a group of islands located across the English Channel from the rest of Europe

Scandinavia a region of islands and peninsulas in far northern Europe

fjord a narrow inlet of the sea set between high, rocky cliffs

geothermal energy energy from the heat of Earth's interior

North Atlantic Drift an ocean current that brings warm, moist air across the Atlantic Ocean

Section Summary
PHYSICAL FEATURES

Northern Europe consists of two regions. The **British Isles** are a group of islands located across the English Channel from the rest of Europe. **Scandinavia** is a region of islands and peninsulas in far northern Europe. Iceland, to the west, is often considered part of Scandinavia.

Fewer people live in the northern portion of the region, which is covered by rocky hills and low mountains. Farmland and plains stretch across the southern part of the region.

Slow moving sheets of ice called glaciers once covered the region. They carved lakes and **fjords**, narrow inlets between high, rocky cliffs. The fjords make the coast of Norway irregular and jagged.

> Underline the sentence that describes the land in the northern portion of the region.

> What two features were created by glaciers?
> _____
> _____

NATURAL RESOURCES

Northern Europe has many natural resources that
have helped make it one of the world's wealthiest
regions. Energy resources include oil and natural
gas in areas of the North Sea controlled by the
United Kingdom and Norway. Hydroelectric energy
is created by machines that are turned by flowing
water channeled from lakes and rivers. Iceland's hot
springs produce **geothermal energy**, or energy
from the heat of the Earth's interior.

Forests in Norway, Sweden, and Finland provide
timber. Fertile farmland in southern areas provides
crops such as wheat and potatoes. The seas and
oceans that surround the region have provided fish
to the people of Northern Europe for centuries.

> Underline the sentences
> that describe energy
> resources located in the
> North Sea.

CLIMATES

Although much of the region is very far north and
close to the Arctic Circle, the climates in Northern
Europe are surprisingly mild. The **North Atlantic
Drift** is a warm ocean current that brings warm,
moist air across the Atlantic Ocean to Northern
Europe. It creates warmer temperatures than other
areas located as far north.

Much of the region has a marine west coast
climate with mild summers and frequent rainfall.
Central Norway, Sweden, and southern Finland
have a humid continental climate with four seasons.
Farther north are subarctic regions, with long, cold
winters and short summers. Tundra and ice cap
climates produce extremely cold temperatures
year-round.

> How does the North
> Atlantic Drift affect the
> climate?
> _____
> _____

CHALLENGE ACTIVITY

Critical Thinking: Making Inferences Fewer
people live in the northern portion of the region
than in the southern portion. List all of the factors
that you can think of which might help explain this
pattern.

Guided Reading Workbook

DIRECTIONS Read each sentence and fill in the blank with the word in the word pair that best completes each sentence.

1. Many lakes in the British Isles were carved by _____ millions of years ago. (volcanoes/glaciers)

2. Northern Europe is made up of the British Isles and _____. (Scandinavia/the Artic Circle)

3. A _____ is a narrow inlet of the sea set between high, rocky cliffs. (fjord/peninsula)

4. Energy produced from the heat of Earth's interior is called

   _____. (geothermal energy/hydroelectric energy)

5. Northern Europe experiences a mild climate due to the

   _____. (Arctic Circle/North Atlantic Drift)

DIRECTIONS Look at each set of four vocabulary terms or places. On the line provided, write the letter of the term that does not relate to the others.

_____ 6. a. glacier
      b. rainfall
      c. fjord
      d. cliff

_____ 7. a. tundra
      b. soil
      c. forest
      d. ocean

_____ 8. a. Northern Europe
      b. British Isles
      c. Scandinavia
      d. Antarctic Circle

_____ 9. a. North Atlantic Drift
      b. mild climate
      c. ocean current
      d. subarctic climate

MAIN IDEAS
1. Invaders and a global empire have shaped the history of the British Isles.
2. British culture, such as government and music, has influenced much of the world.
3. Efforts to bring peace to Northern Ireland and maintain strong economies are important issues in the British Isles today.

Key Terms and Places

constitutional monarchy a type of democracy in which a king or queen serves as head of state, but a legislature makes the laws

Magna Carta a document that limited the powers of kings and required everyone to obey the law

disarm give up all weapons

London the capital of the United Kingdom

Dublin the capital of Ireland

Section Summary
HISTORY

The Republic of Ireland and the United Kingdom make up the British Isles. The United Kingdom consists of England, Scotland, Wales, and Northern Ireland.

The Celts were early settlers of the British Isles. Later, Romans, Angles, Saxons, Vikings, and Normans invaded Britain. Over time England grew in strength, and by the 1500s it had become a world power. England eventually formed the United Kingdom with Wales, Scotland, and Ireland. It then developed a strong economy thanks to the Industrial Revolution and its colonies abroad.

The British Empire stretched around the world by 1900, but later declined. The Republic of Ireland won its independence in 1921. By the mid-1900s Britain had given up most of its colonies.

> **What two countries make up the British Isles?**
> _____

> **Underline the sentence that lists the countries that formed the United Kingdom.**

CULTURE

The United Kingdom is a **constitutional monarchy**, a type of democracy in which a monarch serves as head of state, but a legislature makes the laws. England first limited the power of monarchs during the Middle Ages in a document called **Magna Carta**. Ireland has a president that serves as head of state and a prime minister who runs the government along with Parliament.

The people of the British Isles share many culture traits, but each culture is also unique. The people of Ireland and Scotland keep many traditions alive, and immigrants from all over the world add new traits to the culture of the British Isles.

British popular culture has influenced people around the world. British literature and music are well known and the English language is used in many countries.

> In what ways are the governments of the United Kingdom and Ireland similar and different?
> _____
> _____
> _____

> Underline the sentence that describes how British popular culture has influenced other people.

BRITISH ISLES TODAY

Efforts to bring a long-lasting peace to Northern Ireland remain an important issue. Many Catholics there feel they have not been treated fairly by Protestants. Some hope to unite with the Republic of Ireland. In the late 1990s peace talks led to the creation of a national assembly in Northern Ireland. However, some groups refused to **disarm**, or give up all weapons.

Maintaining powerful economies in the British Isles is a key issue today. **London**, the capital of the United Kingdom, is a center for world trade, and the country has reserves of oil and natural gas in the North Sea. **Dublin**, the capital of Ireland, has attracted new industries like computers and electronics.

> What is one economic issue facing the British Isles today?
> _____
> _____

CHALLENGE ACTIVITY
Critical Thinking: Identify Cause and Effect
Explain the factors that caused the development of a strong economy in the United Kingdom following its formation. Then explain two effects of the decline of the British Empire.

DIRECTIONS Read each sentence and fill in the blank with the word
in the word pair that best completes the sentence.

1. The _____ was characterized by the growth of industries like
   textiles, iron, and steel. (Industrial Revolution/Magna Carta)

2. An _____ led to the creation of a national assembly and a
   cease fire in Northern Ireland in the late 1990s.
   (agreement/Industrial Revolution)

3. _____ is an ancient monument in the British Isles that was
   built 5,000 years ago. (Dublin/Stonehenge)

4. A _____ is a government that has a monarch, but a
   legislative body that makes the laws. (Magna Carta/constitutional monarchy)

5. Peace talks in Northern Ireland were stalled when some groups refused to

   _____. (disarm/agreement)

DIRECTIONS Write three words or phrases that describe the term.

6. London _____

7. Dublin _____

8. Magna Carta _____

MAIN IDEAS
1. The history of Scandinavia dates back to the time of the Vikings.
2. Scandinavia today is known for its peaceful and prosperous countries.

Key Terms and Places

Vikings Scandinavian warriors who raided Europe in the early Middle Ages

Stockholm Sweden's capital and largest city

neutral not taking sides in an international conflict

uninhabitable not able to support human settlement

Oslo the capital of Norway

Helsinki Finland's capital and largest city

geyser a spring that shoots hot water and steam into the air

Section Summary
HISTORY

Vikings were Scandinavian warriors who raided Europe during the Middle Ages. They were greatly feared and conquered the British Isles, Finland, and parts of France, Germany, and Russia.

Vikings were excellent sailors. They were the first Europeans with settlements in Iceland and Greenland and the first Europeans to reach North America. They stopped raiding in the 1100s and focused on strengthening their kingdoms. Norway, Sweden, and Denmark competed for control of the region, and by the late 1300s Denmark ruled all the Scandinavian Kingdoms and territories. Sweden eventually broke away, taking Finland, and later Norway, with it. Norway, Finland, and Iceland became independent countries during the 1900s. Greenland remains part of Denmark as a self-ruling territory.

> Underline the sentence that tells areas that Vikings explored.

> What three countries did not become independent until the 1900s?
> _____
> _____

SCANDINAVIA TODAY

Scandinavians share many things, including culture traits like similar political views, languages, and religions. They enjoy high standards of living, are well-educated, and get free health care. The countries have strong economies and large cities.

Each country is unique as well. Sweden has the largest area and population. Most people live in the south in large towns and cities. **Stockholm** is Sweden's capital and largest city. For about 200 years, Sweden has been **neutral**, choosing not to take sides in international conflicts.

Denmark is the smallest country and the most densely populated. Its economy relies on excellent farmland and modern industries. Greenland is a territory of Denmark but most of it is covered with ice and is **uninhabitable**, or not able to support human settlement.

Norway has one of the longest coastlines in the world. **Oslo** is Norway's capital, a leading seaport and industrial center. Important industries include timber, shipping, and fishing. Oil and natural gas provide Scandinavia with the highest per capita GDP in the region; however, oil fields in the North Sea are expected to run out during the next century.

Finland relies on trade and exports paper and other forest products. Shipbuilding and electronics are also important. **Helsinki** is its capital and largest city.

Iceland has fertile farmland and rich fishing grounds. Tourists come to see its volcanoes, glaciers, and **geysers**, springs that shoot hot water and steam into the air. Geothermal energy heats many buildings.

Underline the sentence that lists culture traits Scandinavians share.

What is the largest country in area? What is the smallest?

Why are tourists attracted to Iceland?

CHALLENGE ACTIVITY

Critical Thinking: Making Inferences How do you think the Scandinavian countries might change if oil fields run out during the next century?

domination	geysers	Helsinki
hot springs	neutral	Oslo
Stockholm	uninhabitable	Vikings

DIRECTIONS Answer each question by writing a sentence that contains at least one word from the word bank.

1. How were longboats used by Scandinavian warriors?

_____

_____

2. Why do most people in Greenland live on the southwest coast?

_____

_____

3. What role did Sweden play in World War I and World War II?

_____

_____

4. How are many homes in Iceland heated?

_____

_____

5. What city in Scandinavia is often called a floating city and why?

_____

_____

Eastern Europe

MAIN IDEAS
1. The physical features of Eastern Europe include wide open plains, rugged mountain ranges, and many rivers.
2. The climate and vegetation of Eastern Europe differ widely in the north and the south.

Key Places

Carpathians a low mountain range stretching from the Alps to the Black Sea area

Balkan Peninsula one of the largest peninsulas in Europe, extends into the Mediterranean

Danube longest river in the region, begins in Germany and flows east across the Great Hungarian Plain

Chernobyl a nuclear power plant in Ukraine

Section Summary
PHYSICAL FEATURES

The landforms of Eastern Europe stretch across the region in broad bands of plains and mountains. The Northern European Plain covers most of northern Europe. The **Carpathians** are south of the plains. These mountains extend from the Alps to the Black Sea area. South of the Carpathians is another large plain, the Great Hungarian Plain, located mostly in Hungary. South of this plain are the Dinaric Alps and Balkan Mountains. These mountain ranges cover most of the **Balkan Peninsula**. The peninsula extends into the Mediterranean.

Eastern Europe has many water bodies that are important routes for transportation and trade. The Adriatic Sea lies to the southwest. The Black Sea is east of the region. The Baltic Sea is in the far north. It remains frozen some part of the year, reducing its usefulness.

The rivers that flow through Eastern Europe are also important for trade and transportation, especially the **Danube**. The Danube crosses nine

> Circle three mountain ranges in Eastern Europe.

> Why are rivers important to the economy of Eastern Europe?
> _____

countries before it empties into the Black Sea. This river is very important to Eastern Europe's economy. Many of the region's largest cities are along its banks. Dams on the river provide electricity for the region. This busy river has become very polluted from heavy use.

> **Why is the Danube so polluted?**
> _____

CLIMATE AND VEGETATION

Types of climates and vegetation in Eastern Europe vary widely. The shores of the Baltic Sea in the far north have the coldest climate. The area does not get much rain, but is sometimes foggy. Its cold, damp climate allows huge forests to grow.

The interior plains have a much milder climate than the Baltic Region. Winters can be very cold, but summers are mild. The western parts of the interior plains get more rain than the eastern parts. Because of its varied climate, the forests cover much of the north and open grassy plains lie in the south. In 1986 Eastern Europe's forests were damaged by a major nuclear accident at **Chernobyl**. An explosion released huge amounts of radiation into the air that poisoned forests and ruined soil across the region.

The Balkan coast has a Mediterranean climate with warm summers and mild winters. Some of its beaches attract tourists. The area does not get much rain so there are not many forests. The land is covered by shrubs and trees that do not need much water.

> **Circle the type of climate found along the Balkan coast.**

> **Why is the vegetation along the Balkan coast different from the vegetation of the Baltic Region?**
> _____
> _____

CHALLENGE ACTIVITY

Critical Thinking: Analyzing Information How has climate affected the vegetation in Eastern Europe? Explain your answer in a brief paragraph.

| Adriatic Sea | Balkan Mountains | Balkan Peninsula | Carpathians |
| Chernobyl | Danube | function | radiation |

DIRECTIONS On the line provided before each statement, write **T** if a statement is true and **F** if a statement is false. If the statement is false, write the correct term from the word bank on the line after each sentence that makes the sentence a true statement.

_____ 1. The Balkan Mountains are a low mountain range that stretch in a long arc from the Alps to the Black Sea area.

_____

_____ 2. The Black Sea serves the same function as the Carpathians; they are both important trade routes.

_____

_____ 3. A nuclear explosion at the Chernobyl power plant released huge amounts of radiation into the air.

_____

_____ 4. The Danube begins in Germany and flows through nine countries before emptying into the Black Sea.

_____

_____ 5. One of the largest landforms in Europe, the Chernobyl extends south into the Mediterranean Sea.

_____

Eastern Europe

MAIN IDEAS
1. History ties Poland and the Baltic Republics together.
2. The cultures of Poland and the Baltic Republics differ in language and religion but share common customs.
3. Economic growth is a major issue in the region today.

Key Terms and Places

infrastructure the set of resources—like roads, airports, and factories—that a country needs in order to support economic activities

Warsaw capital of Poland

Section Summary

HISTORY

The groups who settled around the Baltic Sea in ancient times developed into the Estonians, Latvians, Lithuanians, and Polish. Each group had its own language and culture, but in time they became connected by a shared history. By the Middle Ages, each had formed an independent kingdom. Lithuania and Poland were the largest and strongest. They ruled large parts of Eastern and Northern Europe. Latvia and Estonia were smaller, weaker, and often invaded.

In the 1900s two world wars greatly damaged the Baltic region. In World War I millions died in Poland, and thousands more were killed in the Baltic countries. The region also suffered greatly during World War II. This war began with the invasion of Poland by Germany. While fighting the Germans, troops from the Soviet Union invaded Poland and occupied Estonia, Latvia, and Lithuania.

After World War II ended, the Soviet Union took over much of Eastern Europe, making Estonia, Latvia, and Lithuania part of the Soviet Union. The Soviets also forced Poland to accept a Communist government. In 1989 Poland rejected communism

How did the Baltic Republics lose their independence after World War II?

_____

and elected new leaders. In 1991 the Baltic Republics broke away from the Soviet Union. They became independent countries again.

CULTURE

The Baltic countries differ from each other in languages and religion, but are alike in other ways. The Latvian and Lithuanian languages are alike, but Estonian is like Finnish, the language spoken in Finland. Polish is more like languages of countries farther south. Most Polish people and Lithuanians are Roman Catholics because their trading partners were from Catholic countries. Latvians and Estonians are Lutherans, because these countries were once ruled by Sweden, where most people are Lutherans.

These countries share many customs and practices. They eat similar foods, practice crafts such as ceramics, painting, and embroidery, and enjoy music and dance.

THE REGION TODAY

The economies of Baltic countries grew more slowly than those of Western European nations because the Soviets did not build a decent **infrastructure**. Poland and the Baltic Republics are working hard to rebuild their economies. As a result, cities like **Warsaw** have become major industrial centers. To help their economies grow, many Baltic countries are trying to attract more tourists. Since the Soviet Union collapsed in 1991, the rich cultures, historic sites, and cool summer climates attract visitors.

CHALLENGE ACTIVITY
Critical Thinking: Understanding Effects

Imagine that you are a newly elected leader of a Baltic country. Write a speech that tells what you will do to improve the country's economy.

> **Underline the sentences that tell how the governments of the Baltic countries changed after 1989.**

> **What economic problems did Soviet rule cause for Poland and the Baltic Republics?**
>
> _____
>
> _____

> **What new source of income have the Baltic countries found?**
>
> _____

| Baltic Republics | embroidery | infrastructure |
| Krakow | Poland | Warsaw |

DIRECTIONS Read each sentence and fill in the blank with the word in the word pair that best completes the sentence.

1. The Soviets failed to build a strong _____, which has weakened the economies of the Baltic states. (embroidery/infrastructure)

2. By the Middle Ages, the kingdoms of Lithuania and _____ were large and strong. (Poland/Warsaw)

3. _____ is the capital of Poland. (Warsaw/Krakow)

4. The _____ include(s) Latvia, Estonia, and Lithuania. (infrastructure/Baltic Republics)

5. _____ is a type of decorative sewing that is popular among people in the Baltic region. (Krakow/Embroidery)

DIRECTIONS Choose four of the terms from the word bank. On a separate sheet of paper, use these words to write a short story that relates to the section.

Eastern Europe

Section 3

MAIN IDEAS

1. The histories and cultures of inland Eastern Europe vary from country to country.

2. Most of inland Eastern Europe today has stable governments, strong economies, and influential cities.

Key Terms and Places

Prague capital of the Czech Republic

Kiev present-day city where the Rus built a settlement

Commonwealth of Independent States CIS, an international alliance that meets to discuss issues such as trade and immigration that affect former Soviet republics

Budapest capital of Hungary

Section Summary

HISTORY AND CULTURE

Inland Eastern Europe consists of the Czech Republic, Slovakia, Hungary, Ukraine, Belarus, and Moldova. The region is located on the Northern European and Hungarian plains. The area of the Czech Republic and Slovakia was settled by Slavs, people from Asia who moved into Europe by 1000 BC. In time more powerful countries like Austria conquered these Slavic kingdoms. After World War I, land was taken away from Austria to create the nation of Czechoslovakia. In 1993 Czechoslovakia split into the Czech Republic and Slovakia.

Because the Czech Republic and Slovakia are located in Central Europe, they have long had ties to Western Europe. Many people are Roman Catholic. The architecture of **Prague** and other cities shows Western influences.

In the 900s Magyar people invaded what is now Hungary. The Magyars influenced Hungarian culture, especially the Hungarian language. It developed from the Magyar language.

> What group of people settled the area of the Czech Republic and Slovakia?
>
> _____

> Circle the country that land was taken from to create Czechoslovakia.

> When was Czechoslovakia created and when did it split?
>
> _____
>
> _____

Ukraine, Belarus, and Moldova are more closely tied to Russia than to the West. The Rus people built the settlement that is now **Kiev**. The rulers of Kiev created a huge empire that became part of Russia in the late 1700s. In 1922 Russia became the Soviet Union. Ukraine, Belarus, and Moldova became Soviet republics. After the breakup of the Soviet Union in 1991, these countries became independent. Russia has strongly influenced their cultures. Most people are Orthodox Christians, and the Ukrainian and Belarusian languages are written in the Cyrillic, or Russian, alphabet.

> Underline two ways the cultures of Ukraine, Belarus, and Moldova have been influenced by Russia.

INLAND EASTERN EUROPE TODAY

All inland Eastern European countries were once either part of the Soviet Union or run by Soviet-influenced Communist governments. People had few freedoms. The Soviets did a poor job of managing these economies. Since the collapse of the Soviet Union, Hungary, Slovakia, the Czech Republic, Ukraine, and Moldova have become republics. Although Belarus also claims to be a republic, it is really a dictatorship.

Countries of the region belong to international unions. Belarus, Ukraine, and Moldova belong to the **Commonwealth of Independent States**. Its members meet to talk about such issues as trade and immigration. The Czech Republic, Slovakia, and Hungary seek closer ties to the West and belong to the EU. Slovakia, Hungary, and Ukraine have become prosperous industrial centers.

> How have the governments and the economies of the region changed since the collapse of the Soviet Union?
>
> _____
> _____
> _____
> _____

The capital cities of the region are also economic and cultural centers. Prague, Kiev, and **Budapest** are especially important. They are the most prosperous cities in the region. Many tourists visit these cities.

CHALLENGE ACTIVITY

Critical Thinking: Evaluating Write a brief essay that explains how the location of inland Eastern Europe has affected its culture and history.

Budapest	Kiev	Magyars
Prague	Slavs	
Commonwealth of Independent States		

DIRECTIONS Read each sentence and choose the correct term from the word bank to replace the underlined phrase. Write the term in the space provided and then define the term in your own words.

1. Members of <u>this alliance</u> meet in Minsk to discuss issues such as trade and

    immigration. _____

    _____

    Your definition: _____

2. This <u>group of fierce invaders</u> swept into Hungary and established a strong culture

    there. _____

    Your definition: _____

3. <u>This</u> is the capital city of the Czech Republic. _____

    Your definition: _____

4. The Rus established <u>this city</u> in the 800s, which still stands in Ukraine today.

    _____

    Your definition: _____

5. Ukraine, Belarus, and Moldavia were settled by <u>this group of people</u>.

    _____

    Your definition: _____

MAIN IDEAS
1. The history of the Balkan countries is one of conquest and conflict.
2. The cultures of the Balkan countries are shaped by the many ethnic groups who live there.
3. Civil War and weak economies are major challenges to the region today.

Key Terms

ethnic cleansing effort to remove all members of a group from a country or region

Section Summary

HISTORY

The Balkan Peninsula has been ruled by many different groups. In ancient times, the Greeks founded colonies near the Black Sea. This area is now Bulgaria and Romania. Next the Romans conquered most of the area between the Adriatic Sea and the Danube River. When the Roman Empire divided into west and east in AD 300s, the Balkan Peninsula became part of the Byzantine Empire. Under Byzantine rule many people became Orthodox Christians.

Over a thousand years later, Muslim Ottoman Turks conquered the Byzantine Empire. Many people in the Balkans became Muslims. Ottoman rule lasted until the 1800s, when the people of the Balkans drove the Ottomans out. They then created their own kingdoms. In the late 1800s, the Austria-Hungarian Empire took over part of the peninsula. To protest the takeover, a man from Serbia shot the heir to the Austro-Hungarian throne. This event led to World War I. After the war Europe's leaders combined many formerly independent countries into Yugoslavia. In the 1990s this country broke apart. Ethnic and religious conflict led to its collapse.

> Underline the names of groups or empires that ruled the Balkan Peninsula until the 1800s.

CULTURE

The Balkans are Europe's most diverse region. People practice different religions and speak many different languages. Most people are Christians. They are either Orthodox, Roman Catholic, or Protestant. Islam is also practiced. Most people speak Slavic languages that are related to Russian. People in Romania speak Germanic languages or a language that comes from Latin.

> **What makes the Balkans Europe's most diverse region?**
>
> _____
>
> _____
>
> _____

THE BALKANS TODAY

Balkan countries were once run by Communist governments. Poor economic planning has hurt the economies of the region. It is still the poorest region in Europe today. After the breakup of Yugoslavia, many of the countries that had been a part of this country faced violent ethnic and religious conflicts. These conflicts led to **ethnic cleansing** in some areas. In 1995 troops from all over the world came to Bosnia and Herzegovina to help end the fighting.

> **What caused the violence in the Balkans after Yugoslavia broke apart? What stopped the fighting?**
>
> _____
>
> _____
>
> _____

Seven of the Balkan countries were once part of the former Yugoslavia. Macedonia and Slovenia were the first to break away. When Croatia broke away, fighting started between ethnic Croats and Serbs. Peace did not return until many Serbs left Croatia. Bosnia and Herzegovina also had terrible ethnic fighting. Serbia, the largest country to emerge from the former Yugoslavia, also saw terrible fighting. Both Montenegro and Kosovo separated from Serbia.

The Balkans includes three other countries. Albania and Romania are poor and have serious economic and political problems. Bulgaria has a strong economy based on industry and tourism.

CHALLENGE ACTIVITY

Critical Thinking: Predicting Write a paragraph that explains how ethnic diversity could be an advantage for the Balkan countries in the future.

Balkans	ethnic cleansing	implications
Mostar	Orthodox	Roma
Slavic	Soviet Union	Yugoslavia

DIRECTIONS Look at each set of terms following each number. On the line provided, write the letter of the term that does not relate to the others.

_____ 1. a. Protestant   b. Orthodox   c. Catholic   d. Slavic

_____ 2. a. World War I   b. Serbia   c. Germanic   d. Austro-Hungarians

_____ 3. a. Albania   b. Hungary   c. Croatia   d. Slovenia

_____ 4. a. Macedonia   b. Yugoslavia   c. violence   d. ethnic cleansing

_____ 5. a. Roma   b. Greeks   c. Romans   d. Ottomans

DIRECTIONS Choose at least three of the terms from the word bank. On a separate sheet of paper, use these words to write a summary of what you learned in Section 4.

MAIN IDEAS
1. The physical features of Russia include plains, mountains, and rivers.
2. Climate and plant life change from north to south in Russia.
3. Russia has a wealth of resources, but many are hard to access.

Key Terms and Places

Ural Mountains mountain range where Europe and Asia meet

Caspian Sea the world's largest inland sea, borders the Caucasus Mountains

Siberia a vast region in Russia, stretching from the Urals to the Pacific Ocean

Volga River the longest river in Europe, located in western Russia

taiga a forest of mainly evergreen trees covering much of Russia

Section Summary
PHYSICAL FEATURES

The continents of Asia and Europe meet in Russia's **Ural Mountains**. Together, Asia and Europe form the large landmass of Eurasia. A large part of Eurasia is Russia, the world's largest country in area.

Plains and mountains cover much of Russia and the Caucasus. The fertile Northern European Plain, Russia's heartland, extends across western Russia. Here lies **Moscow**, Russia's capital.

Beyond this plain, the vast region of **Siberia** stretches from the Ural Mountains to the Pacific Ocean. The rivers in this plain flow toward the Arctic Ocean. The West Siberian Plain is a huge, flat, marshy area. East of this plain lies the Central Siberian Plateau. High mountain ranges run through southern and eastern Siberia. Eastern Siberia is called the Russian Far East, which includes the Kamchatka Peninsula and several islands. This area is part of the Ring of Fire, known for its many volcanos, 20 of which are still active.

> **Which two continents meet in the Ural Mountains?**
> _____
> _____

> **What is the capital of Russia?**
> _____

> **What is the Ring of Fire?**
> _____
> _____

South of the peninsula lie the Sakahlin islands seized from Japan after World War II. Japan still claims ownership of the Kuril islands.

Rivers in Russia include the Ob, Yenisey, Lena, and **Volga**, the longest river in Europe. Russia also has some 200,000 lakes, including Lake Baikal, the world's deepest lake.

What is the longest river in Europe?
_____

CLIMATE AND PLANT LIFE

Russia is mainly cold, with short summers and long, snowy winters. Russia's northern coast is tundra, and most of the ground is permafrost, or permanently frozen soil. Plant life includes small plants in the north and the vast **taiga**, a forest of mainly evergreen trees.

NATURAL RESOURCES

Russia has a wealth of natural resources, including rich soils, timber, metals, precious gems, and energy resources. These resources have been poorly managed, however, and many remaining resources lie in remote Siberia.

What are the region's natural resources?
_____
_____

CHALLENGE ACTIVITY

Critical Thinking: Making Generalizations Based on what you've read so far, write a short essay about what it might be like to live in Russia.

Sakhalin islands	tundra	Moscow
Siberia	taiga	Ural Mountains
Volga River	steppe	Lake Baikal

DIRECTIONS Read each sentence and fill in the blank with the word
in the word pair that best completes the sentence.

1. It is in the _____ that the continents of Europe and Asia
   meet. (Sakhalin islands/Ural Mountains)

2. The _____ provides an important transportation route
   through Russia. (Lake Baikal/Volga River)

3. The _____'s rich, black soil has made it Russia's main
   farming area. (steppe/taiga)

4. _____ is a cold, empty land of barren plains and endless
   forests. (Siberia/Moscow)

5. The vast forest of evergreen trees that covers about half of Russia is called the
   _____. (steppe/taiga)

DIRECTIONS Choose four of the terms from the word bank. On a
separate sheet of paper, use these words to write a story or poem that
relates to the section.

Russia

MAIN IDEAS
1. The Russian empire grew under powerful leaders, but unrest and war led to its end.
2. The Soviet Union emerged as a Communist superpower with rigid government control.
3. Russia's history and diversity have influenced its culture.

Key Terms and Places

Kiev early center of Russia, now the capital of Ukraine

Cyrillic a form of the Greek alphabet

czar emperor

Bolsheviks Communist group that seized power during the Russian Revolution

gulags Soviet labor camps

Section Summary

THE RUSSIAN EMPIRE

In the AD 800s, Viking traders from Scandinavia helped create the first Russian state of Kievan among the Slavs. Kievan was centered around the city of **Kiev**, now the capital of Ukraine.

Over time, missionaries introduced Orthodox Christianity and **Cyrillic**, a form of the Greek alphabet which Russians still use today.

In the 1200s, Mongol invaders called Tatars conquered Kiev. Local Russian princes ruled several states under the Mongols. Muscovy became the strongest state, with Moscow its main city. After about 200 years Muscovy's prince, Ivan III, seized control from the Mongols. Then in the 1540s, his grandson Ivan IV crowned himself **czar**, or emperor. He became known as Ivan the Terrible for being a cruel and savage ruler.

Muscovy developed into the country of Russia. Peter the Great and then Catherine the Great ruled as czars, building a huge empire and world power.

What is Cyrillic?
_____
_____

What name was Ivan IV given for being such a cruel and savage ruler?
_____
_____

Unrest, war, and other problems weakened the Russian empire. In 1917, the czar lost support and was forced to give up the throne. The **Bolsheviks**, a Russian Communist group, seized power in the Russian Revolution. Bolshevik leaders formed the Soviet Union in 1922.

What was the name of the Russian Communist group that seized power during the Russian Revolution?
_____
_____

THE SOVIET UNION

The Soviet Union became a Communist country, led by Vladimir Lenin. In this political system, the government controls all aspects of life and owns all property. After Lenin's death in 1924, Joseph Stalin ruled as a brutal dictator. He set up a command economy. The government made all economic decisions, took over all industries and farms, and strictly controlled its people. Anyone who spoke out against the government was sent to **gulags**, harsh Soviet labor camps often located in Siberia.

Who was the first leader of the Soviet Union when it became a Communist country?
_____
_____

After suffering many losses in World War II, Stalin worked to create a protective buffer around the Soviet Union. He set up Communist governments in Eastern Europe. As a result, the Cold War, a period of tense rivalry and arms race between the United States and the Soviet Union, developed. The Soviet Union grew weak in the 1980s, and then it fell apart in 1991.

What was the Cold War?
_____
_____

CULTURE

More than 140 million people live in Russia. Most are ethnic Russians, or Slavs, but Russia also has many other ethnic groups. The main faith is Russian Orthodox Christian. Russia has made many contributions to the arts and sciences, including ballet and space research.

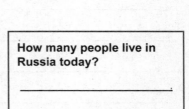

How many people live in Russia today?
_____
_____

CHALLENGE ACTIVITY

Critical Thinking: Drawing Inferences What do you think Russia would be like today if the Soviet Union had not collapsed? Give support for your answer.

Bolsheviks	Cold War	communism
Cyrillic	czar	gulags
Kiev	propaganda	reaction

DIRECTIONS Look at each set of four terms. On the line provided, write the letter of the term that does not relate to the others.

_____ 1. a. Cyrillic   b. Stalin   c. communism   d. gulags

_____ 2. a. Cold War   b. weapons   c. Bolsheviks   d. arms race

_____ 3. a. communism   b. propaganda   c. Soviet Union   d. czar

_____ 4. a. Vikings   b. Bolsheviks   c. Kiev   d. Rus

_____ 5. a. Ivan IV   b. czar   c. Catherine the Great   d. Kiev

DIRECTIONS Choose five of the terms from the word bank. Use these words to write a summary of what you learned in the section.

_____

_____

_____

_____

_____

_____

_____

_____

_____

_____

_____

_____

_____

MAIN IDEAS
1. The Russian Federation is working to develop democracy and a market economy.
2. Russia's physical geography, cities, and economy define its many culture regions.
3. Russia faces a number of serious challenges.

Key Terms and Places

dachas Russian country houses

St. Petersburg city founded by Peter the Great and styled after those of Western Europe

smelters factories that produce metal ores

Trans-Siberian Railroad the longest single rail line in the world, running from Moscow to Vladivostok on the east coast

Chechnya a Russian republic in the Caucasus Mountains, an area of ethnic conflict

Section Summary
THE RUSSIAN FEDERATION

The Russian Federation is governed by an elected president, an appointed prime minister, and a legislature called the Federal Assembly. Since 1991, Russia has been changing from communism to a democracy with a market economy based on free trade and competition. These changes have led to economic growth that is most visible today in Russia's cities. A wide range of goods and services can be found here. Most Russians live in large apartment buildings in cities, but they still enjoy nature. Cities often have large parks and many richer Russians own **dachas**, or country houses.

> What is the Russian legislature called?
> _____

CULTURE REGIONS

Four western culture regions—the Moscow, St. Petersburg, Volga, and Urals regions—make up Russia's heartland. These regions are home to the vast majority of Russia's people.

> What are the four culture regions of Russia's heartland?
> _____

Moscow is Russia's capital and largest city. The Kremlin holds Russia's government offices, beautiful palaces, and gold-domed churches. Moscow is a huge industrial region.

Founded by Peter the Great, **St. Petersburg** was styled after cities of Western Europe and served as Russia's capital for some 200 years. Its location on the Gulf of Finland has made the city an important trade center.

The Volga River of the Volga region is a major shipping route and source of hydroelectric power. Factories here process oil and gas. The Caspian Sea provides black caviar.

The Urals region is an important mining region. **Smelters**, or factories that process metal ores, process copper and iron.

Siberia, another of Russia's culture regions, is east of the Urals. Winters there are long and severe. Siberia has many natural resources, but accessing them is difficult. Lumber, mining, and oil production are the most important industries. Most towns follow the route of the **Trans-Siberian Railroad**, the longest single rail line in the world.

Siberia's coastal areas and islands are known as the Russian Far East. This culture region's resources include timber, rich soils, oil, minerals, and fishing. Vladivostock is the region's main seaport.

Where is St. Petersburg located?

Which river is a major shipping route in the Volga region?

What are winters like in Siberia?

What is notable about the Trans-Siberian Railroad?

RUSSIA'S CHALLENGES

Russia faces economic, employment, health, population, environmental, and ethnic challenges. A major ethnic conflict is in the Russian republic of Chechnya, where some people desire independence.

CHALLENGE ACTIVITY

Critical Thinking: Drawing Inferences Based on what you've learned about each region, which area do you think holds the most potential economically for Russia? Why?

| Chechnya | smelters | dachas |
| St. Petersburg | Sea of Okhotsk | Trans-Siberian Railroad |

DIRECTIONS Read each sentence and fill in the blank with the word
in the word pair that best completes the sentence.

1. Located on the Gulf of Finland, _____ has been called the
   Venice of the North for its many canals. (Chechnya/St. Petersburg)

2. In the Ural Mountains, factories called _____ process the
   copper and iron that is mined in the region. (dachas/smelters)

DIRECTIONS On the line provided before each statement, write **T** if a
statement is true and **F** if a statement is false. If the statement is false,
write the correct term from the word bank on the line after each
sentence that makes the sentence a true statement.

_____ 3. Cities and towns in Siberia are mostly located near the <u>Sea of Okhotsk</u>.

_____

_____ 4. Wealthy Russians go to their <u>dachas</u> to enjoy outdoor activities.

_____

_____ 5. Ethnic conflict is responsible for fighting in <u>St. Petersburg</u>.

_____

The Eurasian Republics

MAIN IDEAS
1. Key physical features of landlocked Central Asia include rugged mountains.
2. Central Asia has a harsh, dry climate that makes it difficult for vegetation to grow.
3. Key natural resources in Central Asia include water, oil and gas, and minerals.

Key Terms and Places

landlocked completely surrounded by land with no direct access to the ocean

Pamirs some of Central Asia's high mountains

Fergana Valley large fertile valley in the plains region of Central Asia

Kara-Kum desert in Turkmenistan

Kyzyl Kum desert in Uzbekistan and Kazakhstan

Aral Sea sea that is actually a large lake, which is shrinking due to irrigation

Section Summary

PHYSICAL FEATURES

Central Asia, the middle part of the continent, is **landlocked**. In the region's east, there are rugged, high mountains. Large glaciers are common in the high mountains. One area of high mountains is called the **Pamirs**.

Because it is landlocked and has such rugged land, Central Asia is isolated. Communication and travel are difficult. The area also has many earthquakes.

From the mountains, the land slowly slopes down to the Caspian Sea in the west. Some land there is 95 feet (29 m) below sea level. The land between the sea and mountains is plains and plateaus. The fertile **Fergana Valley** is in the plains.

Central Asia also has some rivers and lakes. Two important rivers are the Syr Darya (sir durh-YAH) and the Amu Darya (uh-MOO duhr-YAH).

> What two factors make Central Asia isolated?
> _____
> _____

> Underline the sentence that names two important rivers in Central Asia.

They make the Fergana Valley fertile. The rivers flow into the Aral Sea, which is really a large lake. Lake Balkhash is also an important lake. It has freshwater at one end and salty water at the other.

Circle the name of the sea that is really a large lake.

CLIMATE AND VEGETATION

Most of Central Asia has a harsh, dry climate. Temperatures range from very cold to very hot, and there is not much rain. It is hard for plants to grow.

The mountain peaks are cold, dry, and windy. There are harsh desert areas between the mountains and sea. Two major deserts are the **Kara-Kum** and **Kyzyl Kum**. The deserts do have some sources of water. Some areas have rivers crossing them, which lets people live there. People use rivers to irrigate, or supply water to the land.

Underline the names of two major deserts in Central Asia.

Only the far north of Central Asia has a milder climate. Grasses and trees are able to grow there.

NATURAL RESOURCES

Some of Central Asia's natural resources are water, oil, and gas. There is also a supply of minerals, such as gold, lead, and copper.

People use the Syr Darya and Amu Darya rivers to irrigate and make electricity. But water is limited. This has led to conflicts over how to use it. Also, irrigation has kept the rivers from flowing into the **Aral Sea**. As a result, the sea has lost much of its water.

List some of Central Asia's natural resources: _____ _____ _____

Oil and gas can only help the region if the countries can sell it. There are no ocean ports to transport it, so they need to build and maintain pipelines. But this is hard because of the rugged land, as well as economic and political problems.

CHALLENGE ACTIVITY

Critical Thinking: Analyzing Information Write a fact sheet called *Central Asia: Tips for Hikers.* Include key facts that hikers to the region should know and a list of supplies they should bring.

Aral Sea	Caspian Sea	Fergana Valley	Lake Balkhash
Kara-Kum	Kyzyl Kum	landlocked	Pamirs

DIRECTIONS Read each sentence and fill in the blank with the word in the word pair that best completes the sentence.

1. The _____ receives very little rainfall.
   (Kara-Kum/Fergana Valley)

2. Large glaciers can be found in the _____.
   (Kyzyl Kum/Pamirs)

3. The _____ is a major farming area in Central Asia.
   (Kara-Kum/Fergana Valley)

4. The _____ is located in Uzbekistan and Kazakhstan.
   (Caspian Sea/Kyzyl Kum)

5. The _____ has been devastated by the irrigation practices in Central Asia. (Aral Sea/Caspian Sea)

DIRECTIONS Use at least four of the terms from the word bank to write a summary of what you learned in the section.

_____

_____

_____

_____

The Eurasian Republics

MAIN IDEAS
1. Many groups have ruled and influenced the Caucasus during its long history.
2. Today the Caucasus republics are working to improve their economies but struggle with ethnic unrest and conflict.

Key Places

Caspian Sea the world's largest inland sea, borders the Caucasus Mountains

Caucasus Mountains mountain range which forms the Caucasus region's northern border with Russia

Tbilisi the capital of Georgia

Yerevan the capital of Armenia

Baku the capital of Azerbaijan, center of a large oil-refining industry

Section Summary

HISTORY

The Caucasus lies in the **Caucasus Mountains** between the Black Sea and the **Caspian Sea**. The region reflects a range of cultural influences and at one time or another has been ruled or invaded by Persians, Greeks, Romans, Arabs, Turks, Mongols, and Russians.

In the early 1800s, Russia took over much of the Caucasus, but the Ottoman Turks held western Armenia. Before and during World War I, hundreds of thousands of Armenians were killed by the Turks. After the war, Armenia, Azerbaijan, and Georgia were independent, but became part of the Soviet Union in 1922. They regained independence when the Soviet Union fell in 1991.

> **Which groups have ruled or invaded the Caucasus?**
> _____
> _____

THE CAUCASUS TODAY

Although the region has a long history, the Caucasus countries have had to create new governments and economies. Progress has been slowed by ethnic unrest and conflicts. Each country's government has an elected president, an appointed prime minister, and an elected parliament, or legislature.

Georgia is located between the Caucasus Mountains and the Black Sea. **Tbilisi** is the capital. About 70 percent of the people are ethnic Georgians and belong to the Georgian Orthodox Church. Georgian is the official language.

Georgia has struggled with unrest and civil war. Georgians forced out their president in 2003.

Georgia's economy is based on services and farming. Other industries include steel, mining, wine, and tourism.

> **What are Georgia's main industries?**
> _____
> _____

Armenia is a small, landlocked country south of Georgia. **Yerevan** is the capital. Most of the people are Armenian and belong to the Armenian Orthodox Church.

Armenia fought a war with Azerbaijan in the early 1990s. The war involved an ethnic Armenian area of Azerbaijan that is still controlled by Armenian forces today. This conflict has hurt Armenia's economy, but international aid is helping.

> **What country was Armenia at war with in the early 1990s?**
> _____

Azerbaijan is east of Armenia and borders the Caspian Sea. The Azeri make up 90 percent of the population and are mostly Muslim. Oil is the most important part of the economy. **Baku**, the capital, is the center of this industry. Problems include corruption, poverty, and refugees as a result of the conflict with Armenia.

> **What is the most important part of Azerbaijan's economy?**
> _____

CHALLENGE ACTIVITY

Critical Thinking: Compare and Contrast

Describe the similarities and differences between the Caucasus countries.

| agrarian | Caucasus Mountains | Azerbaijan | Baku |
| Black Sea | Caspian Sea | Tbilisi | Yerevan |

DIRECTIONS Write three words or phrases that describe each term.

1. agrarian _____

2. Baku _____

DIRECTIONS Read each sentence and fill in the blank with the word
in the word pair that best completes the sentence.

3. The capital of Armenia is _____. (Baku/Yerevan)

4. _____ is the capital of Georgia. (Yerevan/Tbilisi)

5. Oil is the most important part of _____'s economy.
   (Tbilisi/Azerbaijan)

6. Georgia, Armenia, and Azerbaijan all lie south of _____
   the (Black Sea/Caucasus Mountains).

7. The _____ is the world's largest inland sea.
   (Caspian Sea/Black Sea)

The Eurasian Republics

MAIN IDEAS
1. Throughout history, many different groups have conquered Central Asia.
2. Many different ethnic groups and their traditions influence culture in Central Asia.

Key Terms and Places

Samarqand city along the Silk Road that grew rich from trade

nomads people who move often from place to place

yurt moveable round house made of wool felt mats hung over a wood frame

Section Summary
HISTORY

For hundreds of years, many groups of people came through Central Asia. They left lasting influences.

At one time, there were two trade routes through Central Asia. One route went between Europe and India, through Afghanistan. The other route went through the rest of Central Asia. It was called the Silk Road, because traders from Europe traveled it to get silk and spices from China. **Samarqand** and other cities on the Silk Road grew rich.

By 1500, Europeans stopped using these roads. They discovered they could sail to East Asia on the Indian Ocean. The region became isolated and poor.

The Silk Road brought many people into Central Asia. In AD 500, Turkic-speaking nomads came from northern Asia. From the 700s to 1200s, Arabs ruled. They brought their religion, Islam. Then the Mongols conquered Central Asia. After the Mongols, groups such as the Uzbeks, Kazaks, and Turkmen came in.

In the mid-1800s, Russia conquered this region. Russians built railroads. They also increased oil and cotton production. But people began to resist Russia's rule. After the Soviets took power in Russia, they wanted to weaken resistance to their

> **What places did the two trade routes in Central Asia connect?**
> _____
> _____

> **Underline the reason that Europeans stopped using the trade routes.**

> **Circle the dates that the Arabs ruled Central Asia.**

rule. So they divided Central Asia into republics. They also encouraged ethnic Russians to move in. The Soviets also built huge irrigation projects for more cotton production. In 1991, the Soviet government collapsed. Central Asia's republics became independent countries.

> **What happened to Asia's republics when the Soviet government collapsed in 1991?**
>
> _____
>
> _____

CULTURE

The people who came through Central Asia brought new languages, religions, and ways of life. These mixed with traditional ways.

For centuries, Central Asians raised herds of horses, cattle, goats, and sheep. Many lived as **nomads**. They moved their herds to different pastures in summer and winter. They also moved their houses. The Central Asian nomad's moveable house is called a **yurt**. It is an important symbol today. Even people in cities put up yurts for special events. Nomads are still common in Kyrgyzstan.

> **Unscramble these letters to identify a feature of nomad life: *tury*. Write your answer:**
>
> _____

Today, most of the region's ethnic groups are part of the larger Turkic group. There are ethnic Russians, also. Each group speaks its own language. Some countries have many languages. In some countries Russian is still the official language, because of earlier Russian rule. The Russians also brought Cyrillic, their alphabet. Now most countries use the Latin alphabet, the one for writing English.

> **Circle the name of the Russian alphabet.**

The region's main religion is Islam, but there are also others. Some people are Russian Orthodox, a Christian religion. Today, many religious buildings that were closed by the Soviets have opened again.

CHALLENGE ACTIVITY

Critical Thinking: Drawing Conclusions

Using the dates in the summary, make a timeline of the people who have ruled the region.

Cyrillic	nomads	Pashto
Samarqand	Silk Road	yurt

DIRECTIONS On the line provided before each statement, write **T** if the statement is true and **F** if the statement is false. If the statement is false, write the term that makes the sentence a true statement on the line after each sentence.

_____ 1. Yurts are people who move around often.

_____

_____ 2. A nomad is a movable, round house.

_____

_____ 3. The city of Samarqand was along the Silk Road.

_____

_____ 4. The Russians introduced the Pashto alphabet in Central Asia.

_____

_____ 5. Cyrillic is one of the official languages of Afghanistan.

_____

MAIN IDEAS
1. The countries of Central Asia are working to develop their economies and to improve political stability in the region.
2. The countries of Central Asia face issues and challenges related to the environment, the economy, and politics.

Key Terms and Places

Taliban radical Muslim group that arose in Afghanistan in the mid-1990s

Kabul capital of Afghanistan

dryland farming farming that relies on rainfall instead of irrigation

arable suitable for growing crops

Section Summary
CENTRAL ASIA TODAY

Central Asia is working to recover from a history of invasions and foreign rulers. The region is trying to build more stable governments and stronger economies.

During the 1980s, Afghanistan was at war with the Soviet Union. In the mid-1990s, the **Taliban** took power. This was a radical Muslim group. It ruled most of the country, including **Kabul**, the capital. It based its laws on strict Islamic teachings. Most people disagreed with the Taliban. A terrorist group based in Afghanistan attacked the United States on September 11, 2001. As a result, U.S. and British forces toppled the Taliban government. Now people in Afghanistan have a constitution and more freedom. But some groups still threaten violence.

Kazakhstan was the first area in Central Asia that Russia conquered. It still has many Russian influences. Its economy suffered when the Soviet Union fell. But it is growing again, because of oil reserves and a free market. Kazakhstan has a stable democratic government. People elect a president and parliament.

> What group ruled Afghanistan from the mid-1990s to 2001?
>
> _____

> Underline the sentence that explains why Kazakhstan's economy is growing.

In Kyrgystan, many people farm. They irrigate or use **dryland farming**. This does not bring much money, but tourism may help the economy. In recent years, there have been government protests.

Tajikistan now has a more stable government, after ending conflicts between different groups. Today, the economy relies on cotton farming. But only about 7 percent of the land is **arable**.

Turkmenistan's president is elected for life and has all the power. The economy is based on oil, gas, and cotton farming. The country is a desert, but it has the longest irrigation channel in the world.

Uzbekistan's president is also elected and has all the power. The economy is based on oil and cotton. The economy is stable, but not really growing.

> Why should Tajikistan look for other ways to support its economy?
>
> _____
>
> _____

ISSUES AND CHALLENGES

Central Asia faces challenges in three areas today: environment, economy, and politics.

The shrinking Aral Sea is a serious problem for Central Asia's environment. The seafloor is dry. Dust, salt, and pesticides blow out of it. Its environment also has leftover radiation from Soviet nuclear testing. People's health is a concern. Crop chemicals are also a problem for the environment, harming farmlands.

Central Asia's economy relies on cotton. This has hurt many of their economies. Oil and gas reserves may bring in more money one day. Today there are still challenges, such as old equipment, that need to be overcome for Central Asia's economy to grow.

Central Asia does not have widespread political stability. In some countries, people do not agree on the best kind of government. Some turn to violence or terrorism as a result.

> Underline the main challenges that Central Asia's environment faces.

CHALLENGE ACTIVITY

Critical Thinking: Analyzing Information If you were asked to plan a meeting about protecting the environment in Central Asia, what topics would you put on the agenda? What topic would you want to spend the most time discussing?

Guided Reading Workbook

DIRECTIONS Look at each set of four vocabulary terms following
each number. On the line provided, write the letter of the term that does
not relate to the others.

_____ 1. a. Kabul   b. Astana   c. Tashkent   d. Taliban

_____ 2. a. dryland farming   b. nomads   c. crops   d. arable

_____ 3. a. Issyk-Kul   b. Kazakhs   c. Afghans   d. Kyrgyz

_____ 4. a. Turkmenistan   b. Kabul   c. Uzbekistan   d. Afghanistan

DIRECTIONS Write three words or phrases that describe each term.

5. dryland farming _____

6. arable _____

7. Taliban _____

8. Kabul _____

The Eastern Mediterranean

MAIN IDEAS

1. The Eastern Mediterranean's physical features include the Bosporus, the Dead Sea, rivers, mountains, deserts, and plains.

2. The region's climate is mostly dry with little vegetation.

3. Important natural resources in the Eastern Mediterranean include valuable minerals and the availability of water.

Key Terms and Places

Dardanelles body of water that connects the Sea of Marmara and the Mediterranean Sea; part of the narrow waterway that separates Europe and Asia

Bosporus body of water that connects the Black Sea and the Sea of Marmara; part of the narrow waterway that separates Europe and Asia

Sea of Marmara body of water that connects the Bosporus and the Dardanelles; part of the narrow waterway that separates Europe and Asia

Jordan River river that begins in Syria and flows south through Israel and Jordan, finally emptying into the Dead Sea

Dead Sea lowest point on any continent and the world's saltiest body of water

Syrian Desert a desert of rock and gravel covering much of Syria and Jordan

Section Summary

PHYSICAL FEATURES

The Eastern Mediterranean is part of a larger region called Southwest Asia, or the Middle East. The **Dardanelles**, the **Bosporus**, and the **Sea of Marmara** separate Europe from Asia. A small part of Turkey lies in Europe. The larger Asian part of Turkey is called Anatolia.

The **Jordan River** flows from Syria to Israel and Jordan, then empties into the **Dead Sea**, the world's saltiest body of water.

Two mountain systems stretch across Turkey. The Pontic Mountains lie in the north, and the Taurus Mountains lie in the south. A narrow plain runs from Turkey into Syria. The Euphrates River flows south-east through this plain. Hills, valleys, and plateaus are located farther inland.

> **What three bodies of water separate Europe and Asia?**
> _____
> _____
> _____

> **Which two mountain systems stretch across Turkey?**
> _____
> _____

Two mountain ridges run north–south. One runs
from Syria through western Jordan. The other runs
through Lebanon and Israel.

CLIMATE AND VEGETATION

The Eastern Mediterranean is a mostly dry region.
However, there are important variations. Turkey's
Black Sea coast and the Mediterranean coast to
northern Israel have a Mediterranean climate.
Central Syria and lands farther south have a desert
climate. Much of Turkey has a steppe climate, and a
small area in the northeast has a humid subtropical
climate.

The driest areas are the deserts. The **Syrian
Desert** covers much of Syria and Jordan. The
Negev Desert lies in southern Israel.

> Circle the four words and phrases that describe climates in the eastern Mediterranean.

NATURAL RESOURCES

Because the region is so dry, water is a valuable
resource. Commercial farming relies on irrigation.
Subsistence farming and herding takes place in drier
areas.

Many minerals, including sulfur, mercury, and
copper, are found in the region. Phosphates are
produced in Syria, Jordan, and Israel. They are used
to make fertilizers. The area also exports asphalt,
the dark tarlike material used to pave streets.

> What mineral resources are found in the region?
> _____
> _____
> _____
> _____

CHALLENGE ACTIVITY

Critical Thinking: Drawing Inferences Based on
what you've learned about the climates in the
Eastern Mediterranean region, write an essay
describing which location you think would be best
for farming. What crops would you expect to grow
well there?

| Bosporus | Dardanelles | Dead Sea | Jordan River |
| Negev Desert | phosphates | Sea of Marmara | Syrian Desert |

DIRECTIONS On the line provided before each statement, write **T** if a statement is true and **F** if a statement is false. If the statement is false, write the correct term on the line after each sentence that makes the sentence a true statement.

_____ 1. The Sea of Marmara, the Bosporus, and the <u>Negev</u> separate the European and Asian parts of Turkey.

_____

_____ 2. <u>Phosphates</u> are produced in Syria, Israel, and Jordan.

_____

_____ 3. The <u>Syrian Desert</u> is the lowest point on any continent.

_____

_____ 4. The strategic location of the <u>Bosporus</u> makes it a prized area.

_____

_____ 5. The <u>Dardanelles</u> empties into the Dead Sea.

_____

DIRECTIONS Choose four terms from the word bank. Include these words in a written summary of what you learned in the section.

_____

_____

_____

_____

_____

_____

The Eastern Mediterranean

MAIN IDEAS

1. Turkey's history includes invasion by the Romans, rule by the Ottomans, and a twentieth-century democracy.

2. Turkey's people are mostly ethnic Turks, and its culture is a mixture of modern and traditional.

3. Today, Turkey is a democratic nation seeking economic opportunities as a future member of the European Union.

Key Terms and Places

Ankara the capital of Turkey

Istanbul Turkey's largest city

secular religion is kept separate from government

Section Summary

HISTORY

About 8,000 years ago, the area that is now Turkey was home to the world's earliest farming villages.

The region has been invaded for centuries. The Romans invaded and captured Byzantium, an ancient Greek city on the site of modern **Istanbul,** at the crossroads between Europe and Asia. They changed the name of Byzantium to Constantinople. After the fall of Rome, Constantinople became the capital of the Byzantine Empire.

Seljuk Turks, a nomadic people from Central Asia, invaded the area in the AD 1000s. In 1453 the Ottoman Turks captured Constantinople and made it the capital of the Islamic Empire. The Ottoman Empire was very powerful during the 1500s and 1600s, controlling territory in northern Africa, southwestern Asia, and southeastern Europe. The Ottomans fought on the losing side of World War I and lost most of their territory at the end of the war.

Military officers, led by Mustafa Kemal, took over the government after World War I. Mustafa Kemal later adopted the name Kemal Atatürk,

What did the Romans rename Byzantium?
_____
_____

Who were the Seljuk Turks?
_____
_____

Who was the leader of Turkey after World War I?
_____

which means Father of Turks. Atatürk created the democratic nation of Turkey and moved the capital to **Ankara** from Constantinople, which was renamed **Istanbul**.

Atatürk believed in modernizing Turkey, mainly by adopting some Western methods. He banned certain types of traditional clothing of both men and women, made new laws allowing women to vote and hold office, replaced the Arabic alphabet with the Latin alphabet, and adopted the metric system.

> **Why did Atatürk make so many changes and laws?**
> _____
> _____

PEOPLE AND CULTURE

Most of the people living in Turkey are ethnic Turks. Kurds are the largest minority, making up 20 percent of the population.

Turkey's culture today reflects Kemal Atatürk's changes. He created a cultural split between the urban middle class and rural villagers. In general, middle-class lifestyle and attitude reflect middle-class Europeans, while rural Turks are more traditional and reflect Islamic influences.

> **What is the largest minority living in Turkey today?**
> _____
> _____

TURKEY TODAY

Istanbul is Turkey's largest city, but the government meets in the capital of Ankara. Turkey has a legislature called the National Assembly. A president and prime minister share executive power. Although most of the people living in Turkey are Muslim, Turkey is a **secular** state.

The economy in Turkey is based on important industries, including textiles and clothing, cement, and electronics, as well as agriculture.

> **What is the National Assembly?**
> _____
> _____

CHALLENGE ACTIVITY

Critical Thinking: Drawing Inferences Kemal Atatürk is the founder of modern Turkey. Do you think he had a greater influence on people living in cities or in the countryside? Explain your reasoning.

Ankara	Constantinople	fez	Istanbul
modernize	Ottoman Empire	secular	shish kebab

DIRECTIONS Answer each question by writing a sentence that contains at least one term from the word bank. You should use all the terms.

1. What role did Constantinople have in Turkey's past? What role does the city of Istanbul have now?

_____

_____

_____

2. Describe some of the changes made by Kemal Atatürk.

_____

_____

_____

3. Who controlled Turkey during the 1500s and 1600s? What happened to this power?

_____

_____

_____

4. What Turkish foods do you think you would like or dislike?

_____

_____

_____

5. What is Turkey's government like today? Where does Turkey's government meet?

_____

_____

_____

The Eastern Mediterranean

MAIN IDEAS
1. Israel's history includes the ancient Israelites and the creation of the State of Israel.
2. In Israel today, Jewish culture is a major part of daily life.
3. The Palestinian Territories are areas next to Israel—Gaza and the West Bank—controlled partly by Palestinian Arabs.

Key Terms and Places

Diaspora the scattering of the Jewish population

Jerusalem the capital of Israel

Zionism a movement that called for Jews to reestablish a Jewish state in Palestine

kosher the term used for food allowed under Jewish dietary laws

kibbutz a large farm where people share everything in common

Gaza a small, crowded piece of coastal land disputed over by Jews and Arabs

West Bank a largely populated, rural piece of land disputed over by Jews and Arabs

Section Summary
HISTORY

Israel is often referred to as the Holy Land. It is home to sacred sites for Jews, Muslims, and Christians. The Israelites established the kingdom of Israel about 1000 BC. In the 60s BC the Roman Empire conquered the region, calling it Palestine, and forced most Jews to leave the region. This was known as the **Diaspora**. Arabs then conquered the land, but it was later invaded by Christian Crusaders, who captured the city of **Jerusalem**, but were eventually driven out. Palestine was part of the Ottoman Empire until it came under British control after World War I.

In the late 1800s European Jews began a movement called **Zionism** that called for Jews to reestablish a Jewish state in their ancient homeland. In 1947 the United Nations voted to divide the Palestine Mandate into Jewish and Arab states. Arab countries rejected this plan. Israel and Arab

> **Why is Israel often referred to as the Holy Land?**
> _____
> _____

> **When did the Roman Empire conquer the region?**
> _____

countries have fought in several wars over this issue, and disputes between the two sides continue today.

ISRAEL TODAY

Israel is a modern, democratic country with a diverse economy. About 75 percent of Israel's population is Jewish. The rest of the population is mostly Arab. Tel Aviv is Israel's largest city.

Jewish holidays and traditions are an important aspect of Israeli Jewish culture. Many Jews follow a **kosher** diet based on ancient religious laws. About 100,000 Israeli Jews live in **kibbutzim** (singular *kibbutz*), large farms where people share everything in common.

> **What percentage of Israel's population is Jewish?**
> _____

> **What are kibbutzim?**
> _____
> _____

THE PALESTINIAN TERRITORIES

In 1967 Israel captured land occupied by Palestinian Arabs—**Gaza**, the **West Bank**, and East Jerusalem. These territories are central to the ongoing conflicts between Arabs and Israelis.

In the 1990s Israel agreed to turn over parts of the territories to Palestinians if the Palestinian leadership—the Palestinian Authority—agreed to renounce terrorism and recognize Israel. In 2005, Israelis transferred Gaza to the Palestinian Authority. In 2006, control of the territories was split between two opposing Palestinian political groups. Political tensions in the region remain high.

> **Which areas of land have been the source of the greatest conflict between Arabs and Israelis?**
> _____
> _____

CHALLENGE ACTIVITY

Critical Thinking: Drawing Inferences In what areas of Israel do you think most Arabs live? Draw an outline map of Israel, locating major cities and the areas with the largest Arab populations.

Arabic	Diaspora	Gaza	Hebrew
Jerusalem	kibbutz	Knesset	kosher
Palestinian	West Bank	Yom Kippur	Zionism

DIRECTIONS Read each sentence and fill in the blank with the term in the word bank that best completes the sentence.

1. Arabic and _____ are both official languages of Israel. (Zionism/Hebrew)

2. The movement that called Jewish people to reestablish a country in Palestine is called _____. (Zionism/Hebrew)

3. If you lived on a _____ you would work on the farm and share everything with other people. (kibbutz/kosher)

4. _____ is an important Jewish holiday celebrated in October. (Diaspora/Yom Kippur)

5. Ramallah is a city in the disputed land of the _____. (Gaza/West Bank)

6. _____ is a holy city to Jews, Christians, and Muslims. (Gaza/Jerusalem)

7. The _____ is the name of Israel's parliament, which is part of the government. (Knesset/Diaspora)

8. The forced removal of Jewish people from Palestine by the Romans is called the _____. (Knesset/Diaspora)

The Eastern Mediterranean

MAIN IDEAS

1. Syria is an Arab country that has been ruled by a powerful family and recently torn apart by civil war.

2. Lebanon is recovering from civil war, and its people are divided by religion.

3. Jordan has few resources and is home to Bedouins and Palestinian refugees.

Key Terms and Places

Damascus the capital of Syria

Beirut the capital of Lebanon

Bedouins Arab-speaking nomads who mostly live in the deserts of Southwest Asia

Amman the capital of Jordan

Section Summary

SYRIA

The capital of Syria, **Damascus**, is believed to be the oldest continuously inhabited city in the world. Syria became part of the Ottoman Empire in the 1500s. After World War I, France controlled Syria. Syria gained independence in the 1940s.

> **Which country controlled Syria after World War I?**
> _____

The Syrian government was led by Hafiz al-Assad from 1971 to 2000. Assad's son, Bashar, was elected president after his father's death in 2000. In 2011, anti-government protestors challenged Bashar Assad's rule. Syria used brutal force to crush the protests. By 2012, Syria was divided by a civil war.

> **What caused the civil war in Syria?**
> _____
> _____
> _____

About 24 million people live in Syria. About 90 percent of the population is Arab. The remaining 10 percent include Kurds and Armenians. About 74 percent of Syrians are Sunni Muslim, about 16 are another form of Islam, and about 10 percent are Christian. By September 2013, more than 120,000 Syrian people had died as a result of the civil war. More than 2 million refugees have left the country.

LEBANON

Lebanon is a small, mountainous country. Many ethnic minority groups settled in Lebanon during the Ottoman Empire. After World War I, it was controlled by France. Lebanon finally gained its independence in the 1940s.

Most Lebanese people are Arab, but they are divided by religion. The main religions in Lebanon are Islam and Christianity, with each of these groups divided into smaller groups. Over time, Muslims have become Lebanon's majority religion.

After independence, Christian and Muslim politicians shared power. However, over time tensions mounted and civil war broke out. Warfare between the groups lasted until 1990. The capital, **Beirut**, was badly damaged.

> **When did Lebanon gain its independence?**
> _____

> **What are the two main religious groups in Lebanon?**
> _____
> _____

JORDAN

The country of Jordan was created after World War I. The British controlled the area until the 1940s, when the country gained full independence. King Hussein ruled Jordan from 1952 to 1999. He enacted some democratic reforms in the 1990s.

Many people in Jordan are **Bedouins**, or Arab-speaking nomads who live mainly in the deserts. **Amman**, the capital, is Jordan's largest city. The country's resources include phosphates, cement, and potash. In addition, the tourism and banking industries are growing. Jordan depends on economic aid from oil-rich Arab nations and the United States.

> **When was Jordan created?**
> _____
> _____

> **Underline Jordan's resources.**

CHALLENGE ACTIVITY

Critical Thinking: Analyzing Information Make a table with a column for each country in this section, List information about the people of each country in the appropriate column. Based on your table, which of these nations has the greatest diversity?

Amman	Bedouins	Beirut
Damascus	Palmyra	

DIRECTIONS Read each sentence and fill in the blank with the word in the word pair that best completes the sentence.

1. _____ is the capital of Syria and is thought to be the oldest continuously inhabited city in the world. (Damascus/Beirut)

2. _____, the capital of Lebanon, was badly damaged during a civil war. (Damascus/Beirut)

3. The Romans called this ancient trading center in Syria _____, meaning "city of palm trees." (Bedouins/Palmyra)

4. _____, who mostly live in the deserts of Southwest Asia, are Arabic-speaking nomads. (Bedouins/Palmyra)

5. The capital of Jordan, _____, is also the country's largest city. (Beirut/Amman)

DIRECTIONS On a separate piece of paper, create a crossword puzzle using the words in the word bank. Use the definition or description of each term as a clue. If you wish, you may add other words from the section to create a bigger puzzle.

MAIN IDEAS
1. Major physical features of the Arabian Peninsula, Iraq, and Iran are desert plains and mountains.
2. The region has a dry climate and little vegetation.
3. Most of the world is dependent on oil, a resource that is exported from this region.

Key Terms and Places

Arabian Peninsula region of the world that has the largest sand desert in the world

Persian Gulf body of water surrounded by the Arabian Peninsula, Iran, and Iraq

Tigris River river that flows across a low, flat plain in Iraq and joins the Euphrates River

Euphrates River river that flows across a low, flat plain in Iraq and joins the Tigris River

oasis a wet, fertile area in a desert that forms where underground water bubbles to the surface

wadis dry streambeds

fossil water water that is not being replaced by rainfall

Section Summary
PHYSICAL FEATURES

The region of the **Arabian Peninsula**, Iraq, and Iran has huge deserts. Not all deserts are sand. Some are bare rock or gravel. The region forms a semicircle with the **Persian Gulf** at the center.

The region's main landforms are rivers, plains, plateaus, and mountains. The two major rivers are the **Tigris** and **Euphrates** in Iraq. They create a narrow fertile area, which was called Mesopotamia in ancient times.

The Arabian Peninsula has flat, open plains in the east. In the south, desert plains are covered with sand. Deserts in the north are covered with volcanic rock. The peninsula rises slowly toward the Red Sea. This makes a high landscape of mountains and

> Underline the words that tell you what deserts can be made of.

> List the four main landforms of this region.
>
> _____
>
> _____
>
> _____
>
> _____

flat plateaus. Plateaus and mountains also cover most of Iran.

CLIMATE AND VEGETATION

This region has a desert climate. It can get very hot in the day and very cold at night. The Rub' al-Khali desert in Saudi Arabia is the world's largest sand desert. Its name means "Empty Quarter," because it has so little life.

Some areas with plateaus and mountains get rain or snow in winter. Some mountain peaks get more than 50 inches of rain a year. Trees grow in these areas. They also grow in **oases** in the desert. At an oasis, underground water bubbles up. Some plants also grow in parts of the desert. Their roots either go very deep or spread out very far to get as much water as they can.

> **Is the desert always hot? Explain your answer.**
> _____
> _____
> _____
> _____

> **Underline the sentence that explains how desert plants get water.**

RESOURCES

Water is one of this region's two most valuable resources. But water is scarce. Some places in the desert have springs that give water. Wells also provide water. Some wells are dug into dry streambeds called **wadis**. Other wells go very deep underground to get **fossil water**. This is water that is not replaced by rain, so these wells will run dry over time.

Oil is the region's other important resource. This resource is plentiful. Oil has brought wealth to the countries that have oil fields. But oil cannot be replaced once it is taken. Too much drilling for oil may cause problems in the future.

> **Circle two important resources in this region.**

CHALLENGE ACTIVITY

Critical Thinking: Designing Design an illustrated poster using the term *Persian Gulf*. For each letter, write a word containing that letter that tells something about the region.

Arabian Peninsula	Euphrates River	fossil water	oasis
Persian Gulf	Tigris River	wadis	

DIRECTIONS Read each sentence and fill in the blank with the word in the word pair that best completes the sentence.

1. The countries of the _____ form a semicircle. (Persian Gulf/Arabian Peninsula)

2. The _____ begins in a humid region and flows through a dry area. (Tigris River/fossil water)

3. The _____ joins with the Tigris River before reaching the Persian Gulf. (oasis/Euphrates River)

4. The _____ is in the center of this region. (Persian Gulf/Arabian Peninsula)

5. One water resource for this region is the wells that are dug into

_____, or dry streambeds. (fossil water/wadis)

DIRECTIONS Use all of the terms from the word bank to write a summary of what you learned in the section.

_____

_____

_____

_____

_____

_____

_____

_____

_____

The Arabian Peninsula, Iraq, and Iran

MAIN IDEAS

1. Islamic culture and an economy greatly based on oil influence life in Saudi Arabia.

2. Most Arabian Peninsula countries other than Iraq and Iran are monarchies influenced by Islamic culture and oil resources.

Key Terms

Shia branch of Islam in which Muslims believe that true interpretations of Islamic teachings can only come from certain religious and political leaders

Sunni branch of Islam in which Muslims believe in the ability of the majority of the community to interpret Islamic teachings

OPEC Organization of Petroleum Exporting Countries, an international organization whose members work to influence the price of oil on world markets by controlling the supply

Section Summary

SAUDI ARABIA

Saudi Arabia is the largest country on the Arabian Peninsula. A major center of religion and culture, its economy is one of the strongest in the region.

Most Saudis speak Arabic. Islam is a strong influence on their culture and customs. This religion was started in Saudi Arabia by Muhammad. Most Saudis follow one of two branches of Islam—**Shia** or **Sunni**. About 85 percent of Saudi Muslims are Sunni.

> **What branch of Islam do most Saudis follow?**
> _____
> _____

Islam influences Saudi culture in many ways. It teaches modesty, so traditional clothing is long and loose, covering the arms and legs. Women rarely go out in public without a husband or male relative with them. But women can own and run businesses.

The country's government is a monarchy. Local officials are elected. In 2015 women will be able to vote and run for office.

Saudi Arabia is an important member of **OPEC**, an organization with members from different countries. OPEC works to control oil supplies to influence world oil prices.

Saudi Arabia also has challenges. It has very little fresh water to grow crops, so it has to import most of its food. Population growth has caused unemployment, especially for young people.

> Underline two challenges Saudi Arabia faces.

OTHER COUNTRIES OF THE ARABIAN PENINSULA

There are six smaller countries of this region: Kuwait, Bahrain, Qatar, the United Arab Emirates (UAE), Oman, and Yemen. Like Saudi Arabia, they are all influenced by Islam and most have monarchies and depend on oil.

> List the six smaller countries on the Arabian Peninsula.
> _____
> _____
> _____
> _____
> _____
> _____

Most of these countries are rich. Yemen is the poorest. Oil was only discovered there in the 1980s.

Most of these countries have a monarchy. Some also have elected officials. Yemen's government is elected, but political corruption has been a problem.

Some of these countries support their economy in other ways besides oil. Bahrain's oil began to run out in the 1990s. Banking and tourism are now important. Qatar and the UAE also have natural gas. Oman does not have as much oil as other countries, so it is trying to create new industries.

> Circle three ways besides oil that countries in this region are supporting their economies.

The Persian Gulf War started in 1990 when Iraq invaded Kuwait. The United States and other countries helped Kuwait defeat Iraq. Many of Kuwait's oilfields were destroyed during the war.

CHALLENGE ACTIVITY

Critical Thinking: Compare and Contrast Use a Venn diagram or a Features Chart to compare and contrast Saudi Arabia with at least two other countries of the Arabian Peninsula. Consider features such as religious influences, resources, governments, and economies.

| OPEC | procedure | reserves |
| Shia | Sunni | desalination |

DIRECTIONS Use a word from the word bank to fill in the blank in each sentence below.

1. The majority of Saudis are _____ Muslims.

2. A _____ is a series of steps taken to accomplish a task.

3. _____ Muslims believe that only imams can interpret Islamic teachings.

4. _____ is an international organization that controls the supply of oil to influence prices on world markets.

5. Saudi Arabia uses _____ plants to remove salt from sea water.

6. Saudi Arabia has the world's largest _____, or supplies, of oil.

Guided Reading Workbook

The Arabian Peninsula, Iraq, and Iran

Section 3

MAIN IDEAS
1. Iraq's history includes rule by many conquerors and cultures. Its recent history includes wars.
2. Most of Iraq's people are Arab, and Iraqi culture includes the religion of Islam.
3. Iraq today must rebuild its government and economy, which have suffered from years of conflict.

Key Terms and Places

embargo limit on trade

Baghdad capital of Iraq

Section Summary

HISTORY

The world's first civilization was in Iraq, in the area called Mesopotamia. Throughout history, many cultures and empires conquered Mesopotamia, including Great Britain in World War I. In the 1950s, Iraqi army officers overthrew British rule.

| Circle the location of the world's first civilization. |

Iraq's recent history includes wars and a harsh, corrupt leader. In 1968 the Ba'ath Party took power. In 1979 the party's leader, Saddam Hussein, became president. He restricted the press and people's freedoms. He killed an unknown number of political enemies.

| Why was Saddam Hussein considered a harsh leader? |
| _____ |
| _____ |
| _____ |
| _____ |

Saddam led Iraq into two wars. In 1980, Iraq invaded Iran. The Iran-Iraq War lasted until 1988. In 1990, Iraq invaded Kuwait. Western leaders worried about Iraq controlling too much oil and having weapons of mass destruction. An alliance of countries led by the United States forced Iraq from Kuwait. After the war, Saddam Hussein did not accept all the terms of peace, so the United Nations placed an **embargo** on Iraq. This hurt the economy.

| Underline the word that means a limit on trade. |

In March 2003, the United States invaded Iraq. Saddam Hussein went into hiding and Iraq's government fell. Saddam Hussein was later found and arrested.

When did the United States invade Iraq?
_____

PEOPLE AND CULTURE

Most of Iraq's people belong to two ethnic groups. The majority are Arab, who speak Arabic. The others are Kurd, who speak Kurdish in addition to Arabic. Kurds live in a large region in the north of Iraq.

Most Iraqis are Muslim. About 60 percent are Shia Muslims and live in the south. About one third are Sunni Muslims and live in the north.

Circle the ethnic group that most people in Iraq belong to.

IRAQ TODAY

Today Iraq is slowly recovering from war. **Baghdad**, Iraq's capital of 6 million people, was badly damaged. People lost electricity and running water. After the war, the U.S. military and private companies helped to restore water and electricity and to rebuild homes, businesses, and schools.

In January 2005 the people of Iraq took part in democracy for the first time. They voted for members of the National Assembly. This group's main task was to write Iraq's new constitution.

Iraq is trying to rebuild a strong economy. Oil and crops are important resources. It may take years for Iraq to rebuild structures such as schools, hospitals, and roads. It may be even harder to create a free society and strong economy.

The U.S. census for the year 2010 reports that about 3,800,000 people live in the city of Los Angeles. How does the population of Baghdad compare with this?
_____
_____
_____

Underline the main task of Iraq's National Assembly.

CHALLENGE ACTIVITY

Critical Thinking: Analyzing On a separate piece of paper, create a time line of events in Iraq since 1968.

alliance	Baghdad	embargo
Kurds	Saddam Hussein	uprising

DIRECTIONS Read each sentence and fill in the blank with the word
in the word pair that best completes the sentence.

1. The United Nations placed an _____, or limit on trade, on
Iraq after the 1991 war. (embargo/alliance)

2. _____ is Iraq's capital. (Kurds/Baghdad)

3. _____ was the ruler of Iraq for many years.
(Saddam Hussein/Kurds)

4. The _____ are mostly farmers and live in northern Iraq.
(Kurds/Baghdad)

5. When Shia Muslims attempted an _____, Saddam Hussein's
response was brutal. (alliance/uprising)

DIRECTIONS Use at least four of the words from the word bank to
write a summary of what you learned in the section.

_____

_____

_____

_____

_____

_____

_____

_____

_____

_____

The Arabian Peninsula, Iraq, and Iran

Section 4

MAIN IDEAS
1. Iran's history includes great empires and an Islamic republic.
2. In Iran today, Islamic religious leaders restrict the rights of most Iranians.

Key Terms and Places

shah king

revolution a drastic change in a country's government and way of life

Tehran capital of Iran

theocracy a government ruled by religious leaders

Section Summary

HISTORY

Iran today is an Islamic republic. In the past, the region was ruled by the Persian Empire and a series of Muslim empires.

The Persian Empire was a great center of art and learning. It was known for architecture and many other arts, including carpets. The capital, Persepolis, had walls and statues that glittered with gold, silver, and jewels. When Muslims conquered the region, they converted the Persians to Islam. But most people kept their Persian culture.

In 1921 an Iranian military officer took charge. He claimed the Persian title of **shah**, or king. In 1941 his son took control. This shah was an ally of the United States and Britain. He tried to make Iran more modern, but his programs were not popular.

In 1979 Iranians began a **revolution**. They overthrew the shah. The new government set up an Islamic republic that follows strict Islamic law.

Soon after the revolution began, Iran's relations with the United States broke down. A mob of students attacked the U.S. Embassy in **Tehran**. Over 50 Americans were held hostage for a year.

> **Name and describe the capital of the Persian Empire.**
> _____
> _____
> _____
> _____

> **Underline the phrase that explains what an Islamic republic does.**

IRAN TODAY

Iran is unique in Southwest Asia, where most people are Arabs and speak Arabic. In Iran, more than half the people are Persian. They speak Farsi, the Persian language.

Iran has one of Southwest Asia's largest populations. It has about 80 million people, and the average age is about 28.

Iran is very diverse. Along with Persians, Iranian ethnic groups include Azeris, Lurs, Kurds, Arabs, and Turks. Most Iranians are Shia Muslim. About 10 percent are Sunni Muslim. Others practice Christianity, Judaism, and other religions.

Persian culture influences life in Iran in many ways. People celebrate Nowruz, the Persian New Year. Persian food is an important part of most family gatherings.

Iran's economy is based on oil. There are also other industries, including carpet production and agriculture.

Iran's government is a **theocracy**. Its rulers, or *ayatollahs*, are religious leaders. The country also has an elected president and parliament.

Iran's government has supported many hard-line policies, such as terrorism. Today, the United States and other nations are concerned about Iran's nuclear program as a threat to world security.

> Estimate the number of Iranians under age 28.
> _____

> Circle two ways that Persian culture is part of people's lives today.

CHALLENGE ACTIVITY

Critical Thinking: Analyzing Information Create a table about Saudi Arabia, Iraq, and Iran. For each nation, list information about religion, government, language, ethnic groups, and economy. After you complete your chart, write one or two sentences to summarize the ways these nations are alike and different.

Farsi	Nowruz	revolution
shah	Tehran	theocracy

DIRECTIONS Write three words or phrases related to the term.

1. Nowruz _____

2. revolution _____

3. shah _____

4. Tehran _____

5. theocracy _____

6. Farsi _____

DIRECTIONS Choose three of the words from the word bank. On a separate sheet of paper, use the words to write a paragraph about Iran.

Section 1

MAIN IDEAS
1. Major physical features of North Africa include the Nile River, the Sahara, and the Atlas Mountains.
2. The climate of North Africa is hot and dry, and water is the region's most important resource.

Key Terms and Places

Sahara world's largest desert, covering most of North Africa

Nile River the world's longest river, located in Egypt

silt finely ground, fertile soil good for growing crops

Suez Canal strategic waterway connecting the Mediterranean and Red Seas

oasis wet, fertile area in a desert where a natural spring or well provides water

Atlas Mountains mountain range on the northwestern side of the Sahara

Section Summary

PHYSICAL FEATURES

Morocco, Algeria, Tunisia, Libya, and Egypt are the five countries of North Africa. All five countries have northern coastlines on the Mediterranean Sea. The largest desert in the world, the **Sahara**, covers most of North Africa.

The **Nile River**, the world's longest, flows northward through the eastern Sahara. Near its end, the Nile becomes a large river delta that empties into the Mediterranean Sea. The river's water irrigates the farmland along its banks. In the past, flooding along the Nile left finely ground fertile soil, called **silt**, in the surrounding fields. Today, the Aswan High Dam controls flooding and prevents silt from being deposited in the nearby fields. Farmers must use fertilizer to aid the growth of crops.

East of the Nile River is the Sinai Peninsula, which is made up of rocky mountains and desert.

> **Name the five countries of North Africa.**
> _____
> _____

> **Describe the Nile River.**
> _____
> _____
> _____

Name _____ Class _____ Date _____

Section 1, *continued*

The **Suez Canal**, a narrow waterway connects the
Mediterranean Sea with the Red Sea.

The Sahara has a huge impact on all of North
Africa. It is made up of sand dunes, gravel plains,
and rocky, barren mountains. Because of the
Sahara's harsh environment, few people live there.
Small settlements of farmers are located by **oases**—
wet, fertile areas in the desert that are fed by natural
springs. The Ahaggar Mountains are located in
central North Africa. The **Atlas Mountains** are in
the northwestern part of North Africa.

> Why would an oasis be valuable to someone traveling in the desert?
> _____
> _____

CLIMATE AND RESOURCES

Most of North Africa has a desert climate. It is hot
and dry during the day and cool or cold during the
night. There is very little rain. Most of the northern
coast west of Egypt has a Mediterranean climate.
There it is hot and dry in the summer and cool and
moist in the winter. Areas between the coast and the
Sahara have a steppe climate.

Important resources include oil and gas,
particularly for Libya, Algeria, and Egypt. In
Morocco, iron ore and minerals are important. Coal,
oil, and natural gas are found in the Sahara.

> What kind of climate covers most of North Africa?
> _____

CHALLENGE ACTIVITY

Critical Thinking: Evaluating Why do you think
almost all of Egypt's population lives along the Nile
River? Write a brief paragraph that explains your
answer.

© Houghton Mifflin Harcourt Publishing Company

203

Guided Reading Workbook

Aswan High Dam	Atlas Mountains	delta
Nile River	oasis	Sahara
silt	Sinai Mountains	Suez Canal

DIRECTIONS On the line provided before each statement, write **T** if a statement is true and **F** if a statement is false. If the statement is false, write the term from the word bank that would make the sentence a true statement on the line provided below the sentence.

_____ 1. Built by the French in the 1860s, the <u>Aswan High Dam</u> connects the Mediterranean Sea with the Red Sea.

_____

_____ 2. Flowing for 4,132 miles, the <u>Nile River</u> is the world's longest river.

_____

_____ 3. Annual floods along the northern Nile River left fertile soil called <u>silt</u> in the surrounding fields.

_____

_____ 4. The <u>Sinai Mountains</u>, located on the northwestern side of the Sahara, rise as high as 13,671 feet (4,167 m).

_____

_____ 5. In a desert such as the Sahara, a(an) <u>delta</u> is a wet, fertile area where a natural spring or well provides water.

_____

DIRECTIONS Write three words or phrases that describe each term.

6. Sahara _____

7. Nile River _____

8. silt _____

9. oasis _____

10. Suez Canal _____

North Africa

MAIN IDEAS
1. North Africa's history includes ancient Egyptian civilization.
2. Islam influences the cultures of North Africa and most people speak Arabic.

Key Terms and Places

Alexandria city in Egypt founded by Alexander the Great in 332 BC

Berbers an ethnic group who are native to North Africa and speak Berber languages

Section Summary
NORTH AFRICA'S HISTORY

Around 3200 BC, people along the northern Nile united into a single Egyptian Kingdom. The ancient Egyptians participated in trade, developed a writing system, and built pyramids in which to bury their pharaohs, or kings. The pyramids were made of large blocks of stone that were probably rolled on logs to the Nile and then moved by barge to the building site. The Great Pyramid of Egypt took about twenty years to finish.

> **Where did ancient Egyptians bury their kings?**
> _____
> _____

Hieroglyphs, pictures and symbols that stand for ideas and words, formed the basis for Egypt's first writing system. Each symbol stood for one or more sounds in the Egyptian language. Many writings recorded the achievements of pharaohs.

> **What are hieroglyphs?**
> _____
> _____
> _____

Invaders of North Africa included people from the eastern Mediterranean, Greeks, and Romans. Alexander the Great, the Macedonian king, founded the city of **Alexandria** in Egypt in 332 BC. It became an important port of trade and a great center of learning. Arab armies from Southwest Asia started invading North Africa in the AD 600s. They ruled most or all of North Africa until the 1800s, bringing the Arabic language and Islam to the region.

> **How long did Arabs from Southwest Asia rule North Africa?**
> _____

In the 1800s European countries began invading North Africa. By 1912 Spain and France controlled Morocco, France also controlled Tunisia and Algeria, Italy controlled Libya, and the British controlled Egypt. The countries gradually gained independence in the mid-1900s. Algeria was the last country to win independence in 1962. Today the countries of North Africa are trying to build stronger ties to other Arab countries.

What European countries ruled North Africa in the early 1900s? _____ _____

CULTURES OF NORTH AFRICA

Egyptians, **Berbers**, and Bedouins make up almost all of Egypt's population. People west of Egypt are mostly of mixed Arab and Berber ancestry. Most North Africans speak Arabic and are Muslims.

Grains, vegetables, fruits, and nuts are common foods. Couscous, a pellet-like pasta made from wheat, is served steamed with vegetables or meat. Another favorite dish is *fuul*, made from fava beans.

What language do most North Africans speak? What religion do they practice? _____ _____

Two important holidays are Muhammad's birthday and Ramadan, a holy month during which Muslims fast. Traditional clothing is long and loose. Many women cover their entire body except for the face and hands.

North Africa is known for its beautiful architecture, wood carving, carpets, and hand-painted tiles. The region has produced important writers, including Egypt's Nobel Prize winner Naguib Mahfouz. Egypt also has a thriving film industry. North African music is based on a scale containing more notes than the one common in Western music. This North African scale creates a wailing or wavering sound.

Name two important North African holidays. _____ _____

CHALLENGE ACTIVITY

Critical Thinking: Evaluating Imagine that you are traveling throughout North Africa. Write a letter to a friend at home that describes the people you meet and the places you visit.

Guided Reading Workbook

| Alexandria | Arabic | Berbers | couscous |
| fuul | harissa | hieroglyphics | pharaohs |

DIRECTIONS Look at each set of four terms. On the line provided, write the letter of the term that does not relate to the others.

_____ 1. a. pharaohs   b. pyramids   c. Egyptians   d. Muslims

_____ 2. a. couscous   b. fuul   c. Cleopatra   d. harissa

_____ 3. a. King Tut   b. Berbers   c. herders   d. tribes

_____ 4. a. writing   b. couscous   c. hieroglyphics   d. pictures

_____ 5. a. trade   b. Alexandria   c. Morocco   d. seaport

DIRECTIONS Answer each question by writing a sentence that contains at least one word from the word bank.

6. What languages do North Africans speak?

_____

_____

7. What are some common foods served in North Africa?

_____

_____

North Africa

MAIN IDEAS

1. In 2011, a pro-democracy movement called the Arab Spring brought change to North Africa.
2. Many of Egypt's people are farmers and live along the Nile River.
3. People in the other countries of North Africa are mostly pastoral nomads or farmers, and oil is an important resource in the region.

Key Terms and Places

Arab Spring wave of pro-democracy uprisings that took place in 2011 in North Africa and Southwest Asia

Cairo capital of Egypt, located in the Nile Delta

Maghreb collective name for Western Libya, Tunisia, Algeria, and Morocco

souks large marketplaces

free port a city in which almost no taxes are placed on goods sold there

dictator someone who rules a country with complete power

Section Summary

THE ARAB SPRING

In 2011, a wave of pro-democracy uprisings called the **Arab Spring** shook North Africa and Southwest Asia. Protestors demanded the right to vote and the end of political corruption. Each country touched by the Arab Spring has had a different outcome. **Dictators**, rulers with complete power, were removed in Tunisia, Egypt, and Libya. Other protests were squashed by brute force.

> What did the Arab Spring protestors want?
>
> _____
>
> _____

EGYPT

Massive protests broke out in Egypt in 2011 as a result of ongoing poverty, unemployment, and political corruption. Egypt's military forced President Hosni Mubarak from power, ending his 30-year rule.

In 2012, Mohamed Morsi was elected as president supported by the Muslim Brotherood, a

> Underline the causes of the Egyptian protests in 2011.

conservative organization that believes that Egypt's government should be based on Islamic law. In June 2013 the military removed Morsi from power and banned the Muslim Brotherhood. Today, Egypt's government and society face many challenges.

Egypt is North Africa's most populous country. More than half of all Egyptians live in rural areas. **Cairo,** Egypt's capital, is located in the Nile Delta and suffers from overcrowding, poverty, and pollution. Revenue from the Suez Canal provides important income. The economy depends mostly on agriculture and oil.

OTHER COUNTRIES OF NORTH AFRICA

Western Libya, Tunisia, Algeria, and Morocco are known as the **Maghreb**. The Sahara covers most of this region. Oil is the most important resource, and agriculture is a major economic activity. Tourism is also important, especially in Tunisia and Morocco. Marketplaces called **souks** jam the narrow streets of many North African cities, such as the Casbah in Algiers, the capital of Algeria. Tangier, in Morocco, overlooks the Strait of Gibraltar to Spain and is a **free port.** Almost no taxes are charged on goods sold there.

The countries of North Africa share similar economies and challenges. Until 2011, Mu'ammar al-Ghadfi was Libya's **dictator.** His crackdown on protestors led to a civil war in which his regime toppled. Other countries have made political reforms because of the **Arab Spring.**

> What are important industries for the other countries of North Africa?
>
> _____
> _____
> _____

CHALLENGE ACTIVITY

Critical Thinking: Making Judgments Create a chart that lists four cities in North Africa, and include facts about each one.

Algiers	Cairo	dictator	free port
Maghreb	souks	Arab Spring	Nile Delta

DIRECTIONS Read each sentence and fill in the blank with the word
in the word pair that best completes the sentence.

1. With a population of more than 10 million, _____ is Egypt's
capital and largest city. (Cairo/Tripoli)

2. Western Libya, Tunisia, Algeria, and Morocco make up the

_____. (Algiers/Maghreb)

3. In the Casbah, _____ sell spices, carpets, copper tea pots,
and other goods. (free ports/souks)

4. Tangier is known as a _____, a city in which almost no taxes
are placed on the goods it sells. (free port/souk)

5. The _____ was a wave of pro-democracy protests that
occurred in 2011 in North Africa. (Arab Spring/Nile Delta)

DIRECTIONS Choose five of the terms from the word bank. Use these
words to write a summary of what you learned in the section.

_____

_____

_____

_____

_____

_____

_____

_____

West Africa

MAIN IDEAS
1. West Africa's key physical features include plains and the Niger River.
2. West Africa has distinct climate and vegetation zones that go from arid in the north to tropical in the south.
3. West Africa has good agricultural and mineral resources that may one day help the economies in the region.

Key Terms and Places

Niger River most important river in West Africa

zonal organized by zone

Sahel a strip of land that divides the desert from wetter areas

desertification the spread of desert-like conditions

savanna an area of tall grasses and scattered trees and shrubs

Section Summary
PHYSICAL FEATURES
The main physical features in West Africa are plains and rivers. Most of the region is covered by plains. Plains along the coast have most of the region's cities. People on inland plains usually farm or raise animals. There are a few highlands in the southwest and northeast of the region.

The **Niger River** is the most important river in the region. It brings water to the people of the region for farming and fishing. It also provides a transportation route. It has an inland delta hundreds of miles from the coast where it divides into a network of channels, swamps, and lakes.

> Underline the sentences that describe the importance of the Niger River to the region.

CLIMATE AND VEGETATION
West Africa has four climate regions, which are **zonal**, or organized by zone. They stretch from east to west. The zone farthest north is part of the largest desert in the world, the Sahara.

> Circle the name of the largest desert in the world.

Just to the south of the Sahara is a region called the **Sahel**. It is a strip of land that divides the desert from wetter areas. It has a steppe climate where rainfall varies greatly from year to year. Although it is very dry, enough plants grow there to support some grazing animals.

Because animals have overgrazed the Sahel and people have cut trees for firewood, the wind blows soil away. There has also been drought in the area. This has caused **desertification**, or the spread of desert-like conditions.

To the south of the Sahel is **savanna**, an area of tall grasses and scattered trees and shrubs. When rain falls regularly, it is a good area for farming.

The coasts of the Atlantic Ocean and the Gulf of Guinea have a humid tropical climate. Much rain there supports tropical forests. Many trees have been cut to make room for the growing population.

> **What are two causes of desertification?**
> _____
> _____

> **Why have many trees been cut from tropical rain forests?**
> _____
> _____

RESOURCES

Because of the good farmland and climate in some areas, agricultural products are an important resource. These include coffee, coconuts, peanuts, and cacao, which is used to make chocolate. West Africa also has minerals such as diamonds, gold, iron ore, and bauxite, which is the source of aluminum. Oil is the region's most valuable resource. Nigeria is a major exporter of oil, which is found near its coast.

> **List four mineral resources found in West Africa.**
> _____
> _____

CHALLENGE ACTIVITY

Critical Thinking: Identifying Cause and Effect

Why do you think fewer people live in the northern portion of the region than in the southern portion? Write a paragraph to explain your reasoning.

delta	desertification	Gulf of Guinea	Niger River
Sahara	Sahel	savanna	zonal

DIRECTIONS Read each sentence and fill in the blank with the word
in the word pair that best completes the sentence.

1. Geographers describe West Africa's climates as _____
   because they stretch from east to west in bands. (savanna/zonal)

2. Desertification in the _____ is causing the expansion of the
   Sahara. (Gulf of Guinea/Sahel)

3. The _____ brings life-giving water to West Africa.
   (Niger River/Gulf of Guinea)

4. Hundreds of miles from the coast in Mali, the Niger River divides into a network
   of channels called the inland _____. (Sahara/delta)

5. Very little vegetation grows in the _____, and few people live
   there. (savanna/Sahara)

DIRECTIONS Write three words or phrases that describe each term.

6. savanna _____

   _____

7. Niger River _____

   _____

8. zonal _____

   _____

West Africa

MAIN IDEAS
1. In West Africa's history, trade made great kingdoms rich, but this greatness declined as Europeans began to control trade routes.
2. The culture of West Africa includes many different ethnic groups, languages, religions, and housing styles.

Key Terms

Timbuktu the cultural center of the Songhai Empire in the 1500s

animism the belief that bodies of water, animals, trees, and other natural objects have spirits

extended family a group of family members that includes the father, mother, children, and close relatives in one household

Section Summary

HISTORY

One of the earliest kingdoms in West Africa was Ghana, which became rich and powerful by about 800. It controlled trade in gold and salt across the Sahara. In about 1300, the empire of Mali took over. It controlled the trade routes and supported artists and scholars. The empire of Songhai took control in the 1500s. Its cultural center was **Timbuktu**. It had a university, mosques, and many schools. But invasions weakened it, and trade decreased.

Europeans began the Atlantic slave trade in the 1500s. Europeans who owned large plantations in the Americas wanted cheap labor. European traders sold enslaved Africans to colonists. Families were split up, and many people died. By the time the slave trade ended in the 1800s, millions of Africans had been taken from their homes.

European countries claimed colonies in the late 1800s so they could have access to West African resources. Europeans built schools, roads, and railroads, but they also created problems for West

> Underline the sentence describing Timbuktu.

> When did the Atlantic slave trade begin? When did it end?
>
> _____
>
> _____

Africans. All the countries in West Africa became independent by 1974.

CULTURE

The societies in West Africa have been influenced by African cultures, European culture, and Islam. There are hundreds of ethnic groups in the region. European colonizers drew borders for countries that put different ethnic groups in one country or separated one group into different countries. Many West Africans are more loyal to their own ethnic groups than to their country. The groups speak hundreds of languages. The use of colonial languages or West African languages that many people share helps with communication.

West African religions include Islam in the north and Christianity in the south. Both were introduced by traders coming to the area. Traditional religions are forms of **animism**. Animism is the belief that bodies of water, animals, trees, and other natural objects have spirits.

Some people in the region wear Western-style clothing. Others wear traditional cotton clothing which is loose and flowing. Rural homes are small and often circular. They are made from mud or straw and have straw or tin roofs. Extended families often live close together in a village. An **extended family** includes parents, children, and other relatives. West Africa's cities have modern buildings. Extended families may live together in houses or high-rise apartments.

> Circle three influences on West African societies.

> What religions did traders introduce in West Africa?
> _____
> _____

> What is an extended family?
> _____
> _____
> _____
> _____

CHALLENGE ACTIVITY

Critical Thinking: Drawing Inferences Write a letter to a newspaper to explain the problems that could arise from creating borders that put different ethnic groups in one country or separating ethnic groups into different countries.

| ancestors | animism | archaeology | extended family |
| Hausa | oral history | Songhai | Timbuktu |

DIRECTIONS On the line provided before each statement, write **T** if a statement is true and **F** if a statement is false. If the statement is false, write the correct term on the line after each sentence that makes the sentence a true statement.

_____ 1. Much of our knowledge about early West Africa is based on <u>animism</u>.

_____

_____ 2. The city of <u>Songhai</u> served as a cultural center as Mali declined.

_____

_____ 3. The belief that bodies of water, animals, trees, and other natural objects have spirits is called <u>animism</u>.

_____

_____ 4. Family members—father, mother, children, and close relatives—living in one household are known as <u>ancestors</u>.

_____

_____ 5. <u>Hausa</u> is one of the largest ethnic groups in West Africa as well as a common language people use to communicate.

_____

DIRECTIONS Choose five of the terms from the word bank. Use these words to write a summary of what you learned in this section on a separate piece of paper.

MAIN IDEAS

1. Nigeria has many different ethnic groups, an oil-based economy, and one of the world's largest cities.

2. Most coastal countries of West Africa have struggling economies and weak or unstable governments.

3. Lack of resources in the Sahel countries is a main challenge to economic development.

Key Terms and Places

secede break away from the main country

Lagos the former capital of Nigeria and the most populous city in West Africa

famine an extreme shortage of food

Section Summary

NIGERIA

Nigeria is the second largest country in West Africa. It has the largest population in Africa and the region's strongest economy. The Igbo ethnic group unsuccessfully tried to **secede**, or break away from the main country, in the 1960s. Leaders moved the capital to Abuja where there are few people, partly to avoid ethnic conflicts. The government is now a democracy after the military ruled for many years.

> Underline the name of the capital of Nigeria.

Nigeria's most important resource is oil. It accounts for 95 percent of the country's export earnings. The main industrial center is **Lagos**, which is the most populous city in West Africa and the former capital of Nigeria. Although Nigeria has many resources, many people are poor. It has a very high birthrate and cannot produce enough food. Corrupt government has also contributed to the country's poverty.

> What are two causes of poverty in Nigeria?
>
> _____
> _____
> _____
> _____

OTHER COASTAL COUNTRIES

Small countries along the coast struggle to develop their economies and stabilize their governments. Senegal and Gambia produce peanuts and offer tourism sites. Guinea has some bauxite reserves. Guinea-Bissau has undeveloped mineral resources. Cape Verde is an island country with a democratic government.

Liberia was founded in the 1820s by Americans for freed slaves. A long civil war there ended in 2003. Civil war in Sierra Leone helped destroy the economies in the area and killed thousands. Ghana and Côte d'Ivoire have rich natural resources including gold, timber, and agricultural products, but these countries have also experienced civil war. Unstable governments and poor farming economies have hurt Togo and Benin.

Circle the type of government Cape Verde has.

Underline three natural resources found in Ghana and Côte d'Ivoire.

SAHEL COUNTRIES

Drought and the expanding desert challenge the Sahel countries to feed their own people. Former nomads in Mauritania are now crowded into cities. Ethnic tensions continue to cause problems there. Niger has a very small amount of farmland where people grow staple, or main, crops. Drought and locusts created **famine**, or an extreme shortage of food, there in the early 2000s. Chad depends on farming and fishing in Lake Chad, although much of its water has evaporated in recent years. It began to export oil in 2004.

Underline the causes of famine in Niger.

Much of Mali is desert with some farming in the south. It is one of the poorest countries in the world, but its economy is improving. Burkina Faso is also very poor and has few resources. Conflicts in the region have hurt its economy.

CHALLENGE ACTIVITY

Critical Thinking: Comparing and Contrasting

Write an essay that compares and contrasts the government, resources, and economy of Nigeria with the other countries in the region.

Abuja	Cape Verde	civil war	distribute
famine	Lagos	secede	Togo

DIRECTIONS Read each sentence and fill in the blank with the word in the word pair that best completes the sentence.

1. _____ is West Africa's only island country. (Cape Verde/Togo)

2. Locusts and drought destroy crops, causing widespread _____. (famine/civil war)

3. Palm products, cacao, and coffee are the main crops in Benin and

   _____, where people depend on farming and herding for

   their income. (Cape Verde/Togo)

4. The most populous city in West Africa is _____. (Abuja/Lagos)

5. The Igbo tried to _____ from Nigeria due to ethnic conflicts. (distribute/secede)

MAIN IDEAS
1. East Africa's physical features range from rift valleys to plains.
2. East Africa's climate is influenced by its location and elevation, and the region's vegetation includes savannas and forests.

Key Terms and Places

rift valley places on Earth's surface where the crust stretches until it breaks

Great Rift Valley the largest rift on Earth, made up of two rifts—the eastern rift and the western rift

Mount Kilimanjaro the highest mountain in Africa

Serengeti Plain one of Tanzania's largest plains, home to abundant wildlife

Lake Victoria Africa's largest lake and the source of the White Nile

drought period when little rain falls, and crops are damaged

Section Summary
PHYSICAL FEATURES

The landscape of East Africa is varied and a home to diverse and abundant wildlife. **Rift valleys** cut from north to south across the region. Rift walls are often steep cliffs that can rise as much as 6,000 feet. The **Great Rift Valley** is made up of two rifts.

East Africa has many volcanic mountains. The tallest of these is **Mount Kilimanjaro**. Although the mountain is located near the equator, its peak is covered with ice and snow. Another area of high elevation is the Ethiopian Highlands.

Some areas of East Africa are flat plains. The **Serengeti Plain** in Tanzania is one of the largest. Many kinds of wildlife live here, including elephants, giraffes, lions, and zebras. Tanzania established much of the plain as a national park.

A number of rivers and lakes are found in East Africa. The Nile is the world's longest river. It begins in East Africa. Then it flows north to the Mediterranean Sea. The source of the White Nile is **Lake Victoria**. The Blue Nile begins in the

What is surprising about Mount Kilimanjaro?

_____

_____

_____

_____

Underline examples of wildlife that can be found on the Serengeti Plain.

Circle the name of the world's longest river.

Ethiopian Highlands. Both rivers meet in Sudan to
form the Nile.

Lake Victoria is Africa's largest lake, but many
other lakes also lie along the rift valleys. Some of
these lakes are extremely hot or salty.

Underline the name of Africa's largest lake.

CLIMATE AND VEGETATION

East Africa has a variety of climate and vegetation.
Latitude and elevation affect climate. For example,
areas near the equator receive heavy rains. Farther
from the equator, the weather is drier. When little
rain falls, **droughts** can occur. During a drought,
crops fail, cattle die, and people begin to starve.
There have been severe droughts in East Africa.

What happens during a drought? _____ _____ _____

The climate south of the equator is tropical
savanna. In savannas, plants include tall grasses and
scattered trees. The rift floors have grasslands and
thorn shrubs.

Plateaus and mountains are found north of the
equator. They have a highland climate and thick
forests. The highlands receive a lot of rainfall. The
mild climate makes farming possible. Many people
live in the highlands. Forests are found at higher
elevations.

Circle the reasons that farming is possible in the highlands.

East of the highlands and on the Indian Ocean
coast, the elevation is lower. Desert and steppe
climates are found here. Vegetation is limited to
shrubs and grasses.

CHALLENGE ACTIVITY

Critical Thinking: Making Generalizations Write
a booklet for tourists to read before they embark on
a helicopter tour of East Africa. What might they
find most interesting about the region?

Blue Nile	drought	Ethiopian Highlands
Great Rift Valley	White Nile	Lake Victoria
Mount Kilimanjaro	rift valley	savanna
Serengeti Plain		

DIRECTIONS Read each sentence and fill in the blank with the word
in the word pair that best completes the sentence.

1. _____ are formed when two tectonic plates move away from
each other, stretching and breaking Earth's crust. (Savannas/Rift valleys)

2. The _____ receives water from the Ethiopian Highlands.
(Blue Nile/White Nile)

3. _____ is the highest point in Africa.
(Lake Victoria/Mount Kilimanjaro)

4. The _____ in Tanzania is home to a great variety of wildlife.
(Serengeti Plain/Great Rift Valley)

5. During a _____, little rain falls, and crops and animals die as
a result. (savanna/drought)

DIRECTIONS Look up the words in the word bank in a dictionary.
Write the dictionary definition of the word that is closest to the
definition used in your textbook.

_____

_____

_____

_____

_____

_____

East Africa

MAIN IDEAS
1. The history of East Africa is one of religion, trade, and European influence.
2. East Africans speak many different languages and practice several different religions.

Key Terms and Places

Nubia part of Egypt and Sudan, an early center of Christianity in Africa

Zanzibar an East African island that became an international slave trading center in the late 1700s

imperialism a practice that tries to dominate other countries' government, trade, and culture

Section Summary

HISTORY

Early civilizations in East Africa were highly developed. Later, Christianity and Islam were brought to the region.

Ethiopia was an early center of Christianity. From there, Christianity spread to **Nubia**, in present-day Egypt and Sudan. An early Christian emperor in Ethiopia was Lalibela. He built 11 rock churches in the early 1200s.

> Circle the names of the two early centers for Christianity.

Muslim Arabs from Egypt brought Islam into northern Sudan. Islam also spread to the Indian Ocean coast of present-day Somalia.

> Who brought Islam to East Africa?
>
> _____
>
> _____

The East African slave trade dates back more than 1,000 years. In the 1500s the Portuguese built forts and towns on the coast. The island of **Zanzibar** became a center of the international slave trade. Later, Europeans forced enslaved people to work on plantations in the interior.

Most European nations ended slavery in the early 1800s, and shifted their focus to trading goods such as gold, ivory, and rubber. In the 1880s, European powers divided up most of Africa. They used **imperialism** to keep power. This is a policy of

> How did most European nations control their colonies?
>
> _____
>
> _____

taking over other countries' governments, trade, and culture. The British controlled much of East Africa. Ethiopia, however, was the one country of East Africa that was never colonized.

Large numbers of Europeans settled in Kenya. But most colonial rulers used African deputies to control the countries. Many deputies were traditional chiefs. They often favored their own peoples. This caused conflict between ethnic groups. These conflicts have made it hard for governments to encourage feelings of national identity.

Most East African countries gained independence in the early 1960s. New challenges faced the newly independent countries.

Underline the name of the only East African country that was never colonized.

CULTURE

East Africa has a diversity of people and cultures. For example, people speak many different languages. French is the official language in Rwanda, Burundi, and Djibouti. English is spoken in Uganda, Kenya, and Tanzania. Swahili is an African language spoken by about 80 million East Africans. Other languages include Amharic, Somali, and Arabic.

Circle the three main languages spoken in East Africa.

Religion and family traditions are important in East Africa. Religions vary within and among ethnic groups. Most of the cultures honor ancestors.

Many East Africans are followers of animist religions. They believe the natural world contains spirits. Some Africans also combine ancient forms of worship with Christianity and Islam.

CHALLENGE ACTIVITY

Critical Thinking: Analyzing Information Choose a country in East Africa. Imagine you are a student who has been asked to speak at your country's one-year anniversary celebration. Write a speech that describes the strengths of your country and the challenges that await.

| animist | Arabic | imperialism | Lalibela |
| Nubia | Swahili | Zanzibar | |

DIRECTIONS Write three words or phrases that describe each term.

1. imperialism _____

2. Zanzibar _____

3. Lalibela _____

4. Swahili _____

5. Nubia _____

DIRECTIONS Read each sentence and fill in the blank with the word
in the word pair that best completes the sentence.

6. In East Africa, many people are followers of _____ religions
and believe that the natural world contains spirits. (Swahili/animist)

7. The English practiced _____ in East Africa as they tried to
dominate countries' governments, trade, and cultures. (Swahili/imperialism)

8. The island of _____ was once a slave-trading center.
(Zanzibar/Nubia)

9. Christianity spread into _____ in the AD 500s, about 200
years later than Ethiopia. (Lalibela/Nubia)

10. The word *Swahili* comes from the _____ word meaning
"on the coast." (Arabic/Zanzibar)

East Africa

MAIN IDEAS
1. National parks are a major source of income for Tanzania and Kenya.
2. Rwanda and Burundi are densely populated rural countries with a history of ethnic conflict.
3. Both Sudan and Uganda have economies based on agriculture, but Sudan has suffered from years of war.
4. The countries of the Horn of Africa are among the poorest in the world.

Key Terms and Places

safari an overland journey to view African wildlife

geothermal energy energy produced from the heat of Earth's interior

genocide the intentional destruction of a people

Darfur a region of Sudan

Mogadishu port city in Somalia

Section Summary
TANZANIA AND KENYA TODAY

Tanzania and Kenya rely on agriculture and tourism. Tourists come to see wildlife on **safaris**. Much of Kenya has been set aside as national parkland to protect wildlife.

Tanzania is rich in gold and diamonds. But most of its people are farmers. The mountains of Kenya provide rich soils for coffee and tea. **Geothermal energy**, another important resource, rises up through cracks in the rift valleys.

Dar es Salaam was once Tanzania's capital. Today the capital is Dodoma. Kenya's capital is Nairobi. In 1998, al Qaeda terrorists bombed the U.S. embassies in Dar es Salaam and Nairobi.

> Circle the capital cities of Tanzania and Kenya.

RWANDA AND BURUNDI TODAY

Rwanda and Burundi were once German colonies. Both have experienced conflicts between ethnic groups—the Tutsi and Hutu. This conflict led to **genocide** in Rwanda. Genocide is the intentional

> Underline the names of two ethnic groups in Rwanda and Burundi.

Guided Reading Workbook

destruction of a people. Rwanda and Burundi are densely populated. They export tea and coffee.

SUDAN AND UGANDA TODAY

Sudan is Africa's largest country. During the last several decades Muslims and Christians have fought a civil war. An Arab militia group has killed tens of thousands in a region of Sudan called **Darfur**.

Uganda was a military dictatorship for several decades. The country has become more democratic since 1986. Economic progress has been slow, however. About 80 percent of Ugandans work in agriculture. Coffee is the country's main export.

| Circle the names of the groups fighting a civil war in Sudan. |

THE HORN OF AFRICA

The Horn of Africa is made up of four countries— Ethiopia, Eritrea, Somalia, and Djibouti.

Ethiopia has always been independent. Its people are mostly Christian and Muslim. Agriculture is the main economic activity. Severe droughts during the 1980s led to starvation. Plenty of rain has fallen in recent years, however.

Eritrea was once an Italian colony. Then it became part of Ethiopia. It broke away in 1993. Today tourism and farming are important to the growing economy.

Most Somalis are nomadic herders. Clans have fought over grazing rights. They have fought for control of port cities such as **Mogadishu**. Civil war and drought led to starvation in the 1990s.

Djibouti is a small desert country. It lies on a strait between the Red Sea and the Indian Ocean. Its port is a major source of income. Djibouti was once a French colony. Its people include the Issa and the Afar. They fought a civil war that ended in 2001.

| What four countries make up the Horn of Africa? |
| _____ |
| _____ |
| _____ |

| Underline important industries in Eritrea. |

CHALLENGE ACTIVITY

Critical Thinking: Drawing Conclusions

Suppose you joined a United Nations delegation in East Africa. Propose ways the UN could help people in the region.

DIRECTIONS Look at each set of four terms following each number.
On the line provided, write the letter of the term in each set that does
not relate to the others.

_____ 1. a. safari   b. wildebeest   c. Mogadishu   d.Serengeti Plain

_____ 2. a. Hutu   b. Tutsi   c. genocide   d. Kenya

_____ 3. a. Darfur   b. Rwanda   c. Burundi   d. Uganda

_____ 4. a. Somalia   b. Eritrea   c. Rwanda   d. Djibouti

_____ 5. a. Amharic   b. Ethiopia   c. coastline   d. drought

affect	Darfur	genocide
geothermal energy	Mogadishu	safari

DIRECTIONS On the line provided before each statement, write **T** if a
statement is true and **F** if a statement is false. If the statement is false,
write the correct term on the line after each sentence that makes it a true
statement.

_____ 6. Different clans have fought for control of the port city of <u>Mogadishu</u>.

_____

_____ 7. Energy that is produced from the heat of Earth's interior is called
<u>geothermal energy</u>.

_____

_____ 8. A <u>safari</u> occurred in a region of Sudan, causing millions to flee the area.

_____

_____ 9. Using national parkland as farmland would <u>affect</u> Kenya's economy and
tourism industry.

_____

_____ 10. Ethnic conflict in <u>Tanzania</u> led to thousands of people being killed by an
Arab militia group.

_____

Central Africa

MAIN IDEAS

1. Central Africa's major physical features include the Congo Basin and plateaus surrounding the basin.
2. Central Africa has a humid tropical climate and dense forest vegetation.
3. Central Africa's resources include forest products and valuable minerals such as diamonds and copper.

Key Terms and Places

Congo Basin the basin near the middle of Central Africa

basin a generally flat region surrounded by higher land such as mountains and plateaus

Congo River river that drains the Congo Basin and empties into the Atlantic Ocean

Zambezi River river in the southern part of the region that flows eastward toward the Indian Ocean

periodic market open-air trading market that is set up once or twice a week

copper belt area where copper is found that runs through northern Zambia and southern Democratic Republic of the Congo

Section Summary

PHYSICAL FEATURES

Central Africa lies between the Atlantic Ocean and the Western Rift Valley. Near the middle of the region is the **Congo Basin**. Plateaus and low hills surround the **basin**. The highest mountains in Central Africa are east of the basin along the Western Rift Valley. Lake Nyasa, also called Lake Malawi, and Lake Tanganyika lie along the rift. The **Congo River** is an important transportation route. It drains the Congo Basin and has hundreds of smaller rivers flowing into it. The many rapids and waterfalls prevent ships from traveling from the interior of the region all the way to the Atlantic. The **Zambezi River** flows toward the Indian Ocean. Many rivers in Angola and Zambia and from Lake Nyasa flow into the Zambezi. It also has many waterfalls, including Victoria Falls.

> Where are the tallest mountains in the region found?
>
> _____
>
> _____

CLIMATE, VEGETATION, AND ANIMALS

Because of its position along the equator, the Congo Basin and much of the Atlantic coast have a humid tropical climate with warm temperatures and plenty of rainfall all year. The warm, wet climate has led to the growth of dense tropical forests. These forests are home to such animals as gorillas, elephants, and okapis—relatives of the giraffe. However, large areas of these forests are now being cleared for farming and logging. To protect the forests and the animals that live there, some Central African governments have set up national park areas.

The climate north and south of the Congo Basin is a tropical savanna climate with warm weather all year but with distinct dry and wet seasons. Grasslands, scattered trees, and shrubs are the main vegetation. In the east, the high mountains have a highland climate. The far southern part of the region has dry steppe and desert climates.

> How has the warm and rainy climate of the Congo Basin affected the vegetation?
> _____
> _____

RESOURCES

The tropical climate is good for farming. Most people are subsistence farmers. Many grow crops for sale. In rural areas people sell goods at a **periodic market**. Other natural resources include timber from forests and rivers, which are important to travel, trade, and production of hydroelectricity. Some countries have oil, natural gas, and coal and valuable minerals such as copper, uranium, tin, zinc, diamonds, gold, and cobalt. Most of Africa's copper is in the **copper belt**. However, political problems and poor transportation have kept these resources from being fully developed.

> Name three kinds of natural resources in Central Africa.
> _____
> _____

> Circle the area where most of the copper is mined.

CHALLENGE ACTIVITY

Critical Thinking: Making Inferences Why might the Congo River be important to the development of the region's mineral resources? Write your answer in a sentence.

| basin | Congo Basin | Congo River | copper belt |
| Lake Tanganyika | periodic market | Victoria Falls | Zambezi River |

DIRECTIONS On the line provided before each statement, write **T** if the statement is true and **F** if the statement is false. If the statement is false, write the correct term on the line after each sentence to make the sentence a true statement.

_____ 1. A copper belt is generally a flat region surrounded by higher land such as mountains and plateaus.

_____

_____ 2. The Congo River is fed by hundreds of smaller rivers.

_____

_____ 3. The Zambia River flows eastward toward the Indian Ocean.

_____

_____ 4. A periodic market is an open-air trading market that is set up once or twice a week.

_____

_____ 5. Most of Africa's copper is found in the Congo Basin, which stretches through northern Zambia and the southern Democratic Republic of the Congo.

_____

DIRECTIONS Write two words or phrases that describe each term.

6. Congo Basin: _____

7. Lake Tanganyika: _____

8. Victoria Falls: _____

MAIN IDEAS
1. Great African kingdoms and European colonizers have influenced the history of Central Africa.
2. The culture of Central Africa includes many ethnic groups and languages, but it has also been influenced by European colonization.

Key Terms and Places

Kongo Kingdom one of the most important kingdoms in Central Africa, founded in the 1300s near the mouth of the Congo River

dialects regional varieties of a language

Section Summary

HISTORY

Early humans have lived in Central Africa for many thousands of years. About 2,000 years ago people from outside the region began to migrate into the region. They formed kingdoms. The **Kongo Kingdom** was one of the most important. Its people grew rich from trade in animal skins, shells, slaves, and ivory. They set up trade routes to western and eastern Africa.

> How did the Kongo Kingdom become rich?
> _____
> _____

The arrival of Europeans in the 1400s changed the region. The Europeans first came looking for trade goods. They wanted the region's forest products and other natural resources. Europeans also traded with some Central African kingdoms for slaves. The slave trade lasted about 300 years, with tragic effects for millions of enslaved Africans. They were forced to go to colonies in the Americas. At first some African kingdoms became richer by trading with Europeans, but in time these kingdoms were weakened by the Europeans.

> Underline the sentence that tells why the Europeans first came to the region.

> How did the slave trade affect the people of the region?
> _____
> _____
> _____
> _____

In the late 1800s France, the United Kingdom, Belgium, Germany, Spain, and Portugal divided all of Central Africa into colonies. The colonial borders ignored the homelands of different groups and put groups with different languages and customs together. This led to serious problems and conflicts after these colonies became independent nations.

Central African colonies gained independence after World War II. In some cases they fought bloody wars to do so. Angola was the last colony to win independence. It did not become an independent country until 1975. After independence, fighting continued among ethnic groups within new countries. The Cold War led to more fighting. Both the Soviet Union and the United States supported different groups in small wars that killed many people.

> **What problems did colonial borders create for the people of the region?**
> _____
> _____

> **How did the United States and the Soviet Union add to the conflicts in Africa?**
> _____
> _____

CULTURE

People in Central Africa speak different languages. Many speak different **dialects** of Bantu languages. Most countries also have official languages such as French, English, Portuguese, or Spanish because of the influence of the European colonial powers. The region's colonial history also influenced religion. Many people in former French, Spanish, and Portuguese colonies are Roman Catholics. In former British colonies, many people are Protestants. The northern part of the region near the Sahel has many Muslims. Many Muslims and Hindus live in Zambia.

The traditional cultures of Central Africa's ethnic groups have influenced the arts. The region is famous for sculpture, carved wooden masks, and colorful cotton gowns. The region is also the birthplace of a popular musical instrument called the *likembe*, or thumb piano, and a type of dance music called *makossa*.

> **List four types of Central African arts.**
> _____
> _____
> _____
> _____

CHALLENGE ACTIVITY

Critical Thinking: Evaluating Information Do you think colonial rule helped or hurt the people of Central Africa? Explain your answer in a brief essay.

| dialects | interact | ivory |
| Kongo Kingdom | likembe | makossa |

DIRECTIONS Read each sentence and fill in the blank with the word
in the word pair that best completes the sentence.

1. _____ is considered one of the most important kingdoms
   formed in Central Africa. Founded in the 1300s, it was located near the mouth of
   the Congo River. (Makossa/Kongo Kingdom)

2. _____ is a cream-colored material that comes from
   elephant tusks. (Ivory/Likembe)

3. _____ are regional varieties of a language.
   (Dialects/Makossa)

4. The _____, or thumb piano, was invented in the Congo
   region. (ivory/likembe)

5. A type of dance music called _____ originated in Cameroon
   and has become popular throughout Africa. (interact/makossa)

MAIN IDEAS
1. The countries of Central Africa are mostly poor, and many are trying to recover from years of civil war.
2. Challenges to peace, health, and the environment slow economic development in Central Africa.

Key Terms and Places

Kinshasa capital of the Democratic Republic of the Congo

inflation the rise in prices that occurs when currency loses its buying power

malaria a disease spread by mosquitoes that causes fever and pain

malnutrition the condition of not getting enough nutrients from food

Section Summary
COUNTRIES OF CENTRAL AFRICA

Most Central African countries are very poor. Because of colonial rule and civil wars, they have had problems building stable governments and strong economies. Before independence, the Democratic Republic of the Congo was a Belgian colony. After the Belgians left, the country had few teachers or doctors. Ethnic groups fought for power. For several decades a corrupt dictator, Mobutu Sese Seko, ran the country. The economy collapsed, but Mobutu became very rich. In 1997 a civil war ended his rule. Although the country has resources such as minerals and forest products, civil war, bad government, and crime have scared away foreign businesses. Most people live in rural areas, but many are moving to the capital, **Kinshasa**.

Since independence, other Central African countries have had similar problems. Central African Republic has had military coups, corrupt leaders, and improper elections. Civil wars in the Republic of the Congo and Angola have hurt their governments and economies. In Angola land mines left from its civil war, high **inflation**, and corrupt officials have caused problems.

> Underline two reasons why Central African countries have had trouble building stable governments and strong economies.

> Circle the problems that have stopped foreign businesses from investing in the Democratic Republic of the Congo.

In most countries the majority of people are subsistence farmers. The economies of many countries depend heavily on the sale of natural resources like oil, copper, or diamonds or on export crops like coffee or cocoa. The Republic of the Congo has oil and forest products. Angola has diamonds and large oil deposits. Zambia's economy depends on copper mining. Malawi relies on farming and foreign aid. Oil discoveries in Equatorial Guinea and São Tomé and Príncipe may help their economies improve. Most nations need better railroads or ports for shipping goods to develop their natural resources.

Cameroon's stable government has helped its economy grow. It has good roads and railways. Gabon also has a stable government. Its economy is the strongest in the region. Half of its income comes from oil.

> **What kind of work do most people in Central African countries do?**
> _____
> _____

> **What would help the countries of the region get more out of their natural resources?**
> _____
> _____

ISSUES AND CHALLENGES

The region faces serious challenges from wars, diseases such as **malaria** and AIDS, and threats to the environment. Wars are one cause of the poor economies in the region. Deaths from wars and disease have resulted in fewer older, more skilled workers. Health officials and some national governments are trying to control malaria by teaching people ways to protect themselves. Other issues include rapid population growth, food shortages, and **malnutrition**. Because so many people die of disease, the region has a very young population. Farmers can't meet the demand for food, so food shortages occur. Other threats are the destruction of tropical forests and open-pit mining of diamonds and copper, which destroys the land.

> **What diseases are a problem in Central Africa?**
> _____
> _____

CHALLENGE ACTIVITY

Critical Thinking: Cause and Effect List one challenge facing the region today. Write a sentence describing one effect of this problem on the people or land of the region.

Cabinda	inflation	Kinshasa
malaria	malnutrition	political

DIRECTIONS Read each sentence and fill in the blank with the word in the word pair that best completes the sentence.

1. The capital of the Democratic Republic of the Congo is

   _____. (Kinshasa/Cabinda)

2. A rise in prices that occurs when currency loses its buying power is

   _____. (inflation/political)

3. _____ is a disease spread by mosquitoes that causes fever and pain. (Malnutrition/Malaria)

4. The condition of not getting enough nutrients from food is called

   _____. (malnutrition/inflation)

5. The word _____ means relating to politics. (political/inflation)

Southern Africa

MAIN IDEAS
1. Southern Africa's main physical feature is a large plateau with plains, rivers, and mountains.
2. The climate and vegetation of Southern Africa is mostly savanna and desert.
3. Southern Africa has valuable mineral resources.

Key Terms and Places

escarpment the steep face at the edge of a plateau or other raised area

veld open grassland areas of South Africa

Namib Desert a desert located on the Atlantic coast, the driest place in the region

pans low, flat areas into which ancient streams drained and later evaporated

Section Summary

PHYSICAL FEATURES

Southern Africa is covered with grassy plains, steamy swamps, mighty rivers, rocky waterfalls, and steep mountains and plateaus.

Most of Southern Africa lies on a large plateau. The steep face at the edge of a plateau or other raised area is called an **escarpment**. In eastern South Africa, part of the escarpment is made up of a mountain range called the Drakensberg. Farther north, the Inyanga Mountains separate Zimbabwe and Mozambique.

Many large rivers cross Southern Africa's plains. The Okavango flows from Angola into a huge basin in Botswana. The Orange River passes through the Augrabies Falls and flows into the Atlantic Ocean.

What is an escarpment?
_____
_____

Name two major rivers of Southern Africa.
_____
_____

CLIMATE AND VEGETATION

Southern Africa's climates change from east to west. The east coast of the island of Madagascar is the wettest place in the region. In contrast to the eastern part of Africa, the west is very dry. Deserts along the Atlantic coast give way to plains with semiarid and steppe climates. Much of Southern

Africa is covered by a large savanna region. On this grassland plain, shrubs and short trees grow. These grassland areas are known as the **veld** in South Africa.

The **Namib Desert** on the Atlantic Coast is the driest area in the region. The Kalahari Desert covers most of Botswana. Here ancient streams have drained into low, flat areas, or **pans**. On these pans, a glittering white layer forms when the streams dry up and leave minerals behind.

While the mainland is mostly dry, Madagascar has lush vegetation and tropical forests. Many animals, such as lemurs, are found here and nowhere else in the world. Unfortunately, rain forest destruction has endangered many of Madagascar's animals.

| Which desert covers most of Botswana? |
| _____ |

RESOURCES

Rich in natural resources, Southern Africa has useful rivers, forests, and minerals. Its rivers provide a source of hydroelectric power and irrigation for farming. Forests are a source of timber. Mineral resources include gold, diamonds, platinum, copper, uranium, coal, and iron ore. Mining is very important to Southern Africa's economy. However, mining can harm the surrounding natural environments.

| What are some of Southern Africa's mineral resources? |
| _____ |
| _____ |
| _____ |
| _____ |
| _____ |

CHALLENGE ACTIVITY

Critical Thinking: Summarizing Based on what you've read so far, write a one-sentence summary to go with each of the following headings.

   a. Physical Features of Southern Africa

   b. Climates of Southern Africa

   c. Vegetation of Southern Africa

   d. Resources of Southern Africa

Augrabies Falls	Drakensberg	escarpment	Inyanga Mountains
Limpopo River	Namib Desert	Orange River	Okavango River
pans	veld		

DIRECTIONS Read each sentence and fill in the blank with the word
in the word pair that best completes the sentence.

1. The _____, Botswana's major river, flows into a huge basin
   and forms a swampy inland delta that is home to many animals.
   (Okavango River/Limpopo River)

2. The open grassland areas of South Africa are known as the

   _____. (veld/pans)

3. In the Kalahari, low, flat areas covered with mineral deposits are called

   _____. (veld/pans)

4. The _____ makes up much of Southern Africa's Atlantic
   coast. (Namib Desert/Drakensberg)

5. The _____ passes through the Augrabies Falls as it flows to
   the Atlantic Ocean. (Okavango River/Orange River)

DIRECTIONS Choose five of the terms from the word bank. Use these
terms to write a summary of what you learned in the section.

_____

_____

_____

_____

_____

_____

_____

_____

Southern Africa

Section 2

 MAIN IDEAS
1. Southern Africa's history began with hunter-gatherers, followed by great empires and European settlements.
2. The cultures of Southern Africa are rich in different languages, religions, customs, and art.

Key Terms and Places

Great Zimbabwe the stone-walled capital built by the Shona in the late 1000s

Cape of Good Hope area at the tip of Africa near where a trade station was set up by the Dutch in 1652

Afrikaners Dutch, French, and German settlers and their descendants living in South Africa

Boers Afrikaner frontier farmers who had spread out from the original Cape colony

apartheid the policy of racial separation set up by South Africa's government

township the separate areas where blacks had to live under apartheid

Section Summary

HISTORY

The Khoisan peoples lived in Southern Africa for centuries. They were hunter-gatherers and herders. Bantu farmers moved from West Africa to Southern Africa about 2,000 years ago. The Bantu brought new languages and iron tools.

A Bantu group, the Shona, built an empire that reached its peak in the 1400s. The Shona farmed, raised cattle, and traded gold. They also built **Great Zimbabwe**, a stone-walled capital made of huge granite boulders and stone blocks. The city became a large trading center until the gold trade slowed.

In the late 1400s Portuguese traders set up bases on the Southern African coast. In 1652 the Dutch set up a trade station in a natural harbor near the **Cape of Good Hope**. The Cape sits at the tip of Africa.

> **What group built an empire in Southern Africa?**
> _____
> _____

> **What was the Great Zimbabwe?**
> _____
> _____
> _____

Other Europeans settled on the Cape. In South Africa, the Dutch, French, and German settlers and their descendants were called **Afrikaners**.

The British took over the Cape area in the early 1800s. The **Boers**, Afrikaner frontier farmers, tried to stop the British, but lost. At about this time, the Zulu became a powerful force in the region. The Zulu were a Bantu-speaking group. However, the British defeated them and took over this land, too. Diamonds and gold were found in South Africa in the 1860s.

South Africa was ruled by white Afrikaners and became more racist in the 1900s. Black South Africans who opposed them formed the African National Congress (ANC). The white government set up a policy called **apartheid**, which divided people into four groups: whites, blacks, Coloureds, and Asians. Coloureds and Asians could only live in certain areas. Blacks had to live in separate areas called **townships**. They had few rights.

Who were the Boers?
_____
_____

What resources were found in South Africa in the 1860s?
_____
_____

What were townships?
_____
_____

CULTURE

Southern Africa has a rich and diverse culture. Its people belong to hundreds of different ethnic groups. They speak many languages, most of which are related to Khoisan or Bantu. They practice different religions, including Christianity and traditional African religions. Its arts reflect its many cultures, using traditional ethnic designs and crafts.

CHALLENGE ACTIVITY

Critical Thinking: Drawing Inferences What do you think the culture of Southern Africa would be like today if Europe still ruled over the region?

| Afrikaners | apartheid | Boers |
| Cape of Good Hope | Great Zimbabwe | townships |

DIRECTIONS On the line provided before each statement, write **T** if a statement is true and **F** if a statement is false. If the statement is false, write the correct term on the line after each sentence to make the sentence a true statement.

_____ 1. In 1652 the Dutch set up a trading colony near the <u>Boers</u>.

_____

_____ 2. The Shona built a large empire and constructed stone-walled towns, including <u>Mozambique</u>, the Shona capital.

_____

_____ 3. Dutch, French, and German settlers and their descendants in South Africa were called <u>Afrikaners</u>.

_____

_____ 4. The <u>Zulu</u> were Afrikaner frontier farmers who resisted British authority in the Cape area.

_____

_____ 5. During apartheid, many blacks were forced to live in separate, crowded areas called <u>colonies</u>.

_____

MAIN IDEAS
1. South Africa ended apartheid and now has a stable government and strong economy.
2. Some countries of Southern Africa have good resources and economies, but several are still struggling.
3. Southern African governments are responding to issues and challenges such as drought, disease, and environmental destruction.

Key Terms and Places

sanctions economic or political penalties imposed by one country on another to force a change in policy

Cape Town city in South Africa that attracts many tourists

enclave a small territory surrounded by a foreign territory

Section Summary
SOUTH AFRICA

Today South Africa has made great progress, but challenges remain. Perhaps South Africa's biggest challenge has been ending apartheid. Many people objected to apartheid. As a result, some countries put **sanctions** —penalties to force a change in policy—on South Africa. Protest within the country increased as well. In response, the government outlawed the African National Congress (ANC), a group defending the rights of black South Africans.

In the late 1980s, South Africa moved away from apartheid. In 1990 the government released its political prisoners, including Nelson Mandela. He was elected South Africa's president in 1994. South Africa's new government is a republic. Its constitution stresses equality and human rights.

South Africa has the region's strongest economy, with more resources and industry than most African countries. Large cities such as Johannesburg and **Cape Town** contribute to the economy.

What are sanctions?
_____
_____
_____
_____

What is the ANC?
_____
_____
_____
_____

Who was elected president of South Africa in 1994?
_____
_____

OTHER COUNTRIES OF SOUTHERN AFRICA

Surrounded by South Africa, Lesotho and
Swaziland are both **enclaves**. An enclave is a small
territory surrounded by a foreign territory.

Namibia gained independence in 1990. It is a
republic. Most of its income comes from mineral
resources. Fishing and ranching are also important.

Botswana is rich in mineral resources and has a
stable, democratic government. Cattle ranching and
diamond mining are its main economic activities.

Zimbabwe is politically unstable. In 2000, the
president began a land reform program, taking land
from white farmers and giving it to black residents.
However, food shortages resulted.

Mozambique is one of the world's poorest
countries. The economy was hurt by a civil war. It
relies on taxes collected on products shipped out of
its ports from the interior of Africa.

> **What does Mozambique's economy rely on?**
> _____
> _____

Madagascar has an elected president, but the
economy is struggling. The country is popular with
tourists because of its unique plants and animals.
Comoros is made up of four tiny islands. It is poor
and politically unstable. However, the government
hopes to improve education and promote tourism.

> **What makes Madagascar a tourist destination?**
> _____
> _____

ISSUES AND CHALLENGES

Southern Africa faces many challenges, especially
poverty, disease, and environmental destruction.
The African Union (AU) is working to promote
cooperation among African countries to try to solve
these problems.

> **What is the AU?**
> _____
> _____

CHALLENGE ACTIVITY

Critical Thinking: Comparing and Contrasting

Contrast the economies and governments of
Botswana and Zimbabwe. Write a couple of
sentences to explain how they are different from
one another.

| African National Congress | Cape Town | enclave |
| execute | Johannesburg | sanctions |

DIRECTIONS Answer each question by writing a sentence or two that contains at least one term from the word bank.

1. How did other countries pressure South Africa to end apartheid?

_____

_____

_____

_____

2. How did South Africa respond to antiapartheid protests within its country?

_____

_____

_____

_____

3. How do South Africa's large cities contribute to its economy?

_____

_____

_____

_____

4. Why are Lesotho and Swaziland influenced by South Africa?

_____

_____

_____

_____

The Indian Subcontinent

MAIN IDEAS

1. Towering mountains, large rivers, and broad plains are the key physical features of the Indian Subcontinent.
2. The Indian Subcontinent has a great variety of climate regions and resources.

Key Terms and Places

subcontinent a large landmass that is smaller than a continent

Mount Everest world's highest mountain, located between Nepal and China

Ganges River India's most important river, flows across northern India into Bangladesh

delta a landform at the mouth of a river created by sediment deposits

Indus River river in Pakistan that creates a fertile plain known as the Indus River Valley

monsoons seasonal winds that bring either moist or dry air to an area

Section Summary

PHYSICAL FEATURES

The Indian Subcontinent is made up of the countries Bangladesh, Bhutan, India, Maldives, Nepal, Pakistan, and Sri Lanka. This subcontinent is also known as South Asia. A **subcontinent** is a large landmass that is smaller than a continent. Huge mountains separate the Indian Subcontinent from the rest of Asia—the Hindu Kush in the northwest and the Himalayas along the north. Lower mountains, called the Ghats, run along India's eastern and western coasts. The Himalayas stretch about 1,500 miles across and are the highest mountains in the world. The highest peak, **Mount Everest**, rises 29,035 feet (8,850 m) above sea level. Pakistan's K2 is the world's second tallest peak. Two major river systems originate in the Himalayas. They have flooded the surrounding land, creating fertile plains. The **Ganges River** flows across northern India. The area along the

> Circle the names of the seven countries in South Asia.

> Underline the world's two highest mountain peaks.

Ganges is called the Ganges Plain. It is India's farming heartland. In Bangladesh the Ganges River joins other rivers to form a huge **delta**, a landform created by sediment deposits. Pakistan's **Indus River** also forms a fertile plain, the Indus River Valley. This region was once home to the earliest Indian civilizations. Now, it is the most heavily populated area in Pakistan.

Other features include a hilly plateau south of the Ganges Plain called the Deccan. East of the Indus Valley is the Thar, or Great Indian Desert. In southern Nepal, the Tarai region is known for its fertile farmland and tropical jungles.

> **Which river forms a fertile plain in Pakistan?**
> _____

CLIMATES AND RESOURCES

Nepal and Bhutan, located in the Himalayas, have a highland climate which brings cool temperatures. In the plains south of the Himalayas, the climate is humid subtropical. The rest of the subcontinent has mainly tropical climates. Central India and Sri Lanka have a tropical savanna climate, with warm temperatures year round. Bangladesh, Sri Lanka, Maldives, and parts of southwest India have a humid tropical climate, with warm temperatures and heavy rains. Southern and western India and most of Pakistan have desert and steppe climates. **Monsoons**—winds that bring either dry or moist air—greatly affect the subcontinent's climate. From June to October, summer monsoons from the Indian Ocean bring heavy rains. In winter, monsoons change direction and bring in dry air from the north.

> **Underline the type of climate found in Nepal and Bhutan.**

The subcontinent's fertile soil is a vital resource for the region. It allows farmers to produce tea, rice, nuts, and jute. Other important resources are timber, livestock, iron ore, coal, natural gas, and gemstones.

> **Circle the resources of the Indian Subcontinent.**

CHALLENGE ACTIVITY

Critical Thinking: Organizing Information Make a table with two columns to show major mountain ranges and river valleys of the Indian subcontinent.

Since 2001 Pakistan has helped the United States fight terrorism. Many people, though, think terrorists still remain in Pakistan.

Bangladesh is a small country, but one of the world's most densely populated. It has about 2,734 people per square mile (1,055 per square km). More than 13 million people live in Bangladesh's capital, **Dhaka**. One of the country's main challenges is flooding from rivers and monsoons, which often causes heavy damage. For example, one flood left over 25 million people homeless.

> Underline the sentence that tells one of Bangladesh's main challenges.

Nepal's population is growing rapidly. Its largest city and capital, **Kathmandu**, is poor and overcrowded. Nepal also faces environmental threats. Land cleared to grow food causes deforestation, leading to soil erosion and harming wildlife. Tourists also harm its environment by leaving trash behind and using valuable resources.

> What are two causes of damage to Nepal's environment?
>
> _____
>
> _____
>
> _____

Bhutan is a small, isolated mountain kingdom between India and China. After years of isolation, Bhutan formed ties with Great Britain and India in the 1900s. Bhutan has begun to modernize, building new roads, schools, and hospitals. Most of its people are farmers, growing rice, potatoes, and corn. To protect its environment and way of life, Bhutan limits the number of tourists who may visit.

> Underline the crops Bhutan's farmers grow.

Sri Lanka has been greatly influenced by its close neighbor, India. Two of Sri Lanka's main ethnic groups—the Tamil and the Sinhalese—have Indian roots. The Tamil minority has fought for years to create a separate state. The fighting ended in 2009 when the government defeated the Tamils. In 2004, an Indian Ocean tsunami struck Sri Lanka, killing thousands. More than 500,000 were left homeless. Sri Lanka is still trying to rebuild its fishing and agricultural industries.

> Circle the two main ethnic groups in Sri Lanka.

CHALLENGE ACTIVITY

Critical Thinking: Analyzing Information Make a chart to compare the challenges faced by Nepal, Bhutan, and Sri Lanka.

circumstances	Dhaka	Kashmir
Kathmandu	Sherpas	Tamils

DIRECTIONS Read each sentence and choose the correct term from the word bank to replace the underlined phrase. Write the term in the space provided and then define the term in your own words.

1. They have provided many guides for Himalayan expeditions.

_____

Your definition: _____

_____

2. This city is the capital of Nepal.

_____

Your definition: _____

_____

3. This region is the source of conflict between India and Pakistan.

_____

Your definition: _____

_____

4. They came from India to work on Sri Lanka's plantations.

_____

Your definition: _____

_____

5. Flooding in Bangladesh results from many conditions such as monsoons.

_____

Your definition: _____

_____

China, Mongolia, and Taiwan

MAIN IDEAS

1. Physical features of China, Mongolia, and Taiwan include mountains, plateaus and basins, plains, and rivers.
2. China, Mongolia, and Taiwan have a range of climates and natural resources.

Key Terms and Places

Himalayas the world's tallest mountain range

Plateau of Tibet the world's highest plateau, located in southwest China

Gobi located in Mongolia, the world's coldest desert

North China Plain fertile plain in east China

Huang He the Yellow River, a river in northern China that often floods

loess fertile, yellowish soil

Chang Jiang the Yangzi River, Asia's longest river, flows across central China

Section Summary

PHYSICAL FEATURES

China has a range of physical features. These include the world's tallest mountains, as well as some of the world's driest deserts and longest rivers. Mongolia and Taiwan are two of China's neighbors. Mongolia is a dry, landlocked country. Taiwan is a green tropical island.

> **How are Mongolia and Taiwan different?**
> _____
> _____
> _____

Mountains are found in much of the region. The **Himalayas** run along the border of southwest China. They are the highest mountains in the world. The highest plateau in the world—the **Plateau of Tibet**—is also located in southwest China. Many of the region's mountain ranges are separated by plateaus, basins, and deserts.

> **Where in China are the Himalayas and the Plateau of Tibet located?**
> _____

The Taklimakan Desert is located in western China. Swirling sandstorms are frequent here. Another desert, the **Gobi**, is located in Mongolia. It is the world's coldest desert.

Section 1, *continued*

Most Chinese live in the eastern **North China Plain**. This region is made up of low plains and river valleys. In Taiwan most people live on a plain on the west coast.

Underline the region where most Chinese live.

Two long rivers run west to east across China. One of these, the **Huang He**, or the Yellow River, picks up a yellowish, fertile soil called **loess**. When the river floods, it deposits the loess, enriching the farmland along the banks. But many people are killed by these floods. Another river, the **Chang Jiang**, or the Yangzi River, flows across central China. It is Asia's longest river and a major transportation route.

How does the Huang He both help and harm people? _____ _____ _____

CLIMATE AND RESOURCES

Climate varies widely across the region. The tropical southeast is warm to hot. There, monsoons bring heavy rains in the summer. Violent storms called typhoons bring heavy winds and rain in the summer and fall. The climate in the north and west is mainly dry. Temperatures across this area vary. The climate in the northeast is quite different. It is drier and colder. In the winter, temperatures can drop below 0°F (–18°C).

What is a typhoon? _____ _____

The region has a variety of natural resources. Farmland is an important resource in both China and Taiwan. Taiwan grows a variety of crops, including sugarcane, tea, and bananas. China also has many mineral, metal, and forest resources. Mongolia's natural resources include minerals and livestock.

Circle an important resource in both China and Taiwan.

CHALLENGE ACTIVITY

Critical Thinking: Making Generalizations Write a journal entry describing your travels through a part of the region, such as hiking in the Himalayas, traveling with nomads across the Gobi desert, or visiting a city. What are your general impressions?

Gobi	Himalayas	Chang Jiang (Yangzi River)
loess	North China Plain	Huang He (Yellow River)
Plateau of Tibet		

DIRECTIONS Read each sentence and fill in the blank with the word in the word pair that best completes the sentence.

1. Asia's longest river, the _____, flows through Central China. (Chang Jiang/Huang He)

2. The _____ is the world's coldest desert. (North China Plain/Gobi)

3. The Roof of the World is another name for the _____. (Plateau of Tibet/Himalayas)

4. The Yellow River picks up large amounts of fertile, yellowish soil called _____. (loess/Gobi)

5. Mount Everest, the world's highest mountain, is located in the _____. (Himalayas/North China Plain)

DIRECTIONS Answer each question by writing a sentence that contains at least one word from the word bank.

6. Where are China's main population centers?

_____

_____

_____

7. How do China's rivers both help and hurt the country's people?

_____

_____

_____

China, Mongolia, and Taiwan

MAIN IDEAS
1. Family lines of emperors ruled China for most of its early history.
2. In China's modern history, revolution and civil war led to a Communist government.
3. China has the world's most people as well as a rich culture shaped by ancient traditions.

Key Terms

dynasty a series of rulers from the same family line

dialect a regional version of a language

Daoism belief system that stresses living simply and in harmony with nature

Confucianism a philosophy based on the ideas and teachings of Confucius

pagodas Buddhist temples that have multi-storied towers with an upward curving roof at each floor

Section Summary

CHINA'S EARLY HISTORY

China's civilization has lasted for about 4,000 years. For most of its long history, China was ruled by dynasties. A **dynasty** is a series of rulers from the same family line.

China limited contact with the outside world for much of its history. But many people wanted Chinese goods, such as silk and tea. Some European powers forced China to open up trade in the 1800s.

> Underline the definition of *dynasty*.

CHINA'S MODERN HISTORY

Rebels forced out China's last emperor in 1911. Over time, the Nationalists and the Communists fought a long civil war. The Communists won in 1949, and the Nationalists fled to Taiwan.

Mao Zedong led the new Communist government in China. Some people's lives improved. But people who criticized the government were punished, and freedoms were limited. Some economic programs failed, causing famine and other problems.

> Who won China's civil war? When did the war end?
>
> _____
>
> _____

Guided Reading Workbook

Mao died in 1976. China's next leader was Deng Xiaoping. Deng worked to modernize and improve the economy. The economy began growing rapidly. Later leaders continued economic reforms.

CHINA'S PEOPLE AND CULTURE

China has 1.3 billion people. Most are crowded in the east, on the Manchurian and North China plains. The majority belong to the Han ethnic group. Many speak Mandarin, one of China's official languages. Others speak a **dialect**, a regional version of a language.

Modern China is influenced by many values and beliefs. The main belief systems are Buddhism and Daoism. **Daoism** stresses living simply and in harmony with nature. Buddhists believe moral behavior, kindness, and meditation can lead to peace.

Many Chinese blend elements of these religions with **Confucianism**. This philosophy is based on the ideas and teachings of Confucius. It stresses family, moral values, and respect for one's elders.

The Chinese have rich artistic traditions. Crafts are made from materials such as bronze, jade, ivory, silk, wood, and porcelain. Paintings on silk paper, calligraphy, poetry, and opera are also common. Traditional architecture features wooden buildings with upward-curving roofs. Buddhist temples called **pagodas** have multi-storied towers with roofs that curve upward at each floor. Popular culture includes sports such as martial arts and activities such as visiting karaoke clubs.

CHALLENGE ACTIVITY

Critical Thinking: Making Judgments Imagine that you are a Chinese emperor and that Europeans want to begin trading with China. Would you allow such contact with the outside world? Explain your answer in a brief essay.

> How did China's economy change under Deng Xiaoping?
> _____
> _____

> Circle the name of one of China's official languages.

> What is Confucianism?
> _____
> _____

Confucianism	Daoism	dialect
dynasty	pagodas	

DIRECTIONS On the line provided before each statement, write **T** if a statement is true and **F** if a statement is false. If the statement is false, write the correct term from the word bank on the line after each sentence that makes the sentence a true statement.

_____ 1. Confucianism stresses living simply and in harmony with nature.

_____

_____ 2. The Qin dialect was the first to unify China under one empire.

_____

_____ 3. Many pagodas, or Buddhist temples, can be seen throughout China.

_____

DIRECTIONS Look at each set of four vocabulary terms. On the line provided, write the letter of the term that does not relate to the others.

_____ 4. a. Daoism   b. Buddhism   c. Communism   d. Confucianism

_____ 5. a. dialect   b. dynasty   c. Qin   d. Qing

_____ 6. a. Han   b. Hui   c. Zhuang   d. Mandarin

_____ 7. a. Great Wall   b. civil war   c. Shi Huangdi   d. terra-cotta soldiers

Guided Reading Workbook

China, Mongolia, and Taiwan

MAIN IDEAS

1. China's booming economy is based on agriculture, but industry is growing rapidly.
2. China's government controls many aspects of life and limits political freedom.
3. China is mainly rural, but urban areas are growing.
4. China's environment faces a number of serious problems.

Key Terms and Places

command economy an economic system in which the government owns all businesses and makes all decisions

Beijing China's capital

Tibet the Buddhist region in southwest China

Shanghai China's largest city

Hong Kong important center of trade and tourism in southern China

Section Summary

CHINA'S ECONOMY

Communist China used to have a **command economy**, in which the government owns all the businesses and makes all decisions. Because it had major economic problems, China began allowing some aspects of a market economy in the 1970s. In a market economy people can make their own decisions and keep the profits they earn.

China's mixed economic approach has helped its economy boom. Today it is the world's second-largest economy.

More than half of all Chinese workers are farmers. They are able to produce a lot of food. However, industry and manufacturing are the most profitable part of China's economy. Economic growth has improved wages and living standards in China. Still, many rural Chinese remain poor. Many do not have work.

> How is a command economy different from a market economy?
> _____
> _____

> Underline the reason why China is able to grow a lot of food.

CHINA'S GOVERNMENT

China's citizens have little political freedom. In 1989, a huge protest took place in China's capital, **Beijing**. About 100,000 people gathered in Tiananmen Square to demand more political rights and freedoms. The government crushed the protest.

China has also put down ethnic rebellions. One revolt took place in 1959 in **Tibet**, a Buddhist region. China has since restricted Tibetans' rights.

Other nations have criticized these actions. They have considered stopping or limiting trade with China until it shows more respect for human rights.

> How have some countries responded to China's actions against human rights?
>
> _____
>
> _____
>
> _____
>
> _____

RURAL AND URBAN CHINA

Most of China's people live in small rural villages. But many people are moving to China's growing cities. The country's largest city is **Shanghai**. China's second-largest city is Beijing. Beijing is an important cultural and political center. Two important cities on the southern coast are **Hong Kong** and Macau. These were once under European control but have recently been returned to China.

> Circle the names of two of China's cities that were under European control until recently.

CHINA'S ENVIRONMENT

China's growth has created environmental problems. These include air and water pollution. Forestland and farmland have been lost. China is working to solve these problems.

CHALLENGE ACTIVITY

Critical Thinking: Drawing Conclusions Imagine that you are living in China and that you have a new pen pal who is curious about what it is like to live in your country. Write a brief letter describing life in China.

Beijing	command economy	free enterprise
Hong Kong	Shanghai	Tibet
most-favored-nation status		

DIRECTIONS On the line provided before each statement, write **T** if a statement is true and **F** if a statement is false. If the statement is false, write the correct term from the word bank on the line after each sentence that makes the sentence a true statement.

_____ 1. A <u>free enterprise</u> is a system in which the government owns most businesses and makes most economic decisions.

_____

_____ 2. In 1997 the United Kingdom returned control of <u>Hong Kong</u> to China.

_____

_____ 3. Controlled by China since 1950, <u>Tibet</u> is a Buddhist region located in southwest China.

_____

_____ 4. China's government will not allow <u>most-favored nation status</u>, an economic system in which people can choose their own careers, decide what to make or sell, and keep the profits they earn.

_____

_____ 5. The United States has threatened to cancel China's <u>command economy</u>, which would hurt China's trade benefits.

_____

DIRECTIONS Write three words or phrases that describe each term.

6. Shanghai _____

7. Beijing _____

MAIN IDEAS
1. Mongolia is a sparsely populated country where many people live as nomads.
2. Taiwan is a small island with a dense population and a highly industrialized economy.

Key Terms and Places

gers large, circular, felt tents that are easy to put up, take down, and move

Ulaanbaatar Mongolia's capital and only large city

Taipei Taiwan's capital and main financial center

Kao-hsiung Taiwan's main seaport and a center of heavy industry

Section Summary
MONGOLIA

The people of Mongolia have a proud and fascinating history. In the late 1200s, Mongolia was perhaps the greatest power in the world. The Mongol Empire stretched from Europe to the Pacific Ocean. Over time, the empire declined. China conquered Mongolia in the late 1600s.

Mongolia declared independence from China in 1911. The Communists gained control 13 years later. The Soviet Union was a strong influence in Mongolia. But in the early 1990s, the Soviet Union collapsed. Since then, Mongolians have worked for democracy and a free-market economy.

> Circle the name of the country that had a strong influence in Mongolia for much of the 1900s.

Many Mongolians have a traditional way of life. Nearly half live as nomads, herding livestock. Many live in **gers**. These large, circular, felt tents are easy to put up, take down, and move. Horses play an important role in the lives of the nomads.

> How do many Mongolians live?
> _____

Mongolia has a small population. Only about 2.7 million people live in the entire country. Mongolia's capital and only large city is **Ulaanbaatar**. One in four Mongolians lives there. The country's main industries include textiles, carpets, coal, copper, and

> Circle the name of Mongolia's capital city.

Guided Reading Workbook

oil. Mongolia produces livestock but very little other food. The country faces both food and water shortages.

TAIWAN

Both China and Japan controlled Taiwan at different times. In 1949 the Chinese Nationalists took over the island. They had left the Chinese mainland after the Communists took over. The Nationalists ruled Taiwan under martial law, or military rule, for 38 years. Today, Taiwan's government is a multiparty democracy.

Tension remains between China and Taiwan. China claims that Taiwan is a rebel part of China. Taiwan claims to be China's true government.

Taiwan's history is reflected in its culture. Most Taiwanese are descendants of people from China. As a result, Chinese ways are an important part of Taiwan's culture. Japan's influence is also seen. European and American practices and customs are beginning to be seen in Taiwan's cities.

Taiwan is a modern country with about 23 million people. Most Taiwanese live in cities on the island's western coastal plain. The rest of the country is mountainous. The two largest cities are **Taipei** and **Kao-hsiung**. Taipei is Taiwan's capital. It is a main financial center. Kao-hsiung is a center of heavy industry and Taiwan's main seaport.

> What group came to Taiwan after the Communists took over mainland China?
>
> _____

> What are some cultural influences on Taiwanese culture? Which is the major influence?
>
> _____
> _____
> _____
> _____

> Underline the place where most Taiwanese live. What is the rest of the country like?
>
> _____

CHALLENGE ACTIVITY

Critical Thinking: Making Judgments Imagine that you are a government official from Taiwan visiting Mongolia. Write a report explaining why Mongolia and Taiwan should or should not become trade partners.

Guided Reading Workbook

| Chang Kai-shek | gers | Ghengis Khan | Kao-hsiung |
| Nationalists | nomads | Taipei | Ulaanbaatar |

DIRECTIONS Read each sentence and fill in the blank with the word in the word pair that best completes the sentence.

1. _____ is Taiwan's capital and main financial center. (Taipei/Chang Kei-shek)

2. A powerful warrior and ruler, _____ built up a huge Mongolian Empire. (Kao-hsiung/Genghis Khan)

3. The coastal city of _____ is Taiwan's main seaport. (Kao-hsiung/Taipei)

4. The capital city of _____ is home to more than a quarter of Mongolia's population. (Ulaanbaatar/Kao-hsiung)

5. _____ served as leader of the Chinese Nationalists in 1949. (Ghengis Khan/Chang Kai-shek)

DIRECTIONS Look up the vocabulary terms below in a dictionary. Write the dictionary definition of the word that is closest to the definition used in your textbook.

6. gers _____

_____

7. nomads _____

_____

MAIN IDEAS
1. The main physical features of Japan and the Koreas are rugged mountains.
2. The climates and resources of Japan and the Koreas vary from north to south.

Key Terms and Places

Fuji Japan's highest mountain

Korean Peninsula Asian peninsula that includes both North Korea and South Korea

tsunamis destructive waves caused by large underwater earthquakes

fishery place where lots of fish and other seafood can be caught

Section Summary
PHYSICAL FEATURES

Japan is made up of four large islands and more than 3,000 smaller ones. They stretch across 1,500 miles of ocean, about the length of the Eastern United States coastline. But they include only about as much land area as California. Most people live on the four largest islands, which are Hokkaido, Honshu, Shikoku, and Kyushu. Mountains cover about 75 percent of Japan. The Japanese Alps are Japan's largest mountain range. Japan's highest mountain, **Fuji**, is not in any mountain range, but is an isolated volcanic peak in eastern Honshu. It has become a symbol of Japan, and is considered sacred by some people. Many shrines and temples have been built around it.

The **Korean Peninsula** juts south from the Asian mainland, and is divided between North and South Korea. Rugged mountains run along the eastern coast, and plains can be found on the western coast and in the river valleys. Korea has more rivers than Japan. Most of them flow westward and empty in the Yellow Sea.

> Circle the names of Japan's four largest islands.

> Where on the Korean Peninsula are the mountains located?
>
> _____
>
> _____

Japan is subject to volcanic eruptions, earth-quakes, and **tsunamis**, which are destructive waves caused by underwater earthquakes. Korea does not have many earthquakes or volcanoes. Like Japan, Korea is subject to huge storms, called typhoons, that sweep in from the Pacific Ocean.

> Underline the sentence that explains what a tsunami is.

CLIMATE AND RESOURCES

Just as Japan and the Koreas have many similar physical features, they also have similar climates. In both places, climate varies from north to south. The northern regions have a humid continental climate with cool summers, long, cold winters, and a short growing season. In the south, a humid subtropical climate brings mild winters and as much as 80 inches of rain each year. Most of the rain falls during the hot, humid summers, which is also when typhoons occur.

> In a humid subtropical climate, when does most of the rain fall?
>
> _____

Unlike the rest of the region, North Korea is rich in mineral resources such as iron and coal. Both of the Koreas use their quick-flowing rivers to generate hydroelectric power. Japan has one of the world's strongest fishing economies. The islands lie near one of the world's most productive **fisheries**, which are areas where lots of fish and seafood can be caught. Huge fishing nets are used to catch the large number of fish needed to serve Japan's busy fish markets.

> Which country on the Korean Peninsula has mineral deposits?
>
> _____

CHALLENGE ACTIVITY

Critical Thinking: Analyzing Write a paragraph describing the physical features and climate of Japan.

fishery	Fuji	humid continental
humid subtropical	Korean Peninsula	tsunamis

DIRECTIONS Read each sentence and fill in the blank with the word
in the word pair that best completes the sentence.

1. The northern parts of the region have a _____ climate, in
which the summers are cool, but the winters are long and cold.
(humid continental/humid subtropical)

2. The _____ is covered with rugged mountains.
(fishery/Korean Peninsula)

3. A _____ can be brought on by underwater earthquakes.
(tsunami/fishery)

4. Due to the swift ocean currents near Japan, it has one of the world's most

productive _____. (fisheries/tsunamis)

5. Many Japanese consider _____ a sacred place.
(Fuji/the Korean Peninsula)

DIRECTIONS Choose four of the vocabulary terms from the word
bank. Use these words to write a summary of what you learned in the
section.

_____

_____

_____

_____

_____

_____

Japan and the Koreas

MAIN IDEAS

1. The early histories of Japan and Korea were closely linked, but the countries developed very differently.
2. Japanese culture blends traditional customs with modern innovations.
3. Though they share a common culture, life is very different in North and South Korea.

Key Terms and Places

Kyoto Japan's imperial capital, known before as Heian

shoguns powerful military leaders of imperial Japan

samurai highly trained warriors

kimonos traditional Japanese robes

kimchi Korean dish made from pickled cabbage and spices

Section Summary

HISTORY

China has had much influence on both Japan and the Koreas. One example is Buddhism, which was once the main religion in both countries. Japan's first government was modeled after China's. Japan's emperors made their capital Heian (now called **Kyoto**) a center for the arts. Some of them paid so much attention to the arts that they allowed generals called **shoguns** to take control. Shoguns had armies of warriors called **samurai** who helped them rule Japan until 1868, when a group of samurai gave power back to the emperor. During World War II, the Japanese brought the United States into the war by bombing its naval base at Pearl Harbor. To end the war, the Americans dropped atomic bombs on the Japanese cities of Hiroshima and Nagasaki.

China ruled the Korean Peninsula for centuries. Later, the Japanese invaded. After World War II, Korea became independent. However, the Soviet Union helped Communists take control in the north

> Underline the sentence that explains how the shoguns gained power.

> Which country helped Communists take control in North Korea?
> _____

while the United States helped to form a democratic government in the south. In 1950 North Korea invaded the south, wanting to unite Korea. The United States and other countries helped the South Koreans remain separate.

JAPANESE CULTURE

The Japanese system of writing uses two types of characters. Some characters, called kanji, each represent a single word. Others, called kana, each stand for a part of a word. Most Japanese people combine elements of Shinto and Buddhism in their religious practices. In the Shinto tradition—native to Japan—everything in nature is believed to have a spirit, or *kami*, which protects people. Through Buddhism, people in Japan have learned to seek enlightenment and peace. Most people in Japan wear Western style clothing, but many also wear the traditional **kimono** on special occasions. Traditional forms of art include Noh and Kabuki plays.

> Circle the names of the kinds of characters used to write Japanese.

> What do Japanese people wear most of the time?
> _____

KOREAN CULTURE

People in both North and South Korea speak Korean. Unlike Japanese, written Korean uses an alphabet. In the past, most Koreans were Buddhist or Confucianist. Today, about one fourth of South Koreans are Christian. Communist North Korea discourages people from practicing any religion.

The people of Korea have kept many old traditions, such as **kimchi**, a dish made from pickled cabbage. Traditional Korean art forms remain, especially in North Korea, where the Communists think Korean culture is the best in the world. In the south, people have adopted new ways of life and forgotten some of their traditions.

> Underline the names of religions practiced in Korea.

CHALLENGE ACTIVITY

Critical Thinking: Sequencing Write a paragraph describing three periods or events in Japan's history.

Guided Reading Workbook

abstract	Buddhism	Kabuki	kana
kanji	kimchi	kimonos	Kyoto
Noh	samurai	Shinto	shoguns

DIRECTIONS On the line provided before each statement, write **T** if the statement is true and **F** if the statement is false. If the statement is false, write the correct term on the line after each sentence to make the sentence a true statement.

_____ 1. The imperial capital at Heian, now called <u>Shinto</u>, was a Japanese center of art, literature, and learning for many centuries.

_____

_____ 2. Many Japanese wear traditional robes called <u>kimonos</u> on special occasions, just as samurai did long ago.

_____

_____ 3. <u>Kanji</u> plays tell stories, but often teach lessons about duty and other abstract lessons as well.

_____

_____ 4. Most texts written in Japanese use a combination of <u>kimchi</u> and kana characters.

_____

_____ 5. In the past, most Koreans practiced <u>kami</u> and Confucianism.

_____

DIRECTIONS Write three words or phrases that describe the term.

6. shoguns _____

7. samurai _____

8. kimchi _____

Japan and the Koreas

MAIN IDEAS

1. Since World War II, Japan has developed a democratic government and one of the world's strongest economies.
2. A shortage of open space shapes daily life in Japan.
3. Crowding, competition, and pollution are among Japan's main issues and challenges.

Key Terms and Places

Diet Japan's elected legislature

Tokyo capital of Japan

work ethic belief that work in itself is worthwhile

trade surplus exists when a country exports more goods than it imports

tariff fee a country charges for exports or imports

Osaka Japan's second largest city

Section Summary

GOVERNMENT AND ECONOMY

Although Japan's emperor is the country's official leader, he has little power and his main role is to act as a symbol. In Japan today power rests with an elected prime minister and a legislature, called the **Diet**, that govern from the capital of **Tokyo**.

Today Japan is an economic powerhouse. Japanese companies use the latest manufacturing techniques to make goods such as cars and electronics. The government has helped Japanese companies succeed by controlling production and planning for the future. The strong **work ethic** of Japan's workers has also helped. Most goods made in Japan are for export to places like the United States. Japan exports much more than it imports, causing a huge **trade surplus**, which has added to Japan's wealth. The amount of imported goods is kept low through high **tariffs**, or fees, which are added to their cost.

> Circle the terms that explain who has power in Japan.

> What happens to most goods manufactured in Japan?
> _____
> _____

Guided Reading Workbook

Japan's economic success is due to its manufacturing techniques, not natural resources. Japan must import most of the raw materials it uses to make goods. Japan must also import much of its food.

DAILY LIFE

Japan is densely populated, and cities such as Tokyo are very crowded. Almost 36 million people live near Tokyo, making land scarce and expensive. Tokyo has many tall buildings. Some hotels save space by housing guests in tiny sleeping chambers. For fun, people visit parks, museums, baseball stadiums, an indoor beach, and a ski resort filled with artificial snow.

Other cities include **Osaka,** Japan's second largest city, and Kyoto, the former capital. Japan's major cities are linked by efficient, high-speed trains. Most people live in cities, but some live in villages or on farms. The average farm in Japan is only 2.5 acres, too small for most farmers to make a living, so many farmers look for jobs in cities.

About how many people live in the Tokyo area?
_____

Underline the places people in Tokyo visit for fun.

ISSUES AND CHALLENGES

Japan's lack of space is a growing problem as is economic competition from countries such as China and South Korea, whose companies have taken away Japanese business. Pollution is another problem of growing concern. And in 2011, a massive earthquake struck Japan, causing a tsunami that killed more than 18.000 people. Japan continues to rebuild today.

Underline Japan's issues and challenges.

CHALLENGE ACTIVITY

Critical Thinking: Evaluating Information Write a paragraph about one of the challenges Japan faces today.

Guided Reading Workbook

Diet	Osaka	tariff
Tokyo	trade surplus	work ethic

DIRECTIONS On the line provided before each statement, write **T** if
the statement is true and **F** if the statement is false. If the statement is
false, write the correct term on the line after each sentence to make the
sentence a true statement.

_____ 1. Because Japan exports more than it imports, it has a large <u>tariff</u>.

_____

_____ 2. Japanese companies are successful partly because of their employees'
loyalty and strong <u>work ethic</u>.

_____

_____ 3. <u>Osaka</u> is Japan's capital city.

_____

_____ 4. Located in western Honshu, <u>Tokyo</u> is Japan's second-largest city.

_____

_____ 5. In Japan, the <u>Diet</u> and the prime minister make the laws.

_____

DIRECTIONS Look up three vocabulary terms in the word bank in a
dictionary. Write the dictionary definition of the word that is closest to
the definition used in your textbook.

_____

_____

_____

_____

_____

Japan and the Koreas

MAIN IDEAS
1. The people of South Korea today have freedom and economic opportunities.
2. The people of North Korea today have little freedom or economic opportunity.
3. Some people in both South and North Korea support the idea of Korean reunification.

Key Terms and Places

Seoul the capital of South Korea

demilitarized zone an empty buffer zone created to keep two countries from fighting

Pyongyang the capital of North Korea

Section Summary
SOUTH KOREA TODAY

The official name of South Korea is the Republic of Korea. It is headed by a president and an assembly, both elected by the people. The United States helped create South Korea's government after World War II.

Like Japan, South Korea is densely populated. Its capital, **Seoul**, is a prosperous and modern city with some 44,000 people per square mile. Many people live near the western coastal plain, preferring it to the mountainous interior. In the cities, people live in small apartments and enjoy an extensive subway system. In the country, many South Koreans live on small farms, grow rice, beans, and cabbage, and follow traditional ways of life.

Although South Korea has a strong economy, in the past, the country's industry was controlled by only four families, and some members of these families were corrupt. New laws and greater foreign investment have brought reforms. South Korea is also challenged by its relationship with North Korea. Since the end of the Korean War in the 1950s, the countries have been separated by a **demilitarized** zone, a buffer zone patrolled by soldiers on both sides.

> What is the population density of Seoul?
> _____
> _____

> Underline the sentence that explains what a demilitarized zone is.

NORTH KOREA TODAY

North Korea's official name, the Democratic People's Republic of Korea, is misleading. The country is a totalitarian, Communist state.

From 1948 until 1994 it was led by the dictator Kim Il Sung. At Kim's death, his son, Kim Jong Il, became ruler and ruled until his death in 2011. Kim Jong Il's son Kim Jong Un then took over, adopting his father's domestic policies

North Korea has a command economy in which the government makes all economic decisions. North Korea uses much of its rich mineral resources to make machinery and military supplies in out-of-date factories. Farms are run as cooperatives, but there is little good farmland.

Although most North Koreans live in cities, such as the capital **Pyongyang**, their life is different from that of their neighbors to the south. Most people are poor and they are denied the rights of freedom of the press, speech, and religion.

North Korea has isolated itself since the fall of the Soviet Union. Its economy has caused shortages and poverty. Many countries worry about North Korea's possession of nuclear weapons.

What years did Kim Il Sung rule North Korea?
_____

Circle the rights that are denied to North Koreans.

KOREAN REUNIFICATION

At times, the North and South Korean governments have expressed support for reunification. In 2000, leaders met for the first time since the Korean War. However, South Korea prefers democracy, and North Korea insists on communism.

Underline the sentence that explains the greatest obstacle to the reunification of Korea.

CHALLENGE ACTIVITY

Critical Thinking: Comparing and Contrasting
Draw a Venn diagram to compare and contrast South Korea and North Korea.

| cooperative | demilitarized zone | policy |
| Pyongyang | Seoul | |

DIRECTIONS Read each sentence and choose the correct term from the word bank to replace the underlined phrase. Write the term in the space provided and then define the term in your own words.

1. North Korea is mostly farmed by <u>these</u> groups who work the

   land together. _____

   Your definition: _____

   _____

   _____

2. <u>This densely populated city</u> is the capital of South Korea. _____

   Your definition: _____

   _____

   _____

3. <u>This area</u> lies between North and South Korea to keep the two countries from

   fighting. _____

   Your definition: _____

   _____

   _____

4. Few people in <u>this crowded city</u> own private cars because the North Korean

   government allows only top Communist officials to own cars. _____

   Your definition: _____

   _____

   _____

Section 1

MAIN IDEAS
1. Southeast Asia's physical features include peninsulas, islands, rivers, and many seas, straits, and gulfs.
2. The tropical climate of Southeast Asia supports a wide range of plants and animals.
3. Southeast Asia is rich in natural resources such as wood, rubber, and fossil fuels.

Key Terms and Places

Indochina Peninsula peninsula that makes up part of Mainland Southeast Asia

Malay Peninsula peninsula that makes up part of Mainland Southeast Asia

Malay Archipelago island group that makes up part of Island Southeast Asia

archipelago a large group of islands

New Guinea Earth's second largest island

Borneo Earth's third largest island

Mekong River most important river in Southeast Asia

Section Summary
PHYSICAL FEATURES

Two peninsulas and two large island groups make up the Southeast Asia region. Mainland Southeast Asia is made up of the **Indochina Peninsula** and the **Malay Peninsula**. Island Southeast Asia is made up of the many islands of the Philippines and the **Malay Archipelago**. A large group of islands is called an **archipelago**.

> Underline the two peninsulas that make up Mainland Southeast Asia.

> Circle the two island groups that make up Island Southeast Asia.

Mainland Southeast Asia has rugged mountains, low plateaus, and river floodplains. Island Southeast Asia has more than 20,000 islands, including **New Guinea**, the world's second largest island, and **Borneo**, the world's third largest island. Island Southeast Asia is part of the Ring of Fire, where earthquakes and volcanoes often occur.

For all of Southeast Asia, water is of great importance. The region's fertile river valleys and deltas support farming and are home to many people. The **Mekong River** is the region's most important river.

CLIMATE, PLANTS, AND ANIMALS

Southeast Asia is in the tropics, the area on and around the equator. This region is generally warm all year round.

The climate on the mainland is mostly tropical savanna. Monsoon winds bring heavy rain in summer and drier air in winter there. Savannas—areas of tall grasses and some trees and shrubs—grow here.

The islands and the Malay Peninsula have a mostly humid tropical climate. Here, it's hot, muggy, and rainy all year. This climate supports tropical rain forests. These forests are home to many different plants and animals. Some animals are only found here, such as orangutans and Komodo dragons. Many plants and animals are endangered, however, due to the cutting down of the rain forest.

> **What kinds of plants grow in the region's tropical savanna climate?**
> _____
> _____

> **Why are the plants and animals of the rain forest endangered?**
> _____
> _____

NATURAL RESOURCES

Southeast Asia is rich in natural resources. Farming is very productive here thanks to the region's climate and rich soil. Rice is a major crop. Rubber tree plantations are found on Indonesia and Malaysia. The rain forests supply hardwoods and medicines. The region also has fisheries, minerals, and fossil fuels.

CHALLENGE ACTIVITY

Critical Thinking: Drawing Inferences Write an essay explaining the advantages and disadvantages of Southeast Asia's water resources for its people.

archipelago	Borneo	Indochina Peninsula
Malay Archipelago	Malay Peninsula	Mekong River
New Guinea	tropics	

DIRECTIONS On the line provided before each statement, write **T** if the statement is true and **F** if the statement is false. If the statement is false, write the correct term on the line after each sentence that makes the sentence a true statement.

_____ 1. New Guinea and the <u>Philippines</u> are the world's second- and third-largest islands respectively.

_____

_____ 2. The most important river in Southeast Asia is the <u>Mekong River</u>.

_____

_____ 3. Mainland Southeast Asia is made up of two peninsulas—the <u>Borneo Peninsula</u> and the Indochina Peninsula.

_____

_____ 4. The two large island groups in Southeast Asia are the Philippines and the <u>New Guinea Archipelago</u>.

_____

_____ 5. Southeast Asia lies in the <u>floodplains</u>, the area on and around the equator.

_____

DIRECTIONS Choose four of the terms from the word bank. On a separate piece of paper, use these terms to write a summary of what you learned in the section.

MAIN IDEAS
1. Southeast Asia's early history includes empires, colonial rule, and independence.
2. The modern history of Southeast Asia involves struggles with war and communism.
3. Southeast Asia's culture reflects its Chinese, Indian, and European heritage.

Key Terms and Places

Timor small island that Portugal kept control of after Dutch traders drove them out of the rest of the region

domino theory idea that if one country fell to communism, other countries nearby would follow like falling dominoes

wats Buddhist temples that also serve as monasteries

Section Summary

EARLY HISTORY

The most advanced early civilization was the Khmer Empire in what is now Cambodia. The Khmer built a huge temple, Angkor Wat. This temple showed their advanced civilization and Hindu religion. Later, the Thai settled in the Khmer area. Buddhism began to replace Hinduism in the region.

In the 1500s European countries set up colonies. Led by Portugal, they came to colonize, trade, and spread their religion. Spain claimed the Philippines and spread Roman Catholicism there. Later, the Dutch drove Portugal out of much of the region. **Timor**, a small island, was all that stayed under Portugal's control.

In the 1800s the British and French set up colonies and spread Christianity. The United States came into the region in 1898, when it won the Philippines from Spain in the Spanish-American War. Colonial powers ruled all of the area, except for Siam (now Thailand) by the early 1900s.

> Why did European countries come to this region?
> _____
> _____

> Circle the year the United States entered the region.

Guided Reading Workbook

After World War II, the United States granted the Philippines independence. Other people in the region started to fight for freedom, too. The French left in 1954 after a bloody war in Indochina. The independent countries of Cambodia, Laos, and Vietnam were formed from this area. By 1970, most of Southeast Asia was free from colonial rule.

> **Name the three countries formed out of Indochina.**
>
> _____
>
> _____
>
> _____

MODERN HISTORY

In Vietnam, the fighting against the French divided the country into North and South Vietnam. In South Vietnam, a civil war started. In the 1960s, the U.S. decided to send troops to South Vietnam based on the **domino theory**—the idea that if one country fell to communism, other nearby countries would fall, too. After years of fighting, North and South Vietnam became one Communist country.

In Laos and Cambodia civil wars broke out, too. Fighting lasted in Cambodia until the mid-1990s, when the United Nations helped restore peace.

> **Restate the domino theory in your own words.**
>
> _____
>
> _____
>
> _____

CULTURE

The many different ethnic groups in this region mean that many different languages are spoken here. The main religions are Buddhism, Christianity, Hinduism, and Islam. Many grand Buddhist temples, or **wats**, which also serve as monasteries, are found in Southeast Asia. Traditonal customs are still popular, especially in rural areas. Also, many people still wear traditional clothing such as sarongs, strips of cloth worn wrapped around the body.

CHALLENGE ACTIVITY

Critical Thinking: Understanding Cause and Effect Several European countries had colonies in Southeast Asia for hundreds of years. Make a two-column chart of cultural effects and political effects of colonization on the region.

criterion	domino theory	Dutch East Indies	Khmer
Siam	Timor	wats	

DIRECTIONS Read each sentence and fill in the blank with the word in the word pair that best completes the sentence.

1. The _____ had the most developed society in early Southeast Asian history. (Dutch East Indies/Khmer)

2. _____ is now called Thailand. (Timor/Siam)

3. The _____ are now called Indonesia. (Khmer/Dutch East Indies)

4. The region has many _____, or Buddhist temples. (criterion/wats)

5. The United States sent troops to South Vietnam to prevent the spread of

   communism based on the _____. (domino theory/criterion)

DIRECTIONS Choose four of the terms from the word bank. On a separate piece of paper, use these terms to write a poem or short story that relates to the section.

Southeast Asia

MAIN IDEAS

1. The area today is largely rural and agricultural, but cities are growing rapidly.
2. Myanmar is poor with a harsh military government, while Thailand is a democracy with a strong economy.
3. The countries of Indochina are poor and struggling to rebuild after years of war.

Key Terms and Places

Yangon Myanmar's capital and major seaport

human rights rights that all people deserve, such as rights to equality and justice

Bangkok capital and largest city of Thailand

klongs canals

Phnom Penh Cambodia's capital and chief city

Hanoi capital of Vietnam, located in the north

Section Summary

THE AREA TODAY

Mainland Southeast Asia includes the countries of Myanmar, Thailand, Cambodia, Laos, and Vietnam. Because of war, harsh governments, and other problems, progress has slowed in much of this area. However, in an effort to promote political, economic, and social cooperation throughout the region, most of the countries of Southeast Asia have joined the Association of Southeast Asian Nations.

Most people in the region are farmers, living in small villages and growing rice. This area also has several big cities. They are growing rapidly as people move to them in search of work. Rapid growth, however, has led to crowding and pollution.

> Circle the countries of Mainland Southeast Asia.

> What are the effects of the rapid growth on the area's cities?
> _____
> _____

MYANMAR AND THAILAND

Although Myanmar, also called Burma, has many resources, it is a poor country. **Yangon**, or Rangoon, is its capital and a major port city. A harsh military government rules Myanmar. This

government abuses **human rights**—rights that all
people deserve. One woman, Aung San Suu Kyi, is
working to reform Myanmar so people have more
rights. Suu Kyi and others have been repeatedly
arrested, however. Because of Myanmar's poor
record on human rights, many countries will not
trade with it. As a result, Myanmar's economy has
suffered.

Thailand, once called Siam, has a strong
economy. Its capital and largest city is **Bangkok**, a
city famous for its **klongs**, or canals. Bangkok's
klongs are used for trade and travel, and to drain
floodwater. Thailand has a democratically elected
government and rich resources. These factors have
helped its economy grow.

Why won't some countries trade with Myanmar?
_____
_____

THE COUNTRIES OF INDOCHINA

After decades of war, the countries of Indochina—
Cambodia, Laos, and Vietnam—are working hard
to improve their economies.

The capital and chief city of Cambodia, **Phnom
Penh**, is a center of trade. However, years of war
have left the country with little industry. Although
farming has improved, many landmines still remain
buried.

Laos is the area's poorest country. It is
landlocked, with few roads, no railroads, and little
electricity. Most people are subsistence farmers, just
growing enough food to support their families.

Vietnam's main cities include its capital in the
north, **Hanoi**, and Ho Chi Minh City in the south.
Although still a Communist country, Vietnam's
government has been allowing more economic
freedoms. Industry and services are growing, but
most people still farm.

How has war affected the countries of Indochina?
_____
_____

CHALLENGE ACTIVITY

Critical Thinking: Summarizing Summarize the
information about the countries of Mainland
Southeast Asia, using a graphic organizer.

Guided Reading Workbook

Bangkok	Burma	Hanoi
Ho Chi Minh City	human rights	klongs
pedicabs	Phnom Penh	Yangon

DIRECTIONS Read each sentence and fill in the blank with the word
in the word pair that best completes the sentence.

1. _____ is the capital and largest city of Cambodia.
   (Phnom Penh/Yangon)

2. The capital of Myanmar is _____. (Phnom Penh/Yangon)

3. In Thailand _____ are used for transportation, trade, and draining
   floodwaters. (pedicabs/klongs)

4. Vietnam's largest city, _____, is in the south, in the Mekong delta.
   (Hanoi/Ho Chi Minh City)

5. _____ lies near the mouth of the Chao Phraya River.
   (Bangkok/Burma)

DIRECTIONS Write two words or phrases that describe the term.

6. Bangkok _____

7. Hanoi _____

8. human rights _____

9. klongs _____

10. Yangon _____

MAIN IDEAS
1. The area today has rich resources and growing cities but faces challenges.
2. Malaysia and its neighbors have strong economies but differ in many ways.
3. Indonesia is big and diverse with a growing economy, and East Timor is small and poor.
4. The Philippines has less ethnic diversity, and its economy is improving.

Key Terms and Places

kampong village or city district with traditional houses built on stilts; slums around cities

Jakarta capital of Indonesia

Kuala Lumpur Malaysia's capital and a cultural and economic center

free ports ports that place few if any taxes on goods

sultan supreme ruler of a Muslim country

Java Indonesia's main island

Manila capital of the Philippines

Section Summary
THE AREA TODAY

The countries of Southeast Asia are Malaysia, Singapore, Brunei, Indonesia, Timor-Leste, and the Philippines. Like the mainland countries, these island countries face challenges, too, such as ethnic conflicts, poverty, and environmental problems.

As on the mainland, many people in Island Southeast Asia live in rural areas. They fish or farm. Rice is the main crop. Also like the mainland, many people here are moving to cities for work. In some areas, people live in **kampongs**, places with traditional houses on stilts. The term *kampong* also refers to slums around **Jakarta**, Indonesia's capital, and around other cities of Island Southeast Asia.

> Underline the challenges facing Island Southeast Asia.

> Circle the main crop of this area.

MALAYSIA AND ITS NEIGHBORS

Malaysia has two parts. One is on the Malay Peninsula, where most Malaysians live. Its capital, **Kuala Lumpur**, is there as well. The other part is on Borneo. Malaysia is ethnically diverse, with a strong economy. It has a constitutional monarchy, with a prime minister and elected legislature.

Singapore is located on a tiny island that lies on a major shipping route. It is one of the world's busiest **free ports**—ports with few or no taxes on goods. Singapore is modern, wealthy, and clean. It has a strict government. Brunei is on the island of Borneo. A **sultan**, the supreme ruler of a Muslim country, governs this tiny country. As a result of oil and gas deposits, Brunei has grown wealthy.

> **How does Singapore's location help its economy?**
> _____
> _____

INDONESIA AND TIMOR-LESTE

Indonesia is the world's largest archipelago. It has the world's largest Muslim population and is ethnically diverse. **Java** is Indonesia's main island. More than half its people live there. Indonesia has rich resources, such as rubber, oil, gas, and timber, but religious and ethnic conflicts have led to violence.

Years of fighting for independence from Indonesia have left tiny Timor-Leste poor. Most people there farm.

> **What are some of Indonesia's resources?**
> _____
> _____

THE PHILIPPINES

The Philippines has less ethnic diversity than other island countries. **Manila** is its capital. Most Filipinos are poor farmers who do not own any land. The country is mainly Roman Catholic.

CHALLENGE ACTIVITY

Critical Thinking: Drawing Inferences Choose two island countries of Southeast Asia and write an essay that compares two of the following categories: geography, people, government, economy.

concrete	free ports	Jakarta
Java	kampongs	Kuala Lumpur
Manila	sultan	

DIRECTIONS On the line provided before each statement, write **T** if the statement is true and **F** if the statement is false. If the statement is false, write the correct term on the line after each sentence that makes the sentence a true statement.

_____ 1. Singapore is one of the world's busiest kampongs.

_____

_____ 2. Malaysia's capital, Java, is also a cultural and economic center.

_____

_____ 3. The Philippines has many islands, including Luzon, which is where the capital city of Manila is located.

_____

_____ 4. More than half of Indonesia's people live in its capital, Kuala Lampur.

_____

_____ 5. The supreme ruler of Brunei, a Muslim country, is a sultan.

_____

DIRECTIONS Choose four of the terms from the word bank. On a separate piece of paper, use these terms to write a summary of what you learned in the section.

MAIN IDEAS
1. The physical geography of Australia and New Zealand is diverse and unusual.
2. Native peoples and British settlers shaped the history of Australia and New Zealand.
3. Australia and New Zealand today are wealthy and culturally diverse countries.

Key Terms and Places

Great Barrier Reef largest coral reef in the world, off Australia's northeastern coast

coral reef a collection of rocky material found in shallow, tropical waters

Aborigines first humans to live in Australia

Maori New Zealand's first settlers

Outback Australia's interior

Section Summary
PHYSICAL GEOGRAPHY

Australia has wide, flat stretches of dry land. Low mountains, valleys, and a major river system make up the eastern part of the country. The **Great Barrier Reef**, the world's largest **coral reef**, is located off of Australia's northeastern coast.

New Zealand is made up of North Island and South Island. A large mountain range called the Southern Alps is a key feature of South Island. New Zealand also has green hills, volcanoes, hot springs, dense forests, deep lakes, and fertile plains.

> Underline the two islands that make up New Zealand.

Most of Australia has warm, dry desert and steppe climates. The coastal areas are milder and wetter. New Zealand has a marine climate with plenty of rainfall and mild temperatures. Native animals include Australia's kangaroo and koala and New Zealand's kiwi, a flightless bird. Australia has many valuable mineral resources, and farms raise wheat, cotton, and sheep despite the poor soil. New

> Circle the region's native animals.

Zealand has few mineral resources, but plenty of
rich soil.

HISTORY

Aborigines, the first humans in Australia, came
from Southeast Asia more than 40,000 years ago.
Early Aborigines were nomads who gathered plants,
hunted animals, and fished. The **Maori**, New
Zealand's first settlers, came from other Pacific
islands about 1,200 years ago. They hunted, fished,
and farmed. Captain James Cook visited New
Zealand in 1769. British settlers began arriving in
Australia and New Zealand in the late 1700s and
early 1800s. Australia and New Zealand gained
independence in the early 1900s. Both countries are
in the British Commonwealth and close allies of the
United Kingdom.

> Who were the first humans
> to settle in Australia and
> New Zealand?
>
> _____
> _____

AUSTRALIA AND NEW ZEALAND TODAY

Most people in both countries are of British
ancestry. Sydney and Melbourne are Australia's
two largest cities. Auckland is New Zealand's
largest city. Both countries produce wool, meat, and
dairy products. Mining is important throughout the
Outback. Other industries include steel, heavy
machines, and computers. Manufacturing, banking,
and tourism are important in New Zealand.

Today, Australia and New Zealand face the
challenge of improving the political and economic
status of their native populations.

> Circle the name of New
> Zealand's largest city.

CHALLENGE ACTIVITY

Critical Thinking: Making Judgments Why do
you think the Aboriginal and Maori populations of
Australia and New Zealand declined after British
settlers arrived? Explain your answer in a short
paragraph.

Name _____ Class _____ Date _____

Section 1, *continued*

Aborigines	Auckland	coral reef	fjord
Great Barrier Reef	kiwi	koala	Maori
Melbourne	Outback	Sydney	Uluru

DIRECTIONS Read each sentence and fill in the blank with the word in the word pair that best completes the sentence.

1. The _____ were the first people to inhabit Australia. (Aborigines/Maori)

2. Melbourne and _____ are two large cities in Australia. (Auckland/Sydney)

3. A _____ is a collection of rocky materials found in shallow, tropic waters. (coral reef/fjord)

4. The _____ is a flightless bird unique to New Zealand. (koala/kiwi)

5. The _____ is a well-known rock formation in Australia. (Outback/Uluru)

DIRECTIONS Choose five of the terms from the word bank. Use these terms to write a summary of what you learned in this section.

_____

_____

_____

_____

_____

_____

_____

_____

_____

The Pacific Realm

MAIN IDEAS

1. Unique physical features, tropical climates, and limited resources shape the physical geography of the Pacific Islands.
2. Native customs and contact with the western world have influenced the history and culture of the Pacific Islands.
3. Pacific Islanders today are working to improve their economies and protect the environment.

Key Terms and Places

Micronesia region of Pacific Islands located east of the Philippines

Melanesia region of Pacific Islands stretching from New Guinea to Fiji

Polynesia largest region of Pacific Islands, east of Melanesia

atoll small, ring-shaped coral island surrounding a lagoon

territory an area that is under the control of another government

Section Summary
PHYSICAL GEOGRAPHY

There are three regions of islands in the Pacific. **Micronesia**, consisting of about 2,000 small islands, is east of the Philippines. **Melanesia**, the most heavily populated region, stretches from New Guinea to Fiji. **Polynesia**, the largest region, is located east of Melanesia.

There are two kinds of islands in the Pacific: high islands and low islands. High islands are formed from volcanoes or continental rock. They tend to be mountainous and rocky. They have dense forests, rich soil, and many mineral resources. Low islands are much smaller; they have thin soil, little vegetation, few resources, and low elevations. Many low islands are **atolls**, small ring-shaped coral islands surrounding lagoons.

Most high and low islands have a humid tropical climate. Temperatures are warm and rain falls all year.

> **What three regions make up the Pacific Islands?**
> _____
> _____
> _____

> **Circle the type of climate that most high and low islands have.**

HISTORY AND CULTURE

People began settling the Pacific more than 40,000 years ago. They arrived in Melanesia first. Polynesia was the last region to be settled. Europeans first encountered the Pacific Islands in the 1500s. John Cook, a captain in the British Navy, visited all the main regions in the 1700s. By the late 1800s, Britain, Spain, France, and other European nations gained control of most of the islands. When the United States defeated Spain in the Spanish-American War, it took Guam as a **territory,** an area that is under the authority of another government. After World War I, Japan gained control of many islands. After World War II, the United Nations placed some islands under the control of the United States and its Allies.

More than 9 million people of many cultures and ethnic groups live in the Pacific Islands. Most are descended from the original settlers. Some are ethnic Europeans and Asians. Most islanders are now Christian. Many, however, continue to practice traditional customs ranging from architecture to art styles and various ceremonies.

Circle the name of the Pacific Island region that was first to be settled.

What country took Guam as a territory after the Spanish-American war?

About how many people live in the Pacific Islands?

THE PACIFIC ISLANDS TODAY

The Pacific Islands face important challenges today. They are trying to build stronger economies through tourism, agriculture, and fishing. Some countries, including Papua New Guinea, export gold, copper, and oil. The islands also must cope with the potentially damaging effects of past nuclear testing in the area and global warming.

Underline three ways the Pacific Islands are trying to improve their economies.

CHALLENGE ACTIVITY

Critical Thinking: Drawing Conclusions Which island countries probably have stronger economies: those occupying high islands or those occupying low islands? Support your answer using details from the summary.

atoll	Melanesia	Micronesia
Polynesia	territory	

DIRECTIONS On the line provided before each statement, write **T** if a statement is true and **F** if a statement is false. If the statement is false, write the term from the word bank that makes it true on the line after each sentence.

_____ 1. Melanesia, which means "tiny islands," is a group of 2,000 small islands in the Pacific.

_____

_____ 2. Tonga and Hawaii are part of Polynesia.

_____

_____ 3. Micronesia is the most heavily populated of the three Pacific island groups.

_____

DIRECTIONS Read each sentence and choose the correct term from the word bank to replace the underlined phrase. Write the term in the space provided and then define the term in your own words.

4. Wake Island, located west of the Hawaiian Islands, is an unusual physical feature.

_____

Your definition: _____

_____

5. When the United States defeated Spain in the Spanish-American War, Guam became a U.S. political unit. _____

Your definition: _____

_____

MAIN IDEAS
1. Freezing temperatures, ice, and snow dominate Antarctica's physical geography.
2. Explorations in the 1800s and 1900s led to Antarctica's use for scientific research.
3. Research and protecting the environment are key issues in Antarctica today.

Key Terms and Places

ice shelf ledge of ice that extends over the water

icebergs floating masses of ice that have broken off a glacier

Antarctic Peninsula peninsula that extends north of the Antarctic Circle

polar desert a high-latitude region that receives very little precipitation

ozone layer layer of Earth's atmosphere that protects living things from the harmful effects of the sun's ultraviolet rays

Section Summary
PHYSICAL GEOGRAPHY

Ice covers more than 98 percent of Antarctica. Ice flows slowly toward the coasts of Antarctica. At the coast it forms a ledge over the water called an **ice shelf**. Antarctica's largest ice shelf is the Ross Ice Shelf. Floating masses of ice that break off from ice shelves are called **icebergs**. The **Antarctic Peninsula** is on the western side of the continent.

Antarctica has a freezing ice cap climate. It is a **polar desert**, a high-latitude region that receives little precipitation. It is bitterly cold during the dark winter. Summer temperatures reach near freezing.

Tundra plant life grows in ice-free areas. Insects are the only animals on the land. Penguins, seals, and whales live in the nearby waters. Antarctica has many mineral resources.

EARLY EXPLORATIONS

Antarctica was first sighted in 1775. European explorations investigated Antarctica throughout the

> How is an iceberg related to an ice shelf?
>
> _____
> _____
> _____

1800s. A team of Norwegian explorers became the first people to reach the South Pole in 1911.

Several countries have claimed parts of Antarctica. In 1959, several countries signed the Antarctic Treaty, which bans military activity on the continent and sets it aside for scientific research.

What are the terms of the Antarctic Treaty of 1959?
_____
_____
_____

ANTARCTICA TODAY

Antarctica is the only continent with no permanent human population. Scientists use Antarctica to conduct research and study the environment. Several countries, including the United States, have bases there.

Antarctic research includes study of plant and animal life, analysis of weather conditions and patterns, and examination of issues affecting Earth's environment. Scientists are concerned about the thinning of the **ozone layer**—the layer of Earth's atmosphere that protects living things from the harmful effects of the sun's ultraviolet rays.

Tourism, oil spills, and mining are real and potential threats to Antarctica's environment. An agreement reached in 1991 bans mining and drilling and limits tourism.

Underline three activities that threaten Antarctica's environment.

CHALLENGE ACTIVITY

Critical Thinking: Making Judgments What do you think is the greatest threat to Antarctica's environment? Why? Explain your answer.

| Antarctic Peninsula | Antarctic Treaty | glacier | ice shelf |
| icebergs | motive | ozone layer | polar desert |

DIRECTIONS Answer each question by writing a sentence that contains at least one word from the word bank.

1. Describe the physical geography of Antarctica.

_____

_____

_____

2. What kinds of things are scientists studying in Antarctica?

_____

_____

DIRECTIONS Write three words or phrases that describe the term.

3. icebergs _____

_____

4. polar desert _____

_____

5. Antarctic Peninsula _____

_____

6. ozone layer _____

_____